Praise for
BIG Ideas to BIG Results

"Short, simple, and to the point. Kanazawa and Miles distill decades of corporate transformation experience down to a few, vital messages. Required reading for CEOs."

—**Peter Darbee**, Chairman, CEO, and President,
PG&E Corporation

"Mike and Bob have outlined an extensive and highly valuable set of actions and processes that can be implemented by corporate management to drive significant improvement in organizations. Their approach can be of great benefit not only to CEOs and their executive staffs, but also to vice presidents, general managers, and department heads."

—**Richard Beyer**, President and CEO,
Intersil Corporation

"This book is a must read for CEOs who are looking for time-tested principles and a proven process by which senior teams can realign their organization and its people with their strategic intent. In a fast moving world, nothing is more important."

—**Michael Beer**, Cahners-Raab Professor of Business,
Harvard Business School and author, *Breaking the Code of Change*

"*BIG Ideas to BIG Results* is a must read for CEOs, as well as managers empowered with bringing about meaningful change. Most executives are comfortable with functional change within their own areas of competence and responsibilities, but one of the most challenging realities of the 21st century is that competitive advantage and speed of change require complex cross-functional solutions. I am recommending reading this book to all of my C-level clients."

—**Jerry Black**, President and CEO,
Kurt Salmon Associates

"In the past years as a new General Manager and then as a new CEO, I have had the pleasure of working with Bob and Mike on corporate transformation challenges. They have done an outstanding job of distilling complex corporate turnaround principles into a practical book full of blueprints for CEOs, their executive staffs, and their boards to apply in corporate transformations."

—**Dr. Bami Bastani**, President and CEO,
Anadigics, Inc.

"ACT: an amalgamation of time-tested wisdom, frameworks, processes, and illustrative cases that provides a must read for both successful companies and those that are in transition. Everything is right here in this Little Red Book, for the CEO down to the managers of companies that need to execute."

—**Mas Sakamoto**, Vice President, Corporate Planning and Marketing,
NEC Corporation of America

"*BIG Ideas to BIG Results* is a superb handbook for leaders wanting to transform their organizations. With Bob Miles' expert guidance, our company launched a transformation four years ago, and our Drive for Value business model is now embedded in the way we operate."

—**Shirley Gaufin**, Chief Human Resources Officer,
Black & Veatch

"For the past ten years, leader-led techniques have helped us transform Delta TechOps from a cost center to the largest maintenance repair and overhaul center in North America. Mike and Bob make it simple and easy to execute."
—**Anthony Charaf**, Senior Vice President, TechOps, Delta Air Lines, Inc.

"ACT was employed at the Tour a decade and a half ago to help the new commissioner 'take charge' and most recently to relaunch the Nationwide Tour. It is simple, it gets the job done rapidly, and it can be adapted to any corporate transformation challenge."
—**Worth W. Calfee**, President, Nationwide Tour of the PGA Tour

"An important reading for any executive who wants to revitalize his/her company, and do it efficiently!"
—**Jay W. Lorsch**, Louis E. Kirstein Professor of Human Relations, Harvard Business School

"*BIG Ideas to BIG Results* captures a very simple but powerful methodology for transforming ideas into action. Their recipe for leadership really moves the corporate mountain."
—**John Baker**, CEO and President, Florida Rock Industries, Inc.

"*BIG Ideas to BIG Results* shows how to take strategies and connect them with tactics, align an entire organization around a common set of goals, and get everyone bought in. It is the one ingredient most companies miss, and this is the one that helps you win."
—**Tony Weiss**, Vice President/General Manager, Software, Peripherals, Imaging, Displays, and Dell Direct Retail, Dell, Inc.

"*BIG Ideas to BIG Results* is chock full of practical tools to get your strategy and operations in synch and moving faster down the track —a 'do more on less' guidebook for every executive."
—**Marty Beard**, President, Sybase 365

"Want to improve your valuation? Get your ACT in gear. This book is highly recommended reading for executives who understand that higher market values are commanded by those companies that consistently generate big ideas and convert those ideas into big results."
—**Michael Gardner**, Executive Vice President, Wedbush Morgan Securities

"Having experienced guidance from Mike on his process for strategic transformation in our business unit, I must confess that I am now reconciled with strategic business consultants! This book is a must-read for any executive willing to engage into a reshaping of its organization for a more ambitious future."
—**Olivier Le Peuch**, President, Schlumberger Information Solutions

"Our executive clients consistently ask for tools, rather than theory, that they can immediately implement in order to execute strategy. *BIG Ideas to BIG Results* offers a uniquely clear and practical format for confronting and transforming reality with proven results."

—**Whitney Hischier**, Assistant Dean, Center of Executive Development, Haas School of Business, University of California at Berkeley

"*BIG Ideas to BIG Results* describes a powerful yet simple way for leaders to reposition a company in a highly efficient manner, critical in today's fast-paced, ever-changing, 'flat' world. It produces clear measurable results, energizes and aligns everyone in the organization, and is the only methodology I have experienced where everything you do is an integral part of your job—period!"

—**Javed Patel**, CEO, Sierra Monolithics

"It's one part strategic focus, one part business operations, one part leadership, and one part employee engagement. Mike and Bob show you the streamlined, simple, and potent recipe for combining these elements to turn your big strategic ideas into real business results."

—**Pascal Lenoir**, CEO, NagraStar

"*BIG Ideas to BIG Results* is a must read for every CEO, offering a practical approach to alignment and engagement that will result in unbelievable transformation. This book is easy reading and is full of great case studies that will inspire every person in a business leadership role."

—**Carlo Saggese**, Vice President of Application Development, Vistage International—The world's leading chief executive organization

"Kanazawa and Miles provide an easy to relate account of some often paradoxical issues with large corporations. The authors provide sound advice in a book which can be easily read on a long flight."

—**Peters Suh**, President, Vodafone Asia Pacific Ltd and Vodafone Ventures Ltd

"Mike Kanazawa and Bob Miles lay out a powerful, proven process for leaders at all levels. With a focus on alignment and engaging the entire organization, this book is an excellent resource for leaders who want to drive results."

—**Ann Marie Beasley**, Vice President, Office of Strategy Management, Symantec Corporation

"This is a must-have handbook for any leader guiding an organization through strategic change. It provides practical insights that ensure the entire organization understands its role in fulfilling the strategic aims of the business. Too many transformational frameworks rely on a top-down approach; this book helps you ensure all the oars are in the water and rowing together."

—**Matt DiMaria**, Chief Marketing Officer, Sonic Solutions

"I love the topic the book is addressing. Its approach simplifies the recipe for success for any business, large or small, private or public, from the aspect of making ideas produce results. Too often, we as corporate executives go out of our way to complicate the planning and implementation process. It is obvious that the authors have witnessed this tragedy over and over, as their writing is filled with practical examples of 'how-to' bridge ineffective scenarios to become high-performing environments."

—**Esther de Wolde**, CEO,
Phantom Screens

"Whether your organization numbers 10 or 10,000, you owe it to yourself and your team to read this book! The proven process will enable you to refocus your organization, implement lasting change, and produce sustained superior results."
—**Rob Koteskey**, airline captain, naval officer, and team performance consultant

"Big ideas are the easy part. Getting big results requires the joint efforts of all, and not just going through the motions or going along with the flow. *BIG Ideas to BIG Results* provides the recipe for combining your big ideas with an inspired and engaged team. Simply put, it just works."

—**Larry Mondry**, CEO,
CSK Auto

"*BIG Ideas to BIG Results* strikes a balance that is very difficult to achieve in that it's not so rigid as to seem artificial, yet not so flexible as to lack conviction. This book provides real, sound advice."

—**Bill Hopkins**, Managing Principal,
Odyssey Investment Partners

"*BIG Ideas to BIG Results* provides leaders with a solution that instills confidence, purpose, and alignment throughout an entire organization and spikes it with a bias for speed and ACTion. The ACT 'leader-led' process is a dramatic departure from traditional consulting methods in that it unleashes value creators at every level of an organization."

—**George A. Coll**, SVP, New Services,
Sears Holdings Corporation

BIG IDEAS TO
BIG RESULTS

BIG IDEAS TO BIG RESULTS

REMAKE AND RECHARGE YOUR COMPANY, FAST

Michael T. Kanazawa and Robert H. Miles

Vice President, Publisher: Tim Moore
Associate Publisher and Director of Marketing: Amy Neidlinger
Acquisitions Editor: Martha Cooley
Editorial Assistant: Pamela Boland
Development Editor: Russ Hall
Digital Marketing Manager: Julie Phifer
Marketing Coordinator: Megan Colvin
Cover Designer: Alan Clements
Managing Editor: Gina Kanouse
Project Editor: Anne Goebel
Copy Editor: Karen Annett
Proofreader: Heather Waye Arle
Indexer: Erika Millen
Senior Compositor: Gloria Schurick
Manufacturing Buyer: Dan Uhrig

Published by FT Press
Upper Saddle River, New Jersey 07458

FT Press offers excellent discounts on this book when ordered in quantity for bulk purchases
or special sales. For more information, please contact U.S. Corporate and Government Sales,
1-800-382-3419, corpsales@pearsontechgroup.com. For sales outside the U.S., please contact
International Sales at international@pearsoned.com.

Printed in the United States of America

First Printing February 2008

ISBN-10: 0-13-234478-5
ISBN-13: 978-0-13-234478-4

www.bigideastobigresults.com

Pearson Education LTD.
Pearson Education Australia PTY, Limited.
Pearson Education Singapore, Pte. Ltd.
Pearson Education North Asia, Ltd.
Pearson Education Canada, Ltd.
Pearson Educatión de Mexico, S.A. de C.V.
Pearson Education—Japan
Pearson Education Malaysia, Pte. Ltd.

Library of Congress Cataloging-in-Publication Data

Kanazawa, Michael T.

  Big ideas to big results : remake and recharge your company, fast / Michael T. Kanazawa and
Robert H. Miles.

    p. cm.

  ISBN 0-13-234478-5 (hardback : alk. paper) 1. Organizational effectiveness. 2. Organizational
change. 3. Leadership. I. Miles, Robert H. II. Title.

  HD58.9.K36 2008

  658.4'063—dc22

                          2007037056

To my wife Lisa, who enables and encourages me; my parents, who taught me how to learn; my brother, who showed me the real world; and my three boys, to whom I am still just dad…
Mike

To Jane
Bob

Contents

Chapter 1: A Better Way 1

The Sugar High............................ 3

Get Your ACT Together 6

Make Transformation a Simple Routine 9

Endnotes 11

Chapter 2: Breaking Through Gridlock 13

Gridlock! The Task Overload Epidemic........ 13

Where Did All of This Clutter Come From?.... 14

The New Definition of Big Box Retail 15

Task Overload Undermines Accountability 16

One Company—Not Many.................. 18

Busting Through Gridlock: Getting Started..... 19

The Leader's Challenge: Less Is More........ 20

Fighting Fires Versus Fire Prevention 23

Endnotes 24

Chapter 3: Creating Safe Passage 25

Safe Passage—A Clear Transformation Process . 25

The ACT Process Basics: Powerfully Simple.... 28

This Is Not a New Religion, Just a Better
Way of Managing the Business............... 30

Endnotes 32

Chapter 4: Confronting Today's Reality 33

The Emperor's Ugly Clothes 35

Dialogue Versus Discussion 36

Generating Dialogue as a Leader............. 37

Priming the Pump....................... 39

Canary in a Coal Mine 41

On the Outside Looking In................. 44

Talk with Customers and Noncustomers 47
You Are Here: Map the Market 48
Confronting Reality Work Session 52
Endnotes 54

Chapter 5: Sharpening the Strategy Arrow 55
A One-Page View of the Future 56
Creating a Strategic Vision 60
Business Success Modeling. 63
Due Diligence on Yourself 65
Endnotes 71

Chapter 6: Absolute Alignment 73
Translation to Three Corporate Initiatives. 74
Have You Lost Your Marbles? 76
What NOT to Do 78
Zombie Projects 78
Restack the Whole. 80
Individual Commitments to Action 83
Alignment of Commitments—Reducing Silos. . . 84
Alignment of Values 87
Don't Try to Replicate the Scout Oath 87
Put Your Money Where Your Mouth Is 89
The Bottom Line on Alignment 90
Endnotes 93

Chapter 7: Rapidly Engaging the Full Organization 95
It's All about the Results 96
Quantum Jumps 98
"Back in Black" Friday 99
Employee Engagement Is Not Barbeque 100
High-Engagement. 101
Critical Importance of Dialogue 101
Hear It from My Boss 102
Unbounded, But Grounded in Reality. 102
Putting It All Together 104

Reaching Scale and Speed 109
Lighting 1,000 Fires Only Gets You Burned . . . 110
Endnotes 112

Chapter 8:   **Productive Speed** 113
Get the Train Moving, Now 113
The Benefits of Productive Speed 116
All Aboard at Internet Speed 118
Designing the Process for Speed 121
The No-Slack Launch 123
Quick Starts 127
How Do You Keep Time? 131
Speed as a Leadership Discipline 133
Endnotes 134

Chapter 9:   **Creating Leadership Power at All Levels** 135
The Power Curve 136
The Under-Powered Organization 137
Shifting Up the Power Curve 137
Executive Management 138
    This Is Your Day Job *139*
    Everyone Takes a Half Step Up *140*
Middle Management 141
A Real High Flyer 142
Front-Line Managers 143
Big Ideas from within the Team 145
Sharing Power Creates Power 147
Endnotes 148

Chapter 10:   **Building Operational Traction** 149
Commit with Confidence, Publicly 150
Building Traction 151
Accountability 156
Simple Closed-Loop Accountability 156
Promises Versus Declarations 160
    Shoot for the Moon—Drive Innovation . . .*161*
    Above and Below the Waterline *163*

Don't Get Overly Fixated on the Dashboard. . . 164

Ground Truth: The Real Results *166*

Misguided Incentives 168

Performance Coaching 171

Endnotes 173

Chapter 11:   Over the Hump and Into the Slump 175

Post-Launch Blues 178

Ballast and Keel *179*

Mid-Course Adjustment 181

The Process Is Not a One-Time Overlay 182

Mini-Cascades 184

Launching the New Year. 187

Oh Right, the Behaviors... 191

You Don't Get to Relax 192

Plan to Punctuate the Equilibrium Regularly . . 192

Endnotes 194

Chapter 12:   Are You Up to the Challenge? 195

White-Hot Commitment of the Leader. 196

Change the People, or Change the People 197

You Don't Have All the Answers (And Nobody

Expects You To). 201

Get Real. 203

Go For It!. 204

Endnotes 205

Afterword 207

Acknowledgments 217

About the Authors 221

Index 225

1

A Better Way

Quickly getting an organization from BIG ideas to BIG results is today's most pervasive management challenge. Excellent execution, driving sustained growth, and consistent execution of strategy are the top three challenges noted by CEOs around the world, based on a recent survey of over 750 of the world's corporate leaders.[1] In order to rise to these challenges, leaders at all levels need to execute large-scale breakthroughs, or transformations, while at the same time delivering short-term results every day. Achieving this balance is one of the most difficult challenges you will face as a leader in your career and one of the most rewarding when you get it right.

Transformation has been used to describe everything from high-risk complete overhauls of a business to tactical changes to IT systems. So to be clear, by transformation, we mean a wide variety of actions and opportunities that are required to drive continuous growth in a business. These range from a new leader "taking charge," to launching a new phase in the organization, to entering new markets, to integrating major acquisitions, to breaking down silos to operate as "one company," to boldly launching a major strategic initiative. Put simply, transformation means opening up new possibilities for growth and moving from one state to another, but it is tough work and most efforts fall short.

Imagine you are the leader of an organization and you are about to launch a transformation or shift in strategic direction. Your direct report team has just completed a set of anonymous surveys. You're looking over the results as you prepare for a meeting with the team to launch them into the next phase of growth. In the responses, you see things like the following:

- "We never follow through on anything all the way to see if it will produce results. We launch things and then when they don't immediately turn results, we just start launching more things."
- "We are the best at being second best."
- "There should not be 20 initiatives; we should focus on a very few things."
- "We have organizational attention deficit disorder, starting at the top."

These are actual quotes from vice presidents at profitable, multibillion dollar companies that were calling up a shift to a new level of play. Not too encouraging when you are trying to drive a major strategic shift in direction to achieve breakthrough results. These quotes, while startling in some cases, are exactly what is being said in all corners of organizations today. Why do so many high-achieving leaders feel this sense of dread when confronted with the challenge to take things to the next level? Why all the frustration? People are overwhelmed, overtasked, and stuck in gridlock, similar to a traffic jam on Friday afternoon where no matter how badly each individual wants to get home, the whole system is stuck.

The need for these course corrections and interventions to break the status quo are coming at a constant pace today, given the challenges of rapidly growing earnings, globalization, rapid commoditization of markets, executive turnover rates, challenges by activist investors, and all of the familiar triggers for us as business leaders. In the rush to meet all of these challenges, the solutions we've been applying are actually locking down companies in gridlock even more, where transformation becomes impossible to accomplish and everyone is frustrated and stuck.

How are we doing with this challenge? Not great, based on data from a poll of 11,000 workers showing that fewer than half of employees understand their company's strategic goals, less than 25% feel their organization sets goals that people are enthusiastic about, only 38% believe their planning results in clear assignments for individuals, and 43% feel there is any follow through on the plans anyway.[2] This shows a clear picture that a lot of people are running around doing things that aren't moving the company forward—they are just churning.

The range of methods for attempting to lead transformations is as varied as transformation challenges themselves. Some leaders resort to dramatic communications "campaigns," believing that if people can just "get it," they will get on with it. Others attempt to grease the skids of a transformation launch with a barrage of tactical change-management interventions. Other leaders scorecard everything in sight because of their gut belief in measurement and delegation. And who hasn't heard about transformation attempts that have been borne on the backs of TQM, Six Sigma, Process Reengineering, and massive infusions of new technology?

Clearly, each of these management orthodoxies contains elements that can contribute to execution success. But too much religion or reliance on one versus the others leads to an overengineering of some parts of the business, which actually feeds rather than cuts through the gridlock that holds companies in the status quo. Why? None of these approaches were designed from the outset to handle all of the key moving parts in a transformation. These often-ignored macro transformation elements include:

- Confronting the reality of the current business environment and functioning of the organization
- Focusing on a critical few top priorities
- Aligning all parts of the organization to a single set of initiatives
- Rapidly engaging the full organization in translating these organization-wide constructs into operational tactics and job-level objectives
- Rigorously following through to accelerate the learning and performing cycle while creating leaders at all levels of the organization

The Sugar High

Just in case you are one of the few who has never seen this type of transformation effort play out the wrong way, here is a quick viewing. A major corporation needed to transform to meet new competitive pressures. The executives got the help of management consultant experts who promised access to a best-practices knowledge base of process and systems enhancements. A very small group of internal analysts provided data to the consultants to build a financial model that promised to save millions of dollars in operating expenses, based on applying ratios of the best practices to the company's financials. The millions of dollars, then taken as a given, provided much room for investing in consulting help and systems implementations to achieve those savings. With a huge return on investment expected, the executives signed up for the transformation effort to begin.

Rows of cubicles were set up to make room for the business consultants to come in and do their work. Bright and energetic people showed up who had great credentials and fantastic analysis skills. They polled managers to build process maps of the current state of the business. Then, they applied their "knowledge base" to create a future state of the business, which, of course, included the many systems upgrades they had proposed. They closed on the contracts to build the systems and began implementing the technology solutions. More cubicles were set up for the systems consultants to come in and do their work as well.

Finally, a year into the process, it was time for the systems to be rolled out to the "troops" to use. Ashen-faced managers were now told to "buy-in" and get moving with producing the millions of dollars in savings by implementing the new systems and processes. The money was already spent on the systems and processes, so there was no turning back. Unfortunately, the managers weren't fully engaged in the process and had never agreed with many of the suggested changes. In fact, some of the most high-leverage systems and process changes had not even been addressed because they weren't a part of the consultant's knowledge and solution base. Some solutions were completely impractical and didn't take into consideration how work was actually done at that particular company. The process stalled while the consultants held numerous buy-in meetings to try to listen to the troops' concerns. But, of course, it was too late to really change anything and everyone knew that. Buy-in was a futile process.

Seeing the impasse, the executives decided that an internal person should take point because the troops were beginning to reject the consultants. So, two years into the process, a "czar" was named. The poor, unsuspecting czar, of course, had no operational clout, but still fought valiantly with a last-ditch effort to regain momentum. But, in the end, the effort died a slow death. Some savings showed up as aggressive layoffs and redeployments caused people to do "more with less," and some of the systems changes worked. However, the result was far from transformational. It was just chalked up as another "flavor of the month" to the troops and one more layer of projects and programs adding to the overload and gridlock they already faced. Or as one manager called it, "just another sugar high." A quick peak in energy was followed by an immediate crash. And what happens next? Management sees the lack of results and looks for the next new thing to launch, while employees become even more skeptical and unwilling to "buy-in" blindly each successive time.

Most of us have seen this type of effort play out similarly to the curve shown in Figure 1.1.

Typical Cycle of Failure

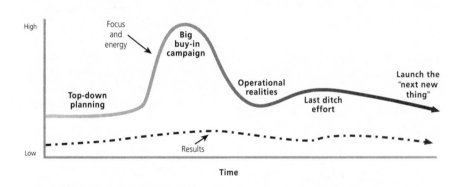

Figure 1.1 Typical stages of a cycle of failure

Nobody is immune to the kinds of rapidly changing market conditions that create the need for these bold calls for action, just as nobody can avoid the macro business cycles that make fortunes rise and fall. And consultants certainly have the ability to help in a more productive way if placed in the correct supporting roles where their true expertise is leveraged. The real question from this description of the all-too-common sugar-high approach: How can we break this cycle? How can we engage our teams more effectively in leading transformations that produce breakthrough results?

Get Your ACT Together

More than 25 years ago, groups of CEOs, division presidents, and their executive teams gathered for two weeks to participate in an innovative program at the Harvard Business School.[3] There, they would work collaboratively on their top business challenge with noncompeting peers and key faculty. Spending time in the hallowed halls of ivy was not at all a time-out from real business for intellectual theorizing. While sequestered on the Harvard campus, they would help each other build action plans that they would implement back home. They would then return nine months later to describe to their peer group how the solutions worked and how they could be improved.

After several years of the program, a clear pattern emerged. The biggest and most common problem facing executives was in leading different types of corporate transformations. They had trouble getting their organizations to execute on their stated strategies quickly. The process that resulted, now known as ACT (Accelerated Corporate Transformation), was conceived through the ideas and trials by these groups of leaders. Over the years,

The Origins of ACT

The ACT (Accelerated Corporate Transformation) process was originally distilled by Dr. Robert H. Miles through the innovative "Managing Organizational Effectiveness" program which he chaired at the Harvard Business School. This process architecture was developed through work with top executives and their teams wrestling with the realities of how to rise to the major challenge confronting their organization. The process was refined through use over the next decade at companies like GE, Office Depot, National Semiconductor, Rockwell, and Symantec. It continues to be refined by Michael Kanazawa and Dr. Miles at Dissero Partners through their collaborative work with executive leaders facing a variety of organizational and strategic challenges.

The ACT process architecture has been designed to quickly focus, align, and engage the full organization and then rigorously follow through for execution. It was also designed to be run by business leaders with light consulting and implementation support the first time through. By design, it allows managers at all levels to effectively lead organizational transformation and strategy execution on their own.

countless leaders and teams have leveraged the same process and refined and streamlined it with their contributions.

By keeping the responsibility for leading the transformation squarely in the hands of business leaders themselves, the result is not only quantum improvement in the targeted initiatives in a shorter-than-expected period of time, but also a fundamental improvement in the leadership acumen from top to bottom in the organization.

Through experience across many situations, it is clear that each of the ACT process steps counts, and, hence, should not be sidestepped. However, how you and your team lead the organization through the steps really makes the difference. For this reason, in the core chapters of this book, the keys to success will be largely conveyed through the stories told by the leaders who have used the ACT process architecture to successfully generate large-scale breakthroughs while driving short-term execution and results.

Following are three examples of the dramatic shifts in performance that are possible, even at a very large scale, within a matter of months (not years). The companies profiled implemented and adopted the ACT process into their operating and management models to quickly generate their breakthrough results. In comparison to the typical cycle of failure, these successful efforts looked like the curve in Figure 1.2 where focus and energy were built early and then sustained, leading to compounding growth in results.

Business Success Cycle

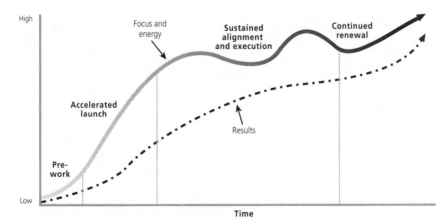

Figure 1.2   Business Success Cycle

- After a planned merger with the #2 competitor in the market was blocked, the new, internally promoted CEO of Office Depot faced a huge challenge—to revitalize the company's sagging retail operations in a single year. The company's leaders resolved to once again make Office Depot the industry's most compelling place to invest, shop, and work. Indeed, these became the major initiatives upon which the company's revitalization was launched. They succeeded. In a year, Office Depot's share price jumped by 156%, customer complaints fell by 50%, and employee retention rates rose by 72%. The company also moved up from the bottom 10% of the Standard & Poor's 500 to number two in terms of percentage increase in shareholder value. "The biggest surprise," then-chief executive Bruce Nelson reflected, "was how quickly people in our company said, 'Count me in. Let's go.' I knew it would happen; I just didn't think we'd get there this fast."[4]

- Southern Company needed to transform its major production function, which consisted of fossil fuel and hydroelectric power plants spread over five geographically dispersed operating companies each with its own union, into a single, new-generation company (or GenCo) called Southern Power. Changing from a staff unit within a regulated public utility into a self-contained, competitive business required Southern Power to learn a whole new way of thinking and acting, all under the white-hot light of national prominence. Parent Southern Company, acclaimed as *Fortune* magazine's "Most Admired" company in the utility industry, was the nation's largest power company at the time, with annual net profit of more than $1 billion. The makeover involved 91 plants and 60,000 union-based employees reporting to five separate subsidiaries, and the feat was accomplished in the middle of a CEO transition. After the repositioning, Southern's costs plunged by more than $100 million in a year, and over $300 million in three years, while accidents were cut by 30% and union grievances fell by 72%. Employee morale soared as well.[5]

- Symantec, once a vibrant Silicon Valley software maker, had stopped growing. Sales were stagnant at about $400 million per year—largely because its past strategy of acquiring companies for growth had run its full course. In fact, all of the best targets in the market had been acquired and future growth would require a different strategy based on internal innovations. With strong leadership and a simple process, Symantec managed to fold its disconnected subsidiaries into one smoothly integrated business focused on customer needs. The new customer focus and highly engaged team revived innovation, inspired new products, and triggered steady sales growth worldwide. In the first year alone, Symantec improved morale, slashing employee turnover by 41%. Meanwhile, Symantec's stock price rose by 53%, its revenue jumped by 24%, and its profitability soared by 290%.

The key differences in these successful efforts compared to the typical failed efforts can be seen by comparing the success versus failure cycles in Figure 1.3. The keys are generating a tight focus and an accelerated, high engagement launch up front, then maintaining alignment and follow through for the remainder of the performance year. Finally, it comes down to consistency in driving the process on an annual basis to continually stretch performance.

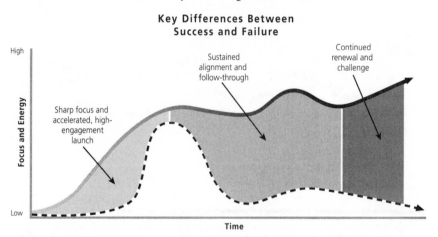

Figure 1.3   Difference between success and failure

Make Transformation a Simple Routine

While running your organization at full speed and in the heat of the most defining moments in your leadership, you will never remember the full checklist of all the little signs and subtleties. What separates those who know what to do from those who actually get it done? Those who succeed follow a proven process and architecture to make sure things don't get overlooked. It is like a preshot routine in golf, lining up on the free-throw line in basketball, preparing to serve in tennis, or going over a preflight checklist on an airplane. Follow a proven routine, get everything set up correctly, get aligned properly, and *then* let it rip.

Unfortunately, there is not one "silver bullet" that will unlock success. There are a lot of moving parts. However, there is a surprisingly simple architecture and process that you can put in place to bring all of the critical principles into play. As a guide through the rest of the book, the Business Success Cycle curve shown in Figure 1.4 shows the primary areas that make the biggest difference in reaching breakthrough results and are covered in detail in each chapter. This icon will appear at the beginning of each chapter as a reminder of where we are in the cycle at each point.

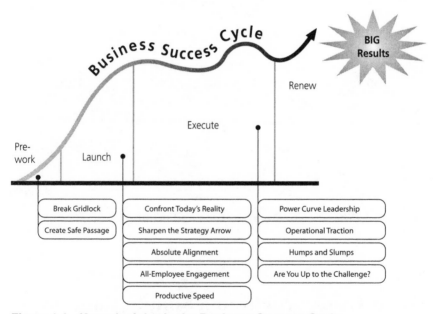

Figure 1.4   Key principles in the Business Success Cycle

Overall, driving transformations and dramatic shifts in performance is hard work. Old habits die hard and there will be tough decisions to make. But if you are intent on breaking your organization free of mediocrity or sending it in a bold, new direction, you can profit from the insights of leaders who have succeeded in doing just that in the chapters that follow. If you put the right process in place, it will handle 90% of all of the lessons, keys to success, and subtle warning flags to which you need to pay attention. Then, you can spend your time thinking strategically, working closely with your leadership team, and communicating clearly with all your employees—the key areas where you provide the most value.

Endnotes

[1] The Conference Board, Annual Conference Board report, "CEO Challenge 2007: Top 10 Challenges," 2007.

[2] FranklinCovey, xQ Report, based on Harris Interactive database, December 2003.

[3] This innovative Harvard Business School executive program, called "Managing Organizational Effectiveness," was chaired by Robert H. Miles during the early 1980s. The lessons learned formed the foundation of the Accelerated Corporate Transformation (ACT) methodology that Miles and Michael Kanazawa have continued to refine for today's practice.

[4] Bruce Nelson, "Anatomy of a Turnaround: How Bruce Nelson Revived Office Depot," *FastTrack Magazine* Summer (2002): 42-47.

[5] Robert H. Miles, "Type I Transformation: Repositioning America's Most Admired Utility," in *Leading Corporate Transformation: A Blueprint for Business Renewal* (San Francisco: Jossey-Bass, 1997), 83–126.

2

Breaking Through Gridlock

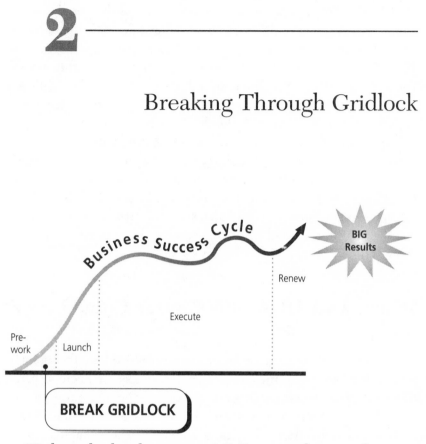

"Task overload and corporate A.D.D. are epidemics in business today."

Gridlock! The Task Overload Epidemic

So much needless complexity has been created in today's businesses that much of what people are assigned to do could be left undone without damage to the bottom line. Organizations are running on extreme task overload. And, in reality, only a critical few initiatives have the potential for making a big difference.

Clearly, this does not mean that a majority of the people have to go or that operating budgets can be cut down to a fraction of today's levels. Because, in reality (and this isn't a well-kept secret), a majority of items on everyone's to-do lists never gets fully attended to anyway. You end up with each person accomplishing a smattering of different tactics that aren't necessarily aligned to others and produce little impact. People and resources should be more focused on the highest impact areas only. Those areas of focus that can contribute the earliest results and the most to the shift in strategic direction must receive an immediate, unfairly generous share of the available resources. Employees need to keep the other routine things that ought to simply get done under "steady strain," that's a given. It's no wonder that so many employees are not clear that their daily work really can contribute significantly to the company's goals.

Where Did All of This Clutter Come From?

In the good name of tuning up core processes and driving efficiency, businesses everywhere have been over-engineered to the point of absurdity. Form has overtaken function. Processes have been pushed to the limits of sanity as people scorecard everything that moves, launch multiple process-change initiatives on every business function simultaneously, and demand that everything is a priority where "failure is not an option!" We are caught in the clutches of organizational attention deficit disorder, with leaders steering rapidly from ditch to ditch, darting off at the next big idea that comes along. This behavior actually kills any momentum the company would have built by staying the course, learning from doing and working out the fundamentals.

Gridlock started simply, innocuously. First, the finance department wanted to put new expense management tools and processes in place to better control overhead costs and comply with regulations. That made sense. Then, human resources launched a new employee-performance system so the organization could better identify the top contributors and work to retain and develop them. Marketing initiated a campaign to help boost sales of newly launched products. Manufacturing launched a Six Sigma program that eventually touched marketing, sales, and finance. And the top executive team embarked on a culture-change effort to boost morale. Ironically, the root cause for low morale was likely that too many initiatives were overloading the system and the people. Individually, all of these projects make sense and taken individually are not necessarily bad or excessive. But when launched simultaneously and not in alignment to and prioritized based on a common strategy, the multiple layers of activity can easily overwhelm an organization, creating gridlock.

The New Definition of Big Box Retail

The vice president of field operations at one major "big box" retailer had an organization that was absolutely buried under the crush of administrative work and tactical rollouts. The company was working to standardize and improve customer experiences across the entire chain of stores. It had focused on some key initiatives at the top, but hadn't fully aligned all of the various programs across functional groups. Each department in the corporate headquarters had a backlog of what they believed to be critically important programs to be rolled out to the field. There were new compensation plans from HR, special sales incentive programs from merchandising, customer service guidelines from marketing, strategy communications and product training from vendors, just to name a few. The functional leaders looking to roll out their programs were quite frustrated with the lack of execution in the field on their programs.

One morning as the senior executive team gathered at headquarters, the field operations VP brought in a huge box of papers and put it on the conference table. People were surprised and curious about the box. Then, he went on to explain that the box contained printouts and copies of every communication from headquarters that had been sent to the field to be rolled out—during just one month! It was immediately clear that there was no way that field managers could read through all of the material, much less execute all of the actions requested in each e-mail, memo, newsletter, "meeting-in-a-box," employee communication, and so forth. Under this condition of complete overload, the field managers had no choice but to selectively implement programs based on their own judgment. The result was a lack of full execution of any of the programs in any given geography and very uneven customer experiences across stores—the very thing the programs were intended to "fix."

In another company, a field operations manager explained the unwritten "two-drawer" method for keeping up with all of the corporate initiatives. A widespread survival technique that had been adopted by field managers, the method involved taking all new memos about corporate initiatives and putting them in a desk drawer. If anyone called or followed up on a particular memo, it was pulled out of the drawer, considered a "real" priority, and tagged for some sort of action. At the end of the month, if nobody called on the rest of the memos, the stack of memos was moved to a second drawer. After two months, if nobody called to follow up about any of those memos in the second drawer, it was okay to throw those memos away. At the end of each month, the rolling two-month file ultimately got thrown away.

The field operations manager swore that after years of following the two-drawer method, only once or twice per month would there be any follow-up from above whatsoever! Instead of spending his day reading and sorting through corporate memos, the manager was able to spend most of his time working in the field, which he thought was more important. Today, this method might be accomplished by "sidelining" e-mails in folders or completely deleting old e-mails that have never been fully read because nothing has come of them. Regardless of the method or technology, the message is still clear. Executives are trying to stuff too much down the organizational pipeline.

These are some of the more vivid realities and examples of task-overload gridlock. They show how managers who wanted to do a good job down in the organization attempted to keep the gridlock beast at bay.

The need to focus—for simplicity—is a tough idea to get across to a team of leaders, each of who is trying to drive his or her own major programs. The simple fact remains: You can launch as many initiatives as you want, but the capacity to execute will become a choke point in reaching results if the programs are not sorted, weeded, prioritized, and sequenced. You'll just be adding more material to the "second drawer" that will get ignored and then tossed out or deleted.

Task Overload Undermines Accountability

Why is this overload and complexity so detrimental to a business? One reason is that it allows people at every level to ignore reality and avoid taking full responsibility for their actions. Too much complexity obscures an organization's strategy and makes it impossible to see what's working and what (or who) isn't.

If there is no clear focus on what is important and too much is happening at once, people who don't deliver results in one area simply point to the other areas where they have gotten the job done. However, the things they accomplished might have been the lowest priorities for the company. Or, worse yet, they rapidly work to "check the box" beside each of their many assigned tasks so at least they can say they did something about everything with which they were charged, focusing on task accomplishment rather than true business impact.

The havoc that an overly complex system can wreak was clearly in evidence at one multibillion-dollar organization. Managers in the company had concocted a many-layered set of incentive programs for their general managers. The managers expected the bonuses and incentives to help focus the team on the most important marketing programs and sales campaigns.

Offering special incentives to juice up the sales team during major campaigns sounds reasonable. Unfortunately, the gremlins of overcomplexity reared their ugly heads, overburdening the company to the point that no one could see that the incentives were counterproductive. Store managers had been receiving special bonuses of all types to prop up the latest sales campaign. The more spectacular the bonus a product manager could create, the more attention his or her initiative would get in the field. At one point, there were even fancy cars as prizes—pretty spectacular. The problem was that these spiffs, bonuses, and campaigns led to strong-arm sales approaches for specific products and stories about salespeople avoiding sales if customers wouldn't buy the proper "bundle" that would qualify for these special sales campaigns. Store managers were receiving hefty bonuses and free trips for their success in selling certain programs while the company was losing both money and customers. Essentially, the complexity of all these incentive programs had been masking simple bookkeeping facts and distorting accountability, thus blocking the very goals the programs had been designed to reach.

One Company—Not Many

Another dimension of the gridlock challenge is that customers build loyalty with companies based on very specific attributes—Volvo for safety, Nordstrom for customer service, Nike for sports performance, Honda for reliable motors. Does that mean that Volvo doesn't have any performance engineering or pay any attention to ergonomics for comfort? Of course not. But when Volvo advertises, they emphasize safety. When they make trade-offs and tough decisions on manufacturing costs and designs, they bias decisions toward the value of safety. Opportunistic companies, in contrast, have no central strategic and market focus and end up taking a stand on everything and, therefore, nothing. The unfocused companies will also launch best-practices efforts on every part of the business, regardless of whether the area is a differentiator in the eyes of customers. This creates more task overload and is overkill in some areas. In a well-focused company, in contrast, you should drive to set (not meet) the standards for best practices in the areas that are the highest value points for your customers—ones that create lasting customer relationships.

Often, companies that grow through acquisitions have a tough time gaining a single market focus. Either a company, over time, builds a unique standing in the eyes of customers, or it is not successful. The challenge in acquisitions is in knowing how to leverage "the best of the best" from each acquired entity to create a new "one company" perspective. As an engineering manager in an acquired division put it, "We are just a bunch of separate companies all with the same business card." His company was in gridlock over R&D funding decisions. Each business fought for its own funding with many overlapping business plans in the marketplace, which you would expect because these were supposed to be complementary businesses. The negotiated outcomes of the R&D budgeting process had resulted in subpar funding for everything, including the portfolios that should have received a "doubling down" of bets. The market's perspective? Jack of all trades, master of none. A lack of focus is a sure way to maintain a mediocre position in the market.

Busting Through Gridlock: Getting Started

Imagine you are leaving a major stadium from a sporting event. When traffic comes to a halt in gridlock, is it because all of the drivers have stopped wanting to move ahead? Of course not. In fact, the more the gridlock sets in, the more frustrated people get and the more they try to push and inch forward—usually at the expense of blocking the progress of others. Because each person has his or her own intentions, eventually too many people with their own agendas meet up at the same intersections. What is needed is some prioritization of traffic flows, the sequencing of longer runs of traffic in specific directions, and a traffic cop to call out the directions clearly. It is the same at a gridlocked organization.

The only way to cure the gridlocked organization and generate the required focus to execute is to be willing to start at the top, set a clear direction, set priorities, and let people's underlying motivations and innovations begin to emerge and build momentum. It takes a leader seeing the pattern of gridlock and stepping up to prioritize efforts and set clear direction to get started.

As put by Len Rodman, chairman and CEO of Black & Veatch, "When I think about what worked in those days at the start of the ACT process, it was the ability to look at a few items and put our energy there. When things are difficult and change needs to happen, it seems that there is a plethora of things to work on—there is always something else that comes up. But we found, by focusing on a very few things everybody could work on, that channeled the mass of the organization in the right direction."[1]

A common fear of many leaders is that if they admit that the organization is doing too much, they will lose their ability to motivate the team to do more. Managers might believe such an admission will build in an excuse for people at all levels to not work harder and to not deliver results. In response, these leaders try to rally the team to step up, thereby adding to the overload rather than prioritizing major initiatives. This just overwhelms an already overtaxed system. And, when the leader keeps raising the bar relentlessly, and calling for more and more effort, it becomes political suicide for any team member to throw up the white flag and call out the issue of task overload. Instead, everyone just hunkers down further in their fox holes, checking the boxes on their tasks as fast as they can.

Focus is not about doing less work overall, but rather doing more on fewer things. You need not give up on the call to grow the organization rapidly or for people to work hard. You just have to be willing to shoulder the risks of clearly articulating a tight focus on what will and won't be done. You need to lead the way to make the tough choices that mean less hedging of bets, and then trust the team to execute with more impact and accountability because they are now called on to drive further against fewer goals. Bill Barnes, a private equity investor at one of the world's largest Swiss banks and former executive at a $30 billion computer manufacturer, describes focus well. He points out that, "Focus comes from clearly understanding the unique elements of your business model and market strengths that are the drivers of your success. And there are times when you can't simultaneously do two things well and will need to focus on your core priorities." Although, he also points out, "You can't get so narrowly focused that you lose sight of how the business environment is changing around you so you'll need to continually reassess your focus."[2]

One of the most damaging business catch phrases in recent history has been "doing more with less." This has become an excuse to reduce resource levels without having the guts to narrow the focus. When there is a need to focus or consolidate resources, you should really say that we are going to be "doing more *on* less"—the critical few activities that will provide the greatest impact.

The Leader's Challenge: Less Is More

The case of a dramatic two-step transformation in the software industry illustrates the point. A new CEO joined a software company in Silicon Valley that had made it to over several hundred million dollars in revenues. He was tasked with looking for how to accelerate growth beyond the billion-dollar mark.

At the point the new CEO was about to step in, the company had already been through one major transformation. The prior CEO had taken a start-up and built it up through a series of acquisitions that resulted in creating a software company that had been able to grow beyond the typically elusive $100 million mark in total revenues for independent software vendors. The acquisition strategy had resulted in the creation of eight relatively independent product units (each looking very much like a pre-acquisition company) that were fragmented in direction. The gridlock—caused by mismatched agendas and priorities across the different independent businesses—was stalling growth. The CEO called for a focusing of the independent units into just three customer-focused business units. Successful execution of this consolidation strategy had resulted in the restoration of double-digit revenue growth and innovations in the core business had begun to move ahead again. But the next hurdle was now approaching—the leap from the few hundred million dollar level to the $1 billion revenue mark.

A mandate was initiated to figure out how to put the company on a path to grow above $1 billion in sales. The company had been built on the strategic advantage of having very far-reaching retail sales channels for desktop software. So, many different types of software products had been acquired and then ramped up through the sales channels. The strategy had worked extremely well, but it was reaching its growth limits. There were essentially no identifiable acquisition targets that had the potential to add enough revenue to make a difference. All of the best ones had already been rolled up into the company. The combined results of each of the business unit's incremental growth within their silos were not adding up to the required growth either. Each business was slightly suboptimized because of limited synergies between the businesses, spreading development and marketing resources thin; there was no clear focus.

The new CEO looked at the challenge he was facing in funding the growth of the company's three consolidated businesses. He had come from a multibillion dollar global technology company and had a very different frame of reference about scaling a business. He realized quickly that one of the business units was focused on a niche market of software tools that would not significantly help the company reach its lofty $1 billion growth target. The business was interesting and growing fast, but ultimately it would always be a small distraction at best.

A second business unit was focused on software for helping small businesses and sales departments manage their contacts better and stay connected to the home office when out on the road. It had a strong brand in the market and was contributing a significant portion of the company's revenue. However, the cost of supporting the contact management application was high and it required a complex sales channel as well. The market was significant in size, but it was limited to small businesses and department-level solutions for sales organizations. The higher-end solutions in the same markets were taken by much larger sales force automation and customer relationship management software vendors, which made an "up-market" move in this business very difficult.

The third business unit was focused on security and system utilities solutions. It had the strongest brand position in the market and strong positioning to move up-market from desktop software into full-enterprise corporate solutions. And the market for computer security solutions was heating up fast as adoption of the Internet was opening new threats to corporate networks.

The new CEO realized that his people and financial resources were being spread too thinly across the three units and needed to be focused on the right market area to create a dominant position that would take the company beyond the $1 billion mark. He recognized that customers had become confused about what the company had become. Was it a software development tools vendor, a boxed retail software player, or an enterprise software solutions company? With a charge from the board of directors to grow revenues, many leaders would not make the choice to exit businesses with major revenue streams attached to them, thus lowering the baseline. However, that is just what the new CEO did.

After selling the software tools and contact management applications businesses, the company had capital to invest. They doubled up their investments in the security business, made some critical acquisitions to gain a larger footprint in serving customer needs in the enterprise security space, and put themselves on a trajectory that took them to over $1 billion in revenues just three years later.

Without the leader's willingness to risk selling off some major revenue streams, the company would not have been able to double its bets on the best market opportunity and eventually grow revenues many times larger than those that were sold off. Although such a bold refocusing was played out at the CEO's level in this example, it resonates just as well at all management levels where leaders have to make tough focusing choices that allow their teams to load up existing resources on the most high-impact areas. No matter what level such bold focusing decisions are made, you, as the leader, must be the one to initiate the challenge for focus.

When you, as a leader, drive for focus, you will set off a whole set of dynamics in the organization that needs to be managed. People will automatically believe that budget and job cuts are coming and shift into battle positions. Each one will immediately start figuring out how to make sure that his or her area stays intact. The notion that your team is full of "team players" can erode quickly if the challenge to focus is not orchestrated properly. More is to come on how to engage your team in this process once you decide to take on this challenge of focus.

Fighting Fires Versus Fire Prevention

A high-flying start-up had gone public, the stock soared from about $6 to $55, and everyone was happy. Then, just as the euphoria was wearing off, a major customer was lost to a competitor, growth stopped, and the stock was back down to $5. A new CEO was brought in to turn things around, quickly. In reflection on the situation, he describes what is true with a lot of start-up companies that go public or become large. The organization starts out functionally organized and, generally, the founders each have strength in certain functional areas. Somebody is strong in finance, somebody's strong in technology, somebody's strong in operations, so there are no decisions to be made at the lower levels—there's no structure at any levels below the top executives. And that was the case at his company. In the founder team, there had been a strong technologist, a strong financial expert, and a strong operator. As the company had grown from $10 to $20 to $30 to $40 to $100 million, there was no organization infrastructure in place, there were no management systems in place, and there were no processes in place.

Everything was event-driven as opposed to process-driven. You could see that as the company had grown beyond the capability for the three founders to make all of the decisions, the company became gridlocked. Especially when the operating founder retired, the two other founders were trying to do the whole job and things were falling apart. This event-driven hub-and-spoke style of management can seem nimble and fast moving when a company is very small. However, as soon as the scale outgrows the few leaders in the "hub," overload sets in. The entire system goes into gridlock, where everyone is stuck waiting for the leaders to make decisions.

The result of the lack of process orientation drove a lack of metrics. Without the ability to anticipate the business, the company always had a fire drill and that had become one of the strengths in the company. It had a very good firefighting engine. The team couldn't prevent fires, and so there were many of them, but they sure were good firefighters. As the CEO saw it, if you could fix other things and maintain the agility and ability to respond to urgent things, then you would have something very good. Firefighting in crisis mode is something many companies have become used to in daily life. Fire prevention is about process, planning, measuring, and following through for improvements. The first moves the CEO made to stabilize the company's free fall were to expand the expectations for leadership and decision making in the VP team and then engage the company in a structured and highly accelerated transformation process. With these in place, they were able to, as the CEO put it, "get in front of the firefighting and start working on fire prevention"—otherwise, they never would have been able to catch up from tactical overload and gridlock to start work on repositioning the company for success.

Tips for Breaking Through Gridlock

- The antidote to organization gridlock is focus. Focus your organization by setting clear direction and priorities starting at the top and through all levels.

- Do more *on* less. Focus everyone on just the critical few things that can contribute the most to turning your big ideas into big results.

- Starting with your senior team, shift from fire fighting to fire prevention mode.

Endnotes

[1] Based on an interview conducted by Robert H. Miles on December 13, 2007, with Len Rodman, chairman, CEO, and president of Black & Veatch, a global engineering services firm.

[2] Based on an interview conducted on October 26, 2007 with William Barnes, VP of private equity investments at one of the largest Swiss banks, who formerly developed the Asia market for a $30 billion computer manufacturing company.

3

Creating Safe Passage

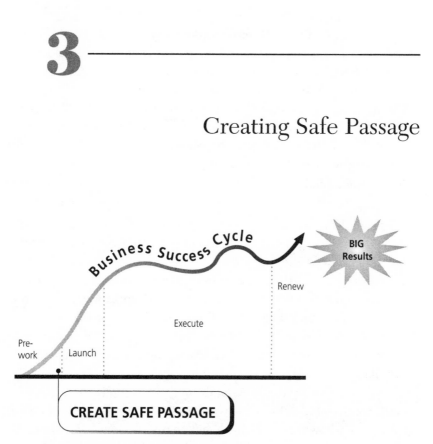

"Lighting a 'burning platform' to initiate change only causes panic if a clear path for safe passage has not been created."

Safe Passage—A Clear Transformation Process

The first key to effectively launching tight execution of a strategy is to make sure that everyone understands the path that will be followed and how and where they fit in. It is fun to say that "we need a burning platform" to get people started moving. It sounds aggressive and decisive. You will get people moving, but in a panic and survival mode. That is not the kind of energy you need to create to be successful.

Before "lighting the fire," you need to make sure that there is a clear and *safe passage* from the state of things today to the new state or strategic direction. Safe passage does not mean that 100% of the people will keep their jobs or that all budgets will remain intact. Everyone knows and understands the realities of making tough trade-offs to focus a business. So, above all, be honest if there are these types of tough decisions that will need to be made. All that is expected by your team is that you lay out a very clear process architecture that shows a few critical pieces: Who will make decisions, when and how people will have input into the decisions, when you will announce final answers, and what will happen as these decisions are made.

To establish safe passage as a leader, you need to do a few things right up front. These are covered in more depth throughout the book, but as a preview of the full concept, here are the essentials. First, lay out a clear roadmap that identifies the major steps and deliverables, and shows how people at all levels in the organization will become involved and engaged in the transformation launch and journey. Second, get the leadership team to agree on a simple set of ground rules to govern how they work together, discuss new ideas, engage in critical thinking, and make decisions. Third, have an objective third party find out what's really on individuals' minds. Commission a round of strictly confidential interviews with each of your key leaders about what's working, what's not, and what thoughts they have about the next phase in the company. Guarantee anonymity, but assemble all of the findings in an unattributed, verbatim fashion to use as a mirror in confronting reality. Fourth, gather fact-based insights from inside and outside the organization to test all the new ideas. And make sure you get insights from non-customers as well as your regular customers. Fifth, convene a well-designed working session in which you and your team can rigorously work your way through all of the new information to develop and refine the vision and supporting business model of the future. Sixth, road test everything down below in the organization before drawing conclusions and finalizing your transformation plan.

There is one qualifier to the term "safe passage" from the perspective of motivating a whole organization to drive the effort. It is not enough to simply lay out your process in advance. Your process needs to be specifically designed for speed and high engagement to be received well and to work.

Many processes don't have both the speed and high-engagement elements covered. The typical belief is that to get speed, you can't spend time on communications and dialogue. While under the gun by a board or boss to quickly focus an organization on a new strategic path, it can seem too messy and time consuming to get too many people involved. Strategy is not done by consensus, that's true, but it can be done quickly with high engagement. As is typically the case with shortcuts, things actually end up taking longer because of repeated revisits of past decisions, continued questioning, lack of alignment, and rework. With the right process for engagement up front, execution actually goes faster and farther in the end.

A story of a new leader who had been placed in such a position comes to mind. Like many new leaders, he was charged with rapidly turning around the performance of his organization. As a first pass, he and one other executive gathered for a few days with an external consultant to the business and hammered out the new strategy for the company. It was bold, well worded, and to the point. He gathered his VP team to share the document and to get some feedback from them before rolling it out to the entire company.

As he finished reading out the new strategy, the room was absolutely silent. This was uncharacteristic for the hard-driving and outspoken team of executives. He said later that it was one of the worst meetings he recalled being in. He tugged at each of the VPs to obtain a few slight changes to some words, but clearly nobody had any energy or excitement. In fact, they seemed completely disinterested. The team left quietly when the meeting was over. This was the impact of trying to change the direction of the company without the engagement of the top leadership team. It certainly was fast to gather just three people to hammer out the document, but the VP team had no ownership, didn't believe that the right things were considered, and had no accountability for making it better. They were being asked to "buy-in" to something that they should have been included in building up front.

From there, the leader moved quickly to launch the new strategy through various corporate events and communications, but the peoples' reception was similar at all levels. Following several months of valuable but lackluster execution time, the executive team decided to double-back to engage the organization in the strategy development process. Not surprisingly, the result was the complete opposite. The engagement effort reenergized the executive team, who began talking with each other about the business, silos began to disappear, and enthusiasm for the future rebounded radically. As one of the executives put it, "People went from feeling like defeatists back into thinking we could win."

Throughout the rest of the book, you'll see how a strategy execution process, like the Accelerated Corporate Transformation (ACT) process, can be deployed to run fast, drive decisive action through leaders at all levels, productively engage the full organization, and achieve breakthrough results—quickly. The only way to create the enormously productive feeling of safe passage is to kick off your transformation or strategy execution effort by showing the organization a well-thought-out roadmap that is simple, makes sense, is market focused, reveals where and how people at all levels will be truly engaged, and doesn't sugarcoat the seriousness of decisions to be made. If you light the burning platform before putting such an architecture in place, you'll just send people running to the exits.

The ACT Process Basics: Powerfully Simple

The ACT process itself does not look too exciting or different on the surface. Many people sharing advice and methodologies have maps that will look almost identical to the untrained eye. However, there are big differences when you go to use them—just as two pieces of music can look very similar on paper, yet one creates beauty when played and the other creates dissonant noise. On the surface, both scores will have notes, bars (the lines where the notes sit), and different markings that are the basics of music. But if the notes aren't in the correct sequence and timing and played in the correct key and note combinations, it will just produce noise. One of the pieces of music in Figure 3.1 is the first part of Mozart's *Eine Kleine Nachtmusik* (A Little Night Music), a beautiful song. The other is noise, given a few subtle changes and errors. Can you tell which is which? Clearly, some musicians and experts will immediately know, but it is tough to tell on the surface. If we played them both through for you, you'd immediately know for sure. The second one sounds really awful.

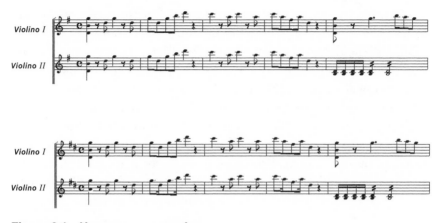

Figure 3.1   Harmony or cacophony

Consider the ACT process a symphony that has continuously been played through, refined, improved, and boiled down to the essentials over years of active work and use. Each time a new leader uses it, he or she puts another crank on streamlining the process—and that's been going on for 25 years. So, the fact that it is simple—and not some Rube Goldberg type of process with a million extra moving parts with fancy names—is intentional and took hard work. Each part has been simplified, sequenced correctly, and plays off the other parts in an intentional way that just flat out works.

The basic process starts with a Launch Phase, compressed into a few months that goes from clarifying the strategy and identifying "Quick Start" initiatives to launch immediately, to creating focus and alignment, to engaging the full organization through a cascade process aimed at creating individual commitments to action throughout the organization.

The launch is followed by a longer Execution Phase that puts in place regular performance checkpoints to hold accountabilities, share best practices across silos, and make course adjustments in a timely way when needed.

Finally, there is a relaunching of the identical process to stretch the organization further for the next performance year, called the Renew Phase. This phase is a more streamlined version of the launch and is all about stretching beyond the prior year's limits.

The top of Figure 3.2 shows a graphic of the full process; the bottom of the figure shows how the organizational energy and focus is built and held high over time. Notice that the process steps are designed and sequenced specifically to maintain the business focus and energy at the correct level to drive results over the course of the first full performance cycle, usually one year. When done correctly, the process creates a building of momentum and acceleration of business performance and culture change as it is integrated into the business operations and management process. In a nutshell, that's the solution. No need to dwell on the process map and architecture now. Each piece will be described in detail throughout the book.

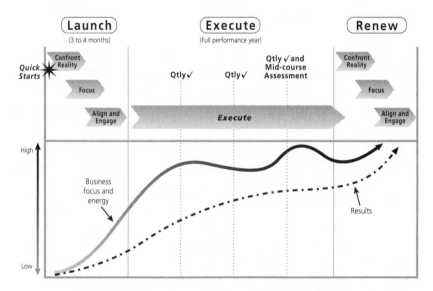

Figure 3.2   Accelerated Corporate Transformation (ACT) process map

This Is Not a New Religion, Just a Better Way of Managing the Business

We do have a word of caution on launching this type of process. There is no need to overhype things, set up revival tent meetings, or preach that the process is a "new religion." It has to be treated as a commonsense way of running the business on a daily basis. Javed Patel, who has served as a senior VP and CEO of public and private companies, explains this important point, "So many other times we would launch programs that were extraneous to our regular jobs. And those other programs were focused just on the executive team. We would come back from one of those off-sites and everyone on the team would be looking at us suspiciously and questioningly, like 'OK, just tell me what you want me to do *now*.'"[1] With an effective transformation process, like ACT, it is not a one-time program, it simply becomes the way the business is managed. Javed continues, "The process just became our normal management practice as a part of daily life from setting strategy to setting individual personal business commitments and following through on performance."

In the ACT process map in Figure 3.2, you see the steps of Confront Reality, Focus, Align and Engage, and Execute in the streamlined process architecture. These items are essential design elements, which characterize the significant difference between cookie-cutter, fixed processes that either serve as an overlay to the existing business or seek to change everything being done already just to fit the new process. The right approach to process architecture is to leverage all of the best existing elements of the management process that are currently working well, make adjustments for any missing elements, adjust the sequence of steps for impact, and then streamline the full process for speed, simplicity, and high engagement. Fixed cookie-cutter processes often require changing too much at once (even things that were working) and are rightly rejected by organizations in most cases.

These ACT design elements make up a proven framework that you can use to test the integrity of the management process you already have in place and to guide the improvements that will generate breakthrough results. Gordon Eubanks, a seasoned CEO of technology start-ups and large companies, points out the importance of a process. "Our transformation process was all about taking charge of our future. The process was an opportunity to look at the business as a whole and ask really tough questions. Instead of defending the status quo, it was more about understanding where the world was going. This type of effort has to be a formal process—otherwise, you won't make the time to address it or the conditions for people to be open-minded and self-critical, which are necessary components."[2] As you will see throughout the book, each application of the framework must be tailored to fit each situation and business challenge, thereby creating safe passage to reach breakthrough results.

Tips for Creating Safe Passage

- Follow a simple, streamlined process that creates "safe passage" for the full team (easy to understand, clear rules of engagement, and internally led by leaders at all levels).

- Don't light your "burning platform" until you have a clear process in place that shows how and when people will be engaged and decisions will be made.

- Leverage a proven process and customize it for your situation.

- Treat your process as simply how business will be done, not as a new "religion."

Endnotes

[1] Based on an interview conducted by Michael Kanazawa on May 11, 2007 with Javed Patel, CEO of a technology company and prior VP of sales and marketing at a publicly traded microchip company. Reprinted by permission.

[2] Based on an interview conducted by Michael Kanazawa on June 1, 2007 with Gordon Eubanks, prior CEO of a market-leading global software company and successful software start-ups. Reprinted by permission.

4

Confronting Today's Reality

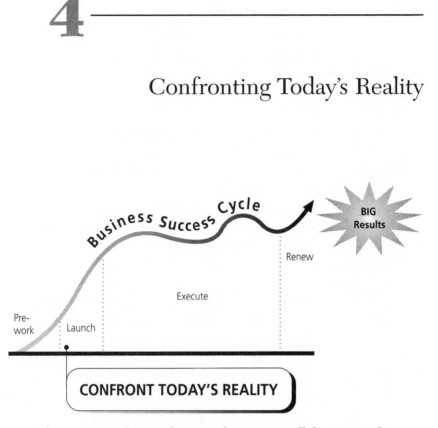

Business Success Cycle

BIG Results

Renew

Execute

Pre-work

Launch

CONFRONT TODAY'S REALITY

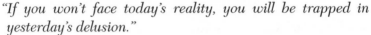

"If you won't face today's reality, you will be trapped in yesterday's delusion."

Denial is the opium of losers. Nothing guarantees fatal errors faster than seeing only what you want to see. Winning is all about realism, accepting truth, and acting on it quickly and more effectively than your competitors. Seeing things from the market or customer perspective, from the outside-in, that's what matters.

History is littered with the defeats of deniers, ranging from Custer at Little Bighorn, to the ideologues of the late Soviet Union, to the leaders of the old network companies who thought they could keep people from using the "wild and unstable" Internet. The challenge here is to determine what it takes to leap from perilous denial to positive realism. At the heart of the matter is your realization that the flip side of denial is courage.

The reality the deniers need to confront is typically right under their noses—in plain sight yet invisible, or at least dismissible, to them. Denial takes many forms; one situation illustrates it well. A multibillion dollar company had just assigned a new CEO and COO. They were looking to reverse a five-year slide in sales.

Two weeks into the assignment to develop the process architecture for helping a company speed its transformation and strategy execution process, a small work team had been given an office on the executive floor to conduct their work. The office had all the appearances of having been hastily vacated. There were still files in the drawers and a large map on the wall, with pins placed on once-promised but long misbegotten conquests. While cleaning out the files, the team noticed a document right on the top of a stack in one of the drawers—perhaps the person had been using the "two-drawer" method before he or she left. Titled "Strategic Options," the file was authored by one of the world's leading strategy consulting firms. It was dated two years prior to the team's arrival and although aspects of the game had changed, it was still worth a look as part of the up-front discovery process.

Flipping past the first few pages, the team stopped at a slide titled Executive Summary Recommendations. There in front of them, with some items circled in red, were all in plain view the straight-up, harsh realities that needed to be addressed currently—only the report had been written and submitted to the previous CEO two years earlier.

The current executive leaders welcomed the team with hopeful comments about the ability to tee up the "real issues" that for so long had been taboo. The prior CEO clearly had access to the report and presumably had reviewed its recommendations. He just hadn't acted on any of them. In contrast, the new CEO and COO were very motivated to confront the realities surrounding the business they had inherited and were quick to put these data on the agenda for executive discussion. This recurrent story of strategies stored as binders on shelves or files in drawers is the all too common and a clear reminder that all of the issues are typically right there in plain sight, but are simply not confronted and addressed.

The Emperor's Ugly Clothes

It is critical for leaders to set a tone that allows the team to confront reality. You would be amazed at how many people are trapped in the "Emperor Has No Clothes" syndrome. Even at the executive levels, certain taboo topics become routinely avoided. There is often a lot of pent-up energy to let out the truth. Surprisingly, it often takes just a bit of structured dialogue (the creation of a safe place to speak openly) and the guidance from the leader for a team to begin driving hard at the real roadblocks to progress. It is a fool's game to try to suppress the real issues. Everyone knows the problems exist whether they speak openly about them or not. People whisper in the halls or joke over drinks after work about these issues. But, until safe passage is provided, most people will not risk mentioning anything about them in front of the boss. If it is not clear how the issues will be accepted or if anything will be done about them, there is only risk for speaking up with no clear benefit.

Sometimes, more than simple dialogue and executive encouragement is needed to suspend taboo status. In addition, it often takes an additional little shock to the system to unlock the conversation, which can come from any level of management. At the worst-performing division of Rockwell International, the team had spent a day and a half denying that they had any problems. Then, one exasperated and brave manager came back from a lunch break and broke the logjam by playing a cassette of the country song, "Pissin' in the Wind." His colleagues immediately realized that what they had been doing all morning amounted to about the same thing.[1] This is not necessarily a best-practice recommendation for everyone, but sometimes one brave soul needs to step up and call the team out onto the ice. Sometimes that will need to be you as a team member and sometimes as the leader.

Encouraging conversations that are critical of the company and leadership to be handled out in the open allows problems to be addressed sooner and new ideas to surface. To suppress these conversations does not make the issues go away; it just drives people into a quiet mode of resentment, cynicism, or just ambivalence. None of those behaviors are useful when looking to constructively confront reality. The ability for leaders to take constructive criticism is the starting point and that means letting your team tell you, the Emperor, that your clothes are ugly at least.

Dialogue Versus Discussion

Over two thousand years ago, Plato got it right when he observed that truth emerges only through dialogue. Socrates soon followed with a general appeal for more time spent through discourse or conversation to get to the bottom of human affairs.

There can be no real understanding, commitment, and, ultimately, engagement in the absence of dialogue. That's why structured dialogue needs to be a core element in leading a transformation or gaining commitment to execute a strategy.

There is a critical distinction in conversations that most of us are typically unconscious of on a daily basis. It is the difference between dialogue and discussion. They are quite different modes of having a conversation. At the core, the purpose of having a dialogue is to search for deeper meaning and understanding. The essence of discussion is to net out differing opinions to get to a final answer. Both are necessary at different times and situations.

The Latin roots of the word *discussion* come from the same place as the words *percussion* or *concussion* and have to do with opposing views being batted back and forth.[2] You know you are in the mode of discussion when, in the midst of a full meeting, two people begin to lock into a rapid back-and-forth with a lot of bystanders to their banter. Discussion is occurring when people are jockeying for airtime, working to have the winning idea, advocating positions, or arguing key points and assumptions. If someone else is speaking and you are trying to break in by saying, "yes, but…, right, but just think about, …let me make a point…", then you are definitely in discussion mode. Or even if you are not speaking up but your mind is conjuring up a rebuttal while the other person is still talking, you're in discussion mode.

Typically, as businesspeople, we will naturally be in discussion mode most of the time. We have all been trained well to debate points, make convincing arguments, and influence others when a decision is due. Discussions are useful in getting to an answer or making a final decision. But discussions are not necessarily useful in generating deep understanding of reality or generating innovative ideas for growth—which are essentials at the beginning of a transformation.

Dialogue, on the other hand, is a form of conversation that is more focused on working to get a deeper understanding and discovering new possibilities within the whole situation. It is about asking the right questions, not coming up with the right answers. Dialogue is often marked by short periods of silence while people are thinking through and internally integrating what has been said. There is no fight for airtime. You are more likely to hear questions such as, "Tell me what you mean by that" or "If we went with that, how would that change things?" As you listen to someone talking, if you are working to internalize what they are saying and to integrate it into your thinking and mindset and building on or adding to their ideas, you are likely in a mode of dialogue.

To be clear, dialogue is not about "feel good" or "self-affirming" conversations, but rather is a tool for getting at very tough truths about the business. Bill Hopkins, a partner in a private equity firm describes the value of dialogue well. "The dialogue is where the answers come from. People don't necessarily answer the (due diligence) questions correctly in the beginning, but through the dialogue we collectively arrive at the right answers. Getting to the right allocations and profit models doesn't come from looking at spreadsheets but by really thinking about how the business actually operates. Once the right numbers are brought together and match reality, management easily comes to the same logical conclusions and they make the decisions."[3]

A critical element of truly engaging your team to confront reality is to know how to design a process that creates a dialogue at all management levels, without the need for external facilitation in every meeting. The key to doing this is addressed in more detail in Chapter 7, "Rapidly Engaging the Full Organization." And the answers won't be about, "Let's all hold hands and sing kum-ba-ya," although that's what some of you might be thinking right now. Dialogues, when done correctly, are actually very powerful work sessions that are carefully structured to facilitate quite courageous conversations and generate breakthrough ideas.

Generating Dialogue as a Leader

Sometimes even when leaders feel they have a real knack for open conversations with their team, they still overpower others with their style. For example, one CEO had a style of engaging in debate.

Debate was his way of getting his team to engage on a topic, to explore different perspectives, and to finally come up with a quality decision. He was quite strong at debating and had more experience at a higher level than anybody else in the room, plus he was competitive. So, he could usually win a debate. Those are all positive traits, but when looking to establish an open dialogue with his team, the end result was that few, if any, people were willing to take him on in a debate. Controversial topics were avoided and there was no true confrontation of reality. Even so, the CEO left those forums wishing that more people had joined in and argued more vigorously. He wanted more of their active participation.

After one session in which he effectively parried several concerns about the current business model based on external data sources that might have been a little dated or that had modeled the environment differently than he would, the team became very quiet. The gremlins of denial were rearing their ugly heads again! At a break during the session, he was told about this dynamic and revisited the fact that what he really wanted was for the team to come to grips with the new market realities and to engage in an open dialogue about their implications. All of that was necessary to begin sharpening the strategy, business model, and culture of the company. Upon reflection, he had to agree that even if the methodologies for collecting the market data weren't perfect, the data were saying exactly what he wanted the team to wrestle with. And he began to realize that his debate-oriented efforts to get them to talk more were having the reverse effect.

After the break, the CEO shared his personal perspective on the data. He explained that he had a natural tendency to debate simply for the sake of argument. He pointed out that he actually believed the conclusions in the studies and had recognized for some time that the company's competitive differentiation had faded. "Look, we can debate and drill down on these data for months," he said. "But the reality is that they will still tell us the same things. It's not necessarily what we want to hear, but we know it's true enough that we need to get on with creating new strategies. Given that things have changed a lot since our heydays, what do you think we need to do?"

The CEO's shift from a debate posture to one of personal sharing and invitation immediately opened up the dialogue in the room. The leaders seeking the change now had executive aircover to elaborate on what had been said and point out their views about market shifts that had occurred and where the company needed to change. The fence-sitters now saw that it was time to get off the fence and engage in discussions that were critical to the business. And, we'd be lying if we said that there were no skeptics remaining in the room. But, it was clearly time for them to deal with the truth and move on as well.

As the leader, your answers, especially if provided too early, always get to be the right ones—at least for that brief moment. You will win every debate and can dominate every discussion. But by knowing when to use those powers and when to step back to let your team dialogue to get to the truth, you will unlock a powerful transformation tool that is essential to confronting reality.

Priming the Pump

Often, leadership teams as well as entire companies fall into the rut of accepting too many "givens" about their business and the way they operate. "They don't want to hear the truth, so why beat your head against a wall." "They've got some sort of agenda and, hey, I just work here!" "Sure there are tough problems, but that's why they get paid the big bucks to solve them." You have probably heard or even made comments like these along the way during your career.

But who are people talking about? Who makes up the "they" group? Almost invariably, the "theys" are those in charge and in control of everything. "They" also sometimes represents the whole system of management in an organization. At an extreme, people imagine it is the "head knockers," the power brokers, the oppressors, and, most certainly, a different and separate group from the "real" workers. This kind of thinking sets up a victim mentality among those who rationalize that it is simply their job to toil under illogical and unfair rules that others have set. In any event, this "they" sort of thinking amounts to a mighty roadblock to transforming a company or a major part of it.

These "we" and "they" distinctions, once established at the top, replicate themselves all the way down the hierarchy. This separation causes authentic communications to break down and creates pent-up frustrations as critical issues fail to be addressed. As each layer of managers holds back the realities just a bit from their boss, a profound sense of false reality begins to flourish at the top. Such an executive disconnect with the business reality freezes innovative thinking throughout the enterprise and inhibits transformation often when needed the most.

How can you unlock the truth to start your transformation with a sharp sense of reality?

The best way to make it safe for people to criticize the status quo is to start with a strictly confidential round of interviews. Many leaders will say up front things like, "On my team we all know each other really well; nobody is shy for sure, so we can just open things up with them in the meeting. I'm not sure we'll learn anything new from the interviews." This perspective is very common. Most times, the interviews reveal that overall the leaders are right about many of the key points. However, the interviews create a feeling that the team owns the issues themselves. More important, most leaders are not perfectly well rounded. Each has his or her own "flat sides," which often become visible and discussable for the first time when strictly confidential interview results are reported out by a third party to jump-start the "real" discussion. This approach simultaneously enables leaders to get to know themselves better while making it safer for their employees to enter into more authentic dialogue about real issues. Finally, the outputs of these confidential interviews, which are designed to be brief, yet provide comprehensive views of the full system, often make up the road map for business and leadership change across the entire transformation.

To be effective, the confidential interviews have to be specifically designed to capture the true underlying issues that are holding the organization back and conducted in a way that produces open conversation. There are three areas to cover in the interviews. The first is to understand individual perspectives on the magnitude and scope of changes required to make the stated shift in direction. Second is a candid perspective on what changes need to be made across the total system in all areas of the organization. Lastly, the interview should cover an assessment of the current leadership and any anticipated issues to address.

These structured interviews should be conducted as private, one-on-one conversations, not emailed surveys, and by a neutral party who is not part of the management team or company staff to ensure full candor. When conducted in this manner, these objective, personal interviews constitute the first major step a leader can take in creating the "safe passage" so essential for the steps that follow in planning and implementation.

Canary in a Coal Mine

In addition to the accountability of leaders to openly confront reality up front, there is an equal accountability for the people at all levels to rise to this challenge throughout an organization. Being selected for input into strategic planning and execution is not a passive right to be "in the know." It is an active role that requires risk taking to engage and an accountability to provide constructive input and ideas for solutions.

A year into the transformation at National Semiconductor, a team of middle managers was convened to evaluate how the effort was going. The team was given several weeks to deliberate and tasked to deliver what its members thought were the biggest obstacles at one of the quarterly leadership meetings.[4]

Most of the executives other than the new CEO were refugees from the company's failed old guard. It was the perception among middle managers that many of these company leaders were attempting to solve current corporate challenges the old way, with reactive restructurings, crisis management, and top-down decision making. They believed many senior executives were not making difficult decisions and sticking with them. Therefore, heading the list of major obstacles to transformation was the very thorny issue of lack of trust and credibility of top management.

When their work was completed, the major challenge to the team had just begun: how to constructively confront their bosses with their major findings and then to work with them to find solutions that could be put into action.

The members of the team felt quite responsible for their task. As one explained, "We now have 400 middle managers who are committed to the change process, and we're afraid of losing momentum."

The ground had been softened by having the senior executives get prepared to receive some hard feedback. The night before the middle manager presentation, the executives explored what was at stake with this intervention, how difficult it might be for their subordinates to speak candidly about the problems on their watch, how to avoid defensive responses to tough feedback, and what next steps they should be prepared to take in doing something constructive about what they learned.

The next morning, the tension was broken by Jerry Baker, the leader of the middle manager team, when he began the presentation by saying, "I feel like a canary going in to test the safety of a mine! (Audience laughter.) If my wings are still flapping after a few minutes, the folks with the real messages will come forward to present their parts of the middle manager feedback." He apologized in advance for focusing on the negatives that would follow, but explained that his team felt that the executive leaders in the room had a duty to deal with the issues being brought forth. And he also explained that the team represented all the company's middle managers and they had promised to deliver feedback to them following the meeting.

At center stage during the presentation was the trust and credibility challenge to the old executive guard. The essence of the challenge to senior leaders was that they were being perceived as risk avoiders who were paying only lip service to the transformation effort. Empowered middle managers, who had left the initial high-engagement cascade experience understanding the need for transformation and having committed to specific actions to support it, had been repeatedly frustrated when they approached their bosses with improvement recommendations.

To help with this important reality confrontation, the encounter was tightly structured. The middle management team was coached to leave emotions at the doorstep of the leadership meeting and to buttress the obstacles they identified with hard facts. They were also counseled about avoiding defensive responses and encouraged to ask executives to only pose questions for clarification during the presentation. Later, they would work on their own to come up with initial responses to the main obstacles.

After the session closed, middle managers were invited to stay overnight while senior executives worked into the evening to develop a response to each obstacle. They prefaced their report out on the key obstacles to middle managers the next morning with a proclamation they had crafted the night before. It read as follows:

> *"The members of this group strongly condemn and disown any action or threat made toward any employee for constructively speaking their mind. Should this have occurred, or occur in the future, we strongly urge that individual to go immediately to the Ombudsman. We value open and honest communication."*

When the senior executive presentation was completed, the assembled group of executives and managers worked to identify the five most critical obstacles to the company's transformation effort, and then five teams, each a mixture of senior and middle managers, were formed, assigned an obstacle, and instructed to identify the most important action steps that needed to be taken to remove it. Throughout the process, the CEO created a safe setting for this important confrontation of reality, and he placed the recommendations of these joint teams on the critical path of the second year of the company's transformation effort.

It was by thoroughly thinking through these process steps that the executives of National Semiconductor were able to effectively confront the reality of the transformation they had been leading and make substantive and timely midcourse corrections. A year later, the company was featured in the *San Francisco Chronicle* as *"Silicon Valley's Comeback Company of the Year."*

The most important outcome of this critical step of confronting reality is providing safe passage that enables a group of leaders to rapidly work through facts and come to grips with the sobering and simple truths. There are time-tested ways of giving lower-level employees the confidence and courage to come out of the shadows to constructively confront higher-ups when they think someone or something is out of line. This is as true both for VPs reporting to the CEO as it is for front-line managers addressing individual contributors. Constructing a simple framework for dialogue, which you'll see more about in the description of Cascades, and planning all the details of this type of engagement with your team is critical. Because, if the canary's wings stop flapping as the first brave soul raises concerns and is ignored or chastised, nobody else will follow them into the conversation.

On the Outside Looking In

A true confronting of reality requires an "outside-in" perspective of the business in addition to the internal view from the team. You need to look at your situation through the eyes of customers and competitors. Their reality is yours.

The best way to generate an outside-in perspective is to, well, go outside. Get outside of having conversations with the internal team in the same old setting. One company's method was to hold executive strategic planning sessions away from the corporate headquarters in less-traveled cities around the country where they had a market presence. The idea was to spend some time together as an executive team while competitively shopping the competition and making unscheduled visits to their own stores as if they were customers. Such visceral experiences go well beyond what you can get from a research presentation of an internally generated competitive analysis or a report by a market research house. Those analyses are useful as well, but they lack the real-world impact of firsthand experience.

However, getting a group of executives together to spend time looking at the market is harder than it sounds. Brad Youmans, a corporate strategist and prior CEO of a start-up software company, points out the challenge. His observation is that there are two types of people you are trying to bring together when you get an executive team together for a strategic outside-in look at the business. And both types of people have valuable views. He explains, "It's like going up for a ride in a helicopter. The strategists say, hey can we take this thing even higher to see way beyond the fence lines? And what do you think is just over that hill? While the operators go up briefly, have a bigger view, and then say, that was nice…now let's get back on the ground where we belong."[5] It is the challenge of balancing those two views and making the work useful in driving real decisions, not just interesting studies from up in the clouds, that makes the difference in an effective confrontation of reality.

One of the more creative ways of confronting reality that worked well for both types of people occurred in the transformation of Southern Company, which launched a transformation while annually being celebrated as *Fortune's* Most Admired Utility, made $1 billion in net profits, and operated across ninety-one fossil fuel and hydroelectric power plants under the umbrella of five different unions. The prospect of being able to actually pull off a major transformation of a company initially doing so well and hemmed in by overlays of complacent managers and union work rules was an extremely challenging situation.

A very creative executive, Rodger Smith, had the task of spurring the transformation of a company that was already on top of its world. The biggest challenge Rodger inherited was finding a way to get people motivated to get engaged in the process. This process would ultimately combine all of the company's plants, which were spread over several states and operated under different union rules, into a new "GenCo," or generating company headed by a single president within the parent company.

Rodger's initial instincts were on the mark. He had to get managers and employees at all levels to understand the need for transformation and to leave their comfort zones. They would need to not only support, but actively lead the effort in their areas of responsibility. Rodger first had to get everyone—managers, union leaders, and employees—to *confront reality*.

The competitive landscape confronting Southern was becoming occupied not by just the large, traditional rivals, with their heavy overheads and long investment horizons, but increasingly by agile new competitors. New independent power producers (IPPs) were beginning to cherry-pick Southern's highest-margin industrial customers. In addition, escalating deregulation of the electric utility industry was opening up the local market to all sorts of new competition from former regional monopolies and independent power brokers.

At one plant location, the urgency of the new reality had become clear to all. Employees at this location could climb to the top of the cooling tower, look out toward the horizon, and see the facilities of two large industrial customers that had been lost to new competitors. But for the vast majority of Southern employees, the need for transformation was not as clear.

Rodger's gut told him that the best way to serve up the new reality would not be from the work of consultants or staffers. Instead, he commissioned diagonal-slice teams, made up of executives, managers, union officials, and rank-and-file employees, to go out and engage with the new business realities. These diverse benchmarking teams researched, toured, and analyzed the operations of several large, rival power generation operations. They scrutinized the capabilities of the new IPPs. Indeed, many of the team members were initially puzzled by the fact that the new rivals would open their doors and books to them. During one of the first visits to one of these new, independent rivals, they asked why the company would be so open to a conversation with a competitor and were astonished by the response they got from its executive leader. He replied,

"You guys are like a big aircraft carrier and I'm a PT boat. You're too big and too cumbersome. You've got too much bureaucracy to turn that thing around as quickly as you need to turn it around. There's a new war that we're fighting, so I'm not concerned about you being a competitor."

The arrogance that IPP executives thought they could beat proud old Southern Company "in its own backyard" was convincing evidence for the benchmarking teams that significant change was not only needed, but essential. As Smith recalled, "What they saw blew their socks off because they discovered a totally different approach to the power generation business. They found the IPP plants well built, efficiently run, and, most important, focused on providing low-cost energy. The competitive spirit, employee empowerment, cost focus, lean staffing, and work culture of these new competitors convinced the teams that fundamental, not the usual incremental, change was required at Southern."[6]

To complete the confronting reality phase, Smith had the teams develop their own reports and present them directly to the Power Generation employees, thereby completing the team members' ownership of the new reality while disseminating it in a credible way to everyone else.

Within two years, Southern had successfully completed the transition in its power generation operations to a GenCo with its own

P&L, eliminated hundreds of millions of dollars in overhead, and had hammered out a "new deal" with its unions to support a more flexible and cost-effective work system.[7]

Talk with Customers and Noncustomers

Seeking the opinions of customers as well as noncustomers is another important way to constructively confront reality. At one high-tech company, there seemed to be no shortage of issues being raised as the new CEO arrived. It was crisis mode and there were lots of opinions on what was wrong. The sales team, in particular, had significant complaints about the product team's slow pace of new product development. In their view, that was the reason they had lost one of the company's largest customers, which, in turn, had driven the tailspin in revenue. The sales team claimed to be the voice of the customer and expected that view to be given heavy weight in the reality top management took into consideration when making key decisions.

The sales team argued that salespeople are on the front line with customers every day. "We know our customers very well and they let us know what they need. Nobody in headquarters has that view of reality." Although, in general, it is true that salespeople are closest to customers in terms of interaction, they also are likely to get a distorted view on what the customers really need. The nature of the sales-client relationship will tend to lead to discussions about features and price—not necessarily other areas such as the quality and integrity of the salespeople themselves, major new product line ideas, and supply-chain challenges. Sensing that the issue wasn't as simple as that of recent delays in product launches, the CEO embarked on a global tour to meet the company's customers himself.

Salespeople around the world geared up by preparing presentations for the CEO to make to their customers and setting up briefing meetings with them for the CEO. However, the CEO quickly put a stop to that activity and let the sales team know that the purpose of the conversations was not to pitch, but to listen. One of the first visits was to a very large customer they had just lost. The CEO went in with no computer presentation and no hard agenda—only with an agenda to find out what had gone wrong. The CEO had the sales relationship manager bring only a blank tablet to take notes. They were definitely uncomfortable in that role. By the time the meeting was over, they had heard about many issues, not the least of which were problems with the sales team's handling of some serious product quality issues. The executives at the customer company commented that they had never had an open-ended meeting like that with a vendor and were shocked that the CEO and his team really just listened.

In addition to talking with all customers, the CEO and his sales reps also conducted interviews with noncustomers, or companies who bought exclusively from competitors. Often, it is uncomfortable to go talk with potential customers with whom you have not been successful with your sales efforts. However, they are quite often great sources of reality for you. They have nothing to lose by making suggestions for improvements and nothing to gain other than helping another potential vendor keep the market competitive—which is in their best interest. In this case, the noncustomers had the same suggestions as those of the large customer that had been lost.

With notepads full of shots of reality from customers and noncustomers, the CEO returned to the office prepared to net out what internal people thought, what different functional groups thought, what customers thought, and what noncustomers thought. Among all of those points of view was reality.

You Are Here: Map the Market

Two of the most useful tools in figuring out how to get to where you want to go are having a map of the area where you are and a big red arrow saying, "You are here." One of the toughest jobs in quickly confronting reality is to create a consistent context and structure to capture all of the various points of view and pieces of data in one way. Too often, there are competing views all presented from a different, and often too narrow, perspective. It becomes impossible to net out any sense of reality. Segmentation schemes are different, product groups and market sizing cuts are different, and, at times, even the internal operating data are inconsistent across groups, coming from various systems all geared to a different structure. Creating a market map is an essential tool in confronting reality.

One example illustrates well the high-level use of market maps. As the music industry was opened up by the forces of the Internet, a number of companies created a market for portable devices to store and playback digital copies of songs stored on your computer and downloaded from the Internet—MP3 players. The service, Napster, opened up the market by creating a capability on the web for anyone to share their music files with anybody else in the world, at no cost. The Napster content was all available online and easy to download so that all the early MP3 devices needed to do was synchronize with a PC, store the music files on the device, and play them back. A host of technology-oriented companies worked to prefect their products for this market, looking only at the customer needs for their portion of the solution. Figure 4.1 shows the initial, narrow market view that set the competitive landscape for the hardware players in this market. As the market matured, they subsegmented the early users of this technology into college students, athletes, and others. Realistically, all of the early customers were gadget geeks of some sort, so when talking to them about their needs, the feedback was the same across customers—faster speed of synchronizing to the PC, more storage, and better playback time or battery life. That's what the companies were hearing, that's what they did well, and so that is what they delivered.

Customer Needs

Narrow Market Map View
• Speed of sync
• Volume of storage
• Playback time (battery life)

Figure 4.1   Narrow market map view

This narrow focus on just providing hardware devices and competing on technical feeds and speeds started to give way when Napster was effectively stopped from letting users share their music for free. Now, an online music source of songs wasn't a given. By that time, people who had never used Napster, because they viewed it as a legal or moral issue, began to see the benefits of online music. Apple looked at the total customer needs of the broader potential market that extended beyond the hardware. These new people were "noncustomers" as far as the traditional gadget geeks were concerned. But there were a lot of these noncustomers, and they were actually quite willing to buy legal copies of online music, wanted an easy way to manage the online experience with the device, and wanted a great-looking and great-sounding product. Figure 4.2 shows the broader market map and customer needs.

Figure 4.2   Expanded market map view

Apple focused on creating the most easy to use, legal, music download site on the Internet. They also invested heavily in the design and controls of their device. By focusing on developing a full and finished solution rather than a tech gadget that required a lot of downloading of special software and tinkering, Apple opened up a whole new market, drove better pricing, and came to dominate the market. Apple solved for the needs of the broader market and turned a niche technology device market into a new music distribution channel. It is easy to get so focused on competing in your narrow space that you ignore the way your customers fully experience and use your product. You can also become blind to entire segments of customers who would use your product if the solution were just a little more complete. You can ignore moves by players who you don't view as competitors because they don't appear to be in your space. The market map is a very useful tool for forcing a customer-oriented view of your strategic landscape where you play.

A market map is simply a two-dimensional chart that typically has a full set of categorized customer needs on the horizontal axis and one of several categorizations for the vertical axis, for example, customer segments. Each axis can have a drill down of detail, allowing for high-level views for strategic planning that can be driven into detail for setting operating tactics. The map forces a customer view of the world, which is where breakthrough ideas come from, and drives a discipline into strategic planning to make more intentional market moves rather than just a collection of random creative tactics.

Brad Youmans, who described the "helicopter" ride earlier, explains, "It is one thing to say you are growing from $1 billion to $2 billion in revenues. It is another to say how you are going to get there. Creating a market map requires rigorous work to get the right segmentation and customer needs model, but once you have it, your ability to find yourself on the map and decide clearly where you want to go becomes easy." And it is not just finding yourself, but clarifying how you'll move forward that is so powerful. Brad continues, "It becomes something like the old game of RISK where you have a map of the world and play to capture all territories. To win, you have to carefully decide how to deploy your resources to not only win, but also to defend your territories over time without getting spread too thin."[8]

With the market map in place, the data, such as customer needs, segmentation, market size/growth, competition, product portfolios, service offerings, and R&D investments, are all plotted on the exact same map. The market map then becomes a view that is continually enriched as more data and points of view are generated in your confrontation of reality. Viewing the market from a market map perspective also allows you to force a broader view of the market as you start with customers' overall needs rather than just a view of what you already provide. This releases you from using the current organizational structure (for example, product groups, divisions, services teams) as the main view of the world, which is limiting.

With this simple construct, a single view of your markets, and the data categorized, you will end up with the information to have a structured conversation and run through a simple set of questions to move from confronting reality to strategic planning:

1. Which segments are driving the most revenue size and growth for the market in the future?
2. Which customer needs areas are underserved?
3. Where do we have a true advantage in serving those under-served customer needs?
4. What moves are competitors making that we should either block or avoid?
5. And, finally, where should we place our bets on the map, which will indicate what customer needs should be served, what segments we'll target, and how we'll compete?

Confronting Reality Work Session

The consolidated and simplified view of reality is made up of different perspectives, including the initial leadership team interviews, views of employees, perspectives from customers and noncustomers, competitive analysis, and market map analysis. This process of gathering and consolidating information can be completed in a short, predetermined time frame with a concerted effort. Then, rather than spend months analyzing and developing presentations, the information, in simple form, is shared with the leadership at a confronting reality work session to spark an intense dialogue.

A typical confronting reality work session will begin with a review of the full transformation process so that it is clear how and when the outputs from the meeting will be used and the importance of getting the right issues on the table immediately. A quick exercise to expand perspectives and raise the level of thinking above the normal tactical drive is often useful to get started. That is followed by a review of the confidential executive interviews that set the stage and begin to test the openness of the conversation. The good, the bad, and the ugly are placed on the table, first, for discussion, and then, to prioritize actions that will enhance the organizational and leadership readiness. Often these issues have to deal with not just the weaknesses in the organization, but also the shortcomings of the leadership team itself. A guided dialogue about these sensitive issues should conclude with a clear set of priorities about what the team is committed to do about them. A quick work exercise to net out the top issues follows and, in many cases, some "quick-start" initiatives are called out right at that point, making for a very fast feedback-action loop that will set the right bias for action throughout the process. That work will likely take a full morning.

The afternoon typically starts with a presentation of fact-based views on the external view of reality. Results of customer and noncustomer visits, market trends, and competitive assessments are reviewed and again netted down to a specific set of areas relating to high-leverage opportunities or major gaps in the business model that need further analysis. Teams of executives are chartered to spend a brief period assessing these areas to be reported back at the next working session in the process, which will focus on setting the strategic direction.

From that confronting reality working session, a common view of reality emerges, which typically raises some high-priority strategic questions that have been buried sometimes for years as "givens" in the organization. If you create the right setting for safe passage, and you are willing to embrace dialogue and challenge, your team will generate breakthroughs in addressing the most critical issues.

Following one very challenging but also invigorating confronting reality session, a CEO commented in private that partway into the process you almost feel like hanging it up. "I felt at one point that people were just wallowing in self-criticism. But later that afternoon as we got to working through the implications, it was amazing. People began to see how we could win again." As your understanding as a leader deepens about reality and you form a more complete picture of the truth, you become even more emboldened and committed to get on with the transformation, and so do the members of your team. There is nothing more powerfully motivating than pursuing a huge dream that is rock-solidly grounded in reality.

Tips for Confronting Today's Reality

■ Follow a simple, streamlined process that creates a "safe passage" for the full team (that is, easy to understand and internally led by leaders at all levels).

- Prime the pump: Start with a strictly confidential round of interviews with all members of the leadership team and make productive use of that input to unlock the organization's internal realities.

- Open the dialogue and embrace challenges.

- Executive team—Let them tell you the emperor's clothes are ugly.

- Subordinates—Include a broad group in a sharing of ideas, not just communicating at them.

- Outside-in thinking—Pull up from the tactical rush and spend time to creatively look at things from customer, noncustomer, and competitor perspectives—beyond reading reports and viewing computer presentations.

- Get your people outside the organization to see firsthand what's really going on.

Endnotes

[1] Robert H. Miles, "Rockwell International Semiconductor Products Division," Case and Video Series, OM88-101 (Atlanta: Emory University, Goizueta Business School, 1988).

[2] Peter Senge, *The Fifth Discipline: The Art & Practice of the Learning Organization* (New York: Doubleday, 2006), 223.

[3] Based on an interview conducted by Michael Kanazawa on April 23, 2007 with Bill Hopkins, managing principal at a private equity investment fund managing $900 million in capital. Reprinted by permission.

[4] Robert H. Miles, *Corporate Comeback: The Story of Renewal and Transformation at National Semiconductor* (San Francisco: Jossey-Bass, 1997), 241–258.

[5] Based on an interview conducted by Michael Kanazawa on May 1, 2007 with Brad Youmans, prior CEO at a software start-up and corporate strategy manager for a nearly $1 billion software division of a global oilfield services company. Reprinted by permission.

[6] Robert H. Miles, "Type I Transformation: Repositioning America's Most Admired Utility," in *Leading Corporate Transformation: A Blueprint for Business Renewal* (San Francisco: Jossey-Bass, 1997), 83–92.

[7] See note 6 above.

[8] See note 5 above.

5

Sharpening the Strategy Arrow

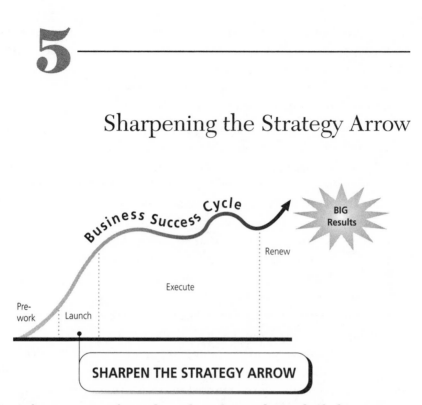

Business Success Cycle

Renew

Execute

Pre-work

Launch

BIG Results

SHARPEN THE STRATEGY ARROW

"If a strategy is formed in a boardroom, but nobody hears it, is it still a strategy?"

Company leaders will often state that they have a strategy up front. On the flip side, a survey of over 11,000 employees revealed that only 48% understand precisely the organizational strategy and goals and 53% feel that all workers are focused on the organizational goals.[1] At roughly 50/50 odds, that is not good. Is it any wonder that company leaders are frustrated that their strategic visions are not being implemented? Any surprise that one of the top three issues for CEOs is how to generate consistent execution of the company strategy?[2] Why the big gap?

As put by the new CEO of a multibillion-dollar retailer, "We thought we had a strategy when I started, but after working with my executive team, we realized that we didn't even know how to spell strategy!" His company had a mission statement, they had a corporate strategy presentation for investors, and they had a list of corporate values posted on the walls of conference rooms. All of the pieces people normally view as signs that a strategy exists were there. The content looked very professional and thoughtful. However, starting at the most senior levels, the company had lost its way. The strategy did not provide clear direction or a specific game plan to win in the marketplace.

So, why is it that company directions are not broadly understood and do not effectively drive action even at the senior management levels? As a starting point, the strategies themselves are often ambiguous, overly complex, and too lofty. They simply aren't taken to a granular enough level to be translated into operational plans. In addition, the core elements of company direction, vision, strategy, and values are often not in alignment. The vision statement is often treated as a marketing exercise to come up with something that "sounds good" as a slogan rather than has meaning. And the strategy development work is conducted as a separate exercise to develop a long, impressive document with lots of arcane analyses that are only shared on a need-to-know basis. Finally, the corporate values are viewed as a human resources "feel-good" exercise that doesn't have much to do with business decision making and execution. As a result, these core elements of transformation don't reinforce each other, come packaged in different vehicles, and, in the end, don't generate focused action.

A One-Page View of the Future

When asked to create a short list of things learned from prior transformation experiences, the CEO of a $16 billion revenues energy company noted that an often-overlooked element in success-fully driving transformations is the "one-page" view of the entire direction. To illustrate the one-pager, he developed with his team a succinct summary of how the vision, values, and business strategy all tied together in a cohesive and exciting direction. "It seems like a minor point, but really it provides a lot of power," he said. "It's mem-orable, easy to communicate, and easy to reference. If people can't remember the strategy, they can't act on it. And it is amazing how many times you need to communicate the same direction over and over again to get it to stick. So, it has to be simple and memorable.

The one-pager does that. And the hard work and real value comes up front in getting the executive team to make the tough decisions that allow you to focus the business so tightly that it can fit on one page."

Figure 5.1 shows a generic form of a one-pager that has served many organizations well. We refer to it as the ACT Arrow.

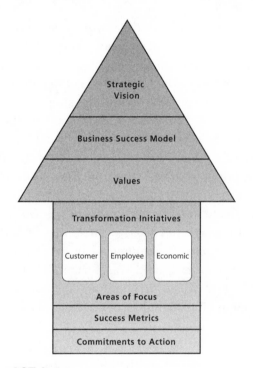

Figure 5.1 The ACT Arrow

The arrowhead consists of the three most fundamental elements required to set direction. The *whats* of transformation are the strategic vision, the business success model, and the values that guide decision making and behaviors during execution. As a starting point, it is critical that these three elements are sharp and simple. This is the most important job the leadership team has to do following a thorough confrontation of reality. Here, they must make the tough decisions to eliminate all of the clutter and net down the focus of the company to a critical few, hard-hitting, high-priority initiatives that they will execute with equal amounts of rigor and courage. These major transformation initiatives populate the shaft of the arrow.

Together with supporting areas of focus and outcome metrics, these few major initiatives are ultimately translated into individual commitments to action throughout the entire organization. So they have to be the right ones and when presented clearly on a single page, like the ACT Arrow, they can be readily understood by all hands at all organizational levels.

This organizing metaphor—the transformation plan-on-a-page—came from Gordon Eubanks, who was CEO at the Silicon Valley–based software company, Symantec.[3] He got the basic idea of focusing on a few important transformation constructs, but was searching for his own way to express them simply and succinctly. He built on a concept from another CEO based in the Valley, Scott McNeally, CEO of Sun Microsystems, who called for everyone in the company to adopt a plan of focused execution of the new Java product line with the following call to action: "Let's put all of our wood behind a signal arrow." With that idea, Gordon developed this simple, easy-to-communicate diagram for putting a full transformation plan on one page, with meaning. The arrow metaphor fit perfectly with the approach to drive focused alignment—the necessary up-front step before launching an accelerated transformation of a company or a major component of it. So, a literal interpretation of McNeally's metaphor was adopted to summarize for everyone in the organization what leadership was trying to do.

The work that goes into developing a sharp point and getting the arrowhead pointed in the right direction starts with a very broad look at the entire system. Then, like a ratchet, you take in the focus one crank at a time. Start with the internal and external views in confronting reality. Next, use a market map to target a strategic vision and decide where in the market you will place your major bets. Finally, you will conduct a total system analysis of the company, compare current to vision states to identify the biggest gaps, and then translate them into a core set of transformation initiatives. The Total System Analysis construct shown in Figure 5.2 is a useful and comprehensive framework for ensuring that all aspects of the business are considered in assessing the gaps. Most transformation initiatives, by their nature, will require changes to multiple areas to be achieved, so the framework ensures that all areas are considered.

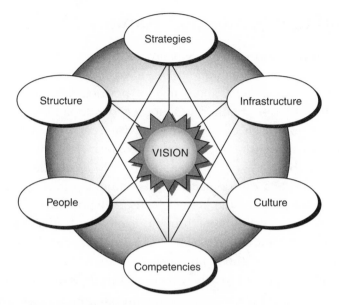

Figure 5.2   Total System Analysis framework
Robert H. Miles, *Leading Corporate Transformation: A Blueprint for Business Renewal* (San Francisco: Jossey-Bass, 1997). Reprinted by permission.

The funnel in Figure 5.3 illustrates the process for narrowing down a strategic vision to a focused set of initiatives. This chapter covers practical ideas and exercises for developing your strategic vision and business success model. The company values and transformation initiatives, which are used to support and drive the vision and business model, will be developed in subsequent chapters.

Figure 5.3   The transformation planning funnel

Creating a Strategic Vision

One of the most commonly heard strategic visions today is, "We want to be a market leader and to be an X billion-dollar player in our market." It's a statement about market position and financial gain. Those are fine aspirations. But, a strategy to be an X billion-dollar player does not work well as a complete vision for focusing and aligning execution. Focusing on an end outcome metric without a clear articulation about the critical requirements to reach the goal allows the leadership team to demand results without providing direction. That does not produce the kind of focused alignment and execution needed to generate the breakthrough results the leaders are hoping to achieve. In addition, a vision that is only financially motivated leaves most people without any passion for achieving it, which is also a necessary component to achieving breakthroughs in performance.

A vision should serve as more than just an aspiration to achieve a numerical goal. Instead, the following are guidelines to use in judging the quality of your vision statement. A vision statement should:

- Be market and customer focused
- Serve as a motivational "cause" for employees
- Clarify the general playing field (set boundary conditions)
- Specify where the company is unique
- Signal an aspiration-driven level of achievement

Some truly great visions over time have never been achieved. Finite thinkers will say its heresy to set a vision that isn't achievable. But visionaries know that a great vision continuously stretches execution by creating a constant tension between current success and greater possibilities. In contrast, finite visions have finite endings.

For example, Nordstrom's company philosophy has remained unchanged for more than 100 years since its establishment in 1901: "Offer the customer the best possible service, selection, quality, and value."[4] This clearly places service first, which is still the hallmark of Nordstrom's business. In another example, Microsoft's original vision was to see "A computer on every desk and in every home, running Microsoft software."[5] This sounded like a pipe dream at one point, but has been almost fully realized today. Just imagine if Microsoft stopped by saying, "We want to be a billion-dollar player and a market-leading operating systems company in the world." That would have been a very limiting vision compared to where the company has gone.

How can you get beyond the dollar targets and know what you and your executive team are really passionate about doing with the company? It's not that complicated. At a new division of a pharmaceuticals company, they were contemplating their objective of becoming a billion-dollar player in the cardiovascular device market. The new division had been put together with several acquired companies and given a young new leader to create the organization. Upon the new leader's arrival, he found that the division lacked a clear sense of direction and unity—just a couple of the many consequences of a dollar-driven vision without focus.

Just before a vision-setting session, the president was reflecting on remarks made by his executive team in a confidential organizational alignment assessment. Responding to the critical remarks about the lack of direction, his gut response was that the division did, in fact, have a vision—and a very focused one at that. He initially chalked this up to a breakdown in communication because he recalled that as the business was launched with the clear statement from his predecessor that, "We're going to take this start-up division and turn it into a billion-dollar business in our market."

At that moment, the company was involved in a vicious fight with larger competitors—which were funding major R&D efforts—to capture big slices of the huge and rapidly growing market for cardiovascular medical devices. For this corporate start-up, which was barely off the ground as a freestanding division and with revenues in the low hundreds of millions, the dream of hitting a billion dollars in revenue in a relatively short time was nothing if not bold.

In reflecting on the current state of the business and the executive comments, he began to view the vision as being too loose without a clearly defined business success model. It seemed that each department could justify fitting almost any pet project under the banner of working toward being a billion-dollar company. And a wide range of incremental initiatives had, in fact, been launched. Some department heads were spending R&D dollars when it was still not clear that their marketing and sales functions had an ability to reach the right customers.

In short, the company's potential range of directions for growth was too broad. Trying to simultaneously move forward on all of them, and then totaling up the revenues to reach the billion-dollar mark, simply wouldn't work. The division's resources were being spread too thin, and none of the best ideas were being well-served in the end. The major bets on clinical trials, R&D resources, and manufacturing capacity needed a disproportionately larger allocation of resources to be successful.

But where, exactly, should the company focus? They began with an executive session to find that focus with a simple, but telling, exercise. The team took a few minutes to write a response to the following, "If *Forbes* or *Fortune* wrote an article about the success of your company three to five years from now, what would it say?" This incredibly simple exercise quickly uncovered differences of opinion on direction and the real motivations that drove the executive team to strive for excellence.

Not entirely surprising, the answers fell into two major categories, which, for simplicity's sake, we'll label "technical" and "humanitarian." The technical vision emphasized how the company had outmaneuvered the competitive field by skipping a generation of products with technology innovations, leaving competitors far behind. The humanitarian vision saw success as delivering complete solutions that extended and increased the quality of peoples' lives.

It didn't take long for the group to realize that these two views weren't mutually exclusive, but complementary. And there it was: the team's version of a motivating strategic vision. It was clear now where the passion was coming from, even for the executive team. The team was there to improve patients' lives by solving critical health issues by developing breakthrough technologies. Out of this exercise emerged the essence of what became the company's shared vision. Over the next months, the words underwent some revision, but not the spirit of putting technology to work in bettering peoples' lives.

The billion-dollar objective, of course, remained as a key way of measuring success, but it was not the prime focal point. In the end, people do need to know how you define winning as an outcome.

With the right senior team gathered, sometimes all it takes to get visioning started is a simple, projective exercise that involves members of the leadership team writing about what they believe their organization will have achieved or will look like in the future if the transformation they are planning is successful. This relatively quick and straightforward exercise usually enables the assembled, experienced decision makers to immediately identify the key strategic vision elements, which can then be quickly refined to populate the very tip of the arrowhead and make it sharp. With such a simple intervention following a thorough confronting reality step, the strategic vision can be generated quickly, without having to waste months of committee work and elaborate brainstorming sessions that cause this second major step in the transformation planning process to bog down.

The process of developing a strategic vision must be both creative and grounded in analysis. Projective techniques like the one discussed stimulate the creative process, which then needs to be grounded in an understanding of customers, competitors, and what employees are passionate about and capable of doing.

Business Success Modeling

To be effective, creative strategic visions must be grounded in a rigorous business success model, and, from that model, distilled into a few specific initiatives—each of which is tied to bold, but unambiguous outcome measures. Therefore, the next part of setting clear direction is to define the business success model. Put plainly, this is how the company will allocate resources, keep score, and, ultimately, make money within the intent and scope of a particular strategic vision.

The old Albert Einstein saying goes something like this, "The definition of insanity is continuing to do the same thing and expecting a different outcome." Similarly, in the work of leading transformations, you're not going to get very far along the path to a bold, new vision if you continue to allocate resources the same way you have done in the past. The essential vehicle for effectively reallocating your limited resources is to create a business success model that is uniquely designed to test and support your new vision. If developed at the company level, this success model should also reveal how you will grow the earnings stream so that you can increasingly improve your ability to access debt and equity sources to accelerate transformation progress. Finally, such a model can also reveal what businesses or activities need to be eliminated to free resources to support the momentum to the vision state.

In short, the business success model is the engine that fuels the ability for the organization to reach the strategic vision and is the basis for both resource allocation and competitive differentiation. Figure 5.4 shows a simple, but very clear articulation of a business success model. It reveals how the company will allocate resources differently, where it will invest for competitive advantage, and how that fits within the context of the overall corporate value chain. In this case, the business success model supports a strategic vision for a company looking to differentiate based on staying ahead of competitors with technology and providing more value in customer service. They will put incremental funding into technology (5%) and customer service (2%). To fund those differentiators, a focus on cost savings in the supply chain (-5%) and leveraging channel partners (-4%) will generate enough savings to net the company a 2% profitability advantage that can be used to go straight into earnings or to have additional pricing flexibility when needed compared with competitors. This simple articulation of the business model makes clear to all employees what their part of the organization specifically needs to contribute. In this case, the technology division's primary focus will be on innovation and speed to market. In strategic supply, the primary focus will be on cost savings. In the channels organization, creating large-scale partnerships will be critical; and for customer service, the focus will be on high-quality customer service.

Value Chain

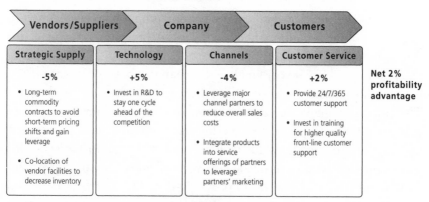

Figure 5.4   Business success model

Due Diligence on Yourself

A great example of what can be done to figure out the best business model quickly can be found in the work of private equity investment firms. These firms buy complete companies using their own capital and debt, stay on as primary owners for several years while turning around or supercharging performance, and then sell the company at a gain. The cycle time for assessing the true value of a company and determining how much to pay for it is very short. This is known as the due diligence period. During that time, a very small team from the private equity firm will dig into the details of the target company's financials, operations, sales channels, customer service, and other supporting organizations to see where the real value is generated and where there might be pockets that are underleveraged. They also look for high risk areas.

This is the same information that corporations need to understand to develop their business success model. It's the simple question of: "How does this business and industry really work, how does it create value, and what are the likely financial consequences of the model's success?" Often, the last step in business modeling is the development of a set of high-level pro forma financial statements that highlight the key success metrics. Sometimes in highly uncertain situations, the best you can do is lay out a set of alternative scenarios—each associated with performance consequences.

This up-front due diligence process has been referred to as similar to a physical exam, a *full* physical exam to be precise. It's not very enjoyable, but is very effective in telling you what is working and what is not. In a matter of days or weeks, the private equity firms are able to come up with a very accurate picture of the target business and the underlying drivers of value.

How can they answer those tough questions so quickly? First, there is a short, relatively fixed time frame for them to make up their minds on a bid for a company. In the case of private equity, the deal will be lost to others if decisions can't be made quickly. In the case of corporate executives, what is at stake is a delay in driving focus into the way the team is executing. Corporate executives often underestimate the speed possible in quickly moving from planning to execution, as the chapter on Speed will reveal. Based on experience, it should only take a few weeks for a small group of people to develop an initial working vision and business success model needed to launch the next phase of growth in an organization. The vision and business success model will always need to be refined and adjusted over time for changes in the environment, so there is no need to over-work them on the front end.

Why do so many executive teams never reach the same level of depth and specificity of direction that private equity investors find in a matter of weeks? According to Bill Hopkins, managing principal in a private equity firm managing $900 million in capital, "There are a few common reasons we've found for management missing some of the drivers of value available to them. Often, people have not gone back and challenged cost allocations in the business and the business has changed. As a result, they don't know where the real profitability is coming from. At times, people may have incentives to make a particular part of the business look better than it is. In addition, too much can be taken for granted in profit and cost expectations around the business based on high-level statements made by past executives and owners. People have a tendency to make things overly complex and usually the real answers are pretty simple."[6]

There is no reason that company executives cannot conduct rapid due diligence on themselves. That is the essence of the front end of the ACT process. The following are some tips for doing this yourself.

First, the analysis team needs to be set up the right way for success. It needs to have a clear mandate and high-level support so that its members can raise and analyze all of the tough questions that others have been afraid to ask. One good way to cover all of the difficult questions is to follow a due diligence checklist that is typically used in buyout situations to guide the work of the due diligence team. These lists are preset items that must be validated and include items such as the following:

- Market
  - Market size and growth of key business lines
  - Market trends and changes (e.g., economic cycles, regulations, technology)

■ **Customers**

- Customer loyalty and willingness to re-up contracts
- Value and quality of core products and technologies from external perspective
- Confirmation of differentiators from external sources

■ **Competition**

- Market share trends and competitive positioning
- Reasons for any recent competitive losses

■ **Company**

- Profitability by business unit
- Capabilities and loyalty of key employees

Leveraging this type of checklist allows the team to focus on finding specific answers with operational leaders, as opposed to probing randomly for problems, which usually only turns up what people want you to see anyway. Also, staff managers in the company who might be tasked with conducting portions of the due diligence job might not know the right questions to ask to get to the truth. The checklist ensures that the tough questions get addressed squarely and in the right depth. When investing money directly in a business, the due diligence teams will take nothing as a given without clear validation with facts. Not surprisingly, internal managers know where the skeletons are and will often try to protect certain data from seeing the light of day. However, a quick set of confidential one-on-one interviews with each of the executives at the company typically reveals those issues immediately and is an important step. In addition, due diligence teams conduct customer as well as and noncustomer interviews to serve as a vital reality check to balance against the internal-only views of people, processes, and technologies.

Finally, such due diligence teams will insist upon open access to and full candor with all members of the top executive team. In a transformation effort, often the internal due diligence team will consist of some operational vice presidents or directors with financial analysts in support. Then, after the confronting reality session, and fueled with the facts from the due diligence, the full executive team is able to determine the biggest levers available for improving the business success model. Based on the experience and knowledge within the executive team, members are broken into smaller teams to take on a prioritized set of issues associated with the business success model for the purpose of fully assessing them and developing recommendations. Within a matter of 3–4 weeks, the senior team regroups to collectively wrestle with the various recommendations to improve the business success model before they conclude on the highest-impact changes that need to be made. This prioritizing and focusing step is critical before moving on to make the more operational decisions.

This is how a variation of due diligence played out in one company in which there were two business units. One business unit manufactured handheld pricing guns to apply price stickers to products and another unit manufactured bar-code printers. The company was struggling to increase earnings and was looking for ways to improve the business. When asked, the leaders represented that each of the business units generated roughly half of the company's earnings. Upon a closer look, questions were raised about the cost allocations between the two businesses. The pricing gun business had a majority market share, needed few salespeople, and had very little to no R&D given the simplicity of the product. The bar-code printer business, on the other hand, required significant R&D expenditures and needed a direct sales force. Despite these differences, the overall cost allocations from the company had been evenly split between the divisions.

After taking into consideration the true differences in these elements of the business model, a quick rebalancing of the cost allocations in line with true costs was made. It clearly revealed that the bar-code printer business was really just breaking even at best, whereas the pricing gun business was generating almost all of the company's earnings. Beyond that, upon closer scrutiny it became apparent that the tape (consumables) loaded into the guns generated about two-thirds of the total company earnings. From that adjustment in understanding profitability, long-overdue decisions about resource and cost allocations across the portfolio mix became much easier to make.

The other aspect of creating a winning business success model is that it needs to be tested for its limits. No amount of advance benchmarking or building of elaborate spreadsheets can tell you for sure what the real limits are. You just need to press out for the edges by taking action. Many business models are underleveraged because companies don't realize how much power they really have in the marketplace and don't know how to exert that leverage for greater profits. Business managers don't always feel that they have the latitude or the support to test the limits because it can sometimes mean failing when you reach the outer edge of performance.

According to Bill Hopkins, "Private equity investors are often much more willing to push things to the edge to find the performance limits of a business than existing owners, which is another reason private investors can find new value in old companies. They typically are more willing to encourage management to take the risk of testing traditional limits."[7]

One business model shift in the highly commoditized business of renting construction equipment illustrates the edge well. The CEO and private investors believed that prices were too low. Management knew that the company was in a cyclical, commodity business and had been driving toward raising rates that brought it back to the levels of prior peaks. Some operating managers were concerned that increasing prices any further would start to drive down utilization rates, leaving equipment unrented. The CEO and investors felt that the market was too tight with supply and the building markets were coming back quickly—leading to even more opportunities for pricing improvements than had been historically available.

To test the limits, management agreed to set a floor in pricing that none of their local outlets could go below. To drive alignment, incentives in the field were reworked to encourage optimizing earnings rather than just high levels of utilization of the equipment. It was concerning to hold firm on higher prices based on a belief that competitors would undercut pricing. However, the market was strong enough that the rental companies who jumped at the low prices sold out their inventory quickly, whereas our sample company waited and was able to sell through its inventory later, but at a 20% to 25% price premium that all went straight to the bottom line. That is how you test the edge. It takes a strong stomach to take the risk; but if you don't risk going over the edge once in a while, you'll never know what is possible.

After you have refined your strategic vision and developed and tested the supporting business model, it is time to complete the focusing and alignment steps in your transformation planning process. You must clearly identify the key transformation initiatives— the *hows* that reside in the shaft of the transformation arrow. Or, as McNeally said, "Put all our wood behind a single arrow."

Tips for Sharpening the Strategy Arrow

- Establish a strategic vision for the organization that

  - Motivates employees

  - Focuses on the customer

  - Clarifies the general playing field (sets boundary conditions)

  - Specifies where the company is unique

  - Signals an aspiration-driven level of achievement

- Translate the vision into a business success model that:

  - Targets specific market and product areas

  - Provides priorities to guide investment and funding decisions

  - Indicates how profitability will be created across the company

- Conduct due diligence on your own company (even when no transaction is pending) to quickly:

  - Identify untapped sources of growth and value

  - Establish a true picture of profitability by unit or product line to drive decisions on focus and resource allocation

  - Create a fact-based foundation for better business execution

- Actively test the limits of your business model

Endnotes

[1] Franklin Covey, xQ Report, based on Harris Interactive database, December 2003.

[2] Linda Barrington, "CEO Challenge 2006: Top 10 Challenges," (The Conference Board, Inc., 2005).

[3] Based on an interview conducted by Michael Kanazawa on June 1, 2007 with Gordon Eubanks, prior CEO of a market-leading global software company and successful software start-ups. Reprinted by permission.

[4] Nordstrom, Inc., "Company History—Nordstrom.com," Nordstrom website. www.nordstrom.com, accessed Sep 21, 2007.

[5] PBS, "Getting Real: How Microsoft Plans to Dominate Digital TV." I, Cringely Weekly Column: May 7, 1998. www.pbs.org/cringely/pulpit/1998/pulpit_19980507_000569.html, accessed Oct 2, 2007.

[6] Based on an interview conducted by Michael Kanazawa on April 23, 2007 with Bill Hopkins, managing principal at a private equity investment fund managing $900 million in capital. Reprinted by permission.

[7] See note 6 above.

6

Absolute Alignment

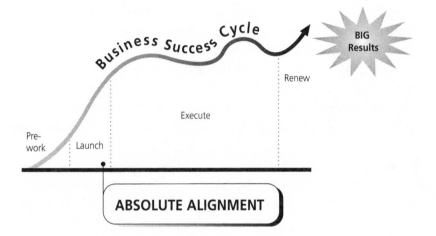

"Alignment doesn't just happen by making a presentation to the troops, it requires deliberate and sustained leadership and action."

Arrows—strategic or otherwise—don't fly very far or true without the support of a well-honed shaft.

In our case of targeting breakthrough results, the shaft consists of a few well-articulated company-wide Transformation Initiatives, each of which is supported by a limited number of carefully selected Areas of Focus and Outcome Metrics, all of which are tied to specific Commitments to Action for every soul in every component and at every level in the enterprise. How to set this up is the purpose of this chapter.

Translation to Three Corporate Initiatives

An organization can only pursue a maximum number of three, possibly four corporate-wide initiatives to achieve quantum improvement in a short time period. It is common that the three initiatives revolve around customers, employees, and financial performance. Therefore, within those top initiatives, there needs to be a clear articulation of areas of intense focus that—when tied to specific outcome metrics—will truly focus the execution of your particular effort. In fact, when it comes to the areas of focus within each initiative, we strongly recommend that they be strictly limited at the company or departmental level to just three, but not more than four for each initiative. When you start multiplying the number of initiatives times the number of areas of focus, you quickly realize that any more additions will overload the system. Then, the components that you have so carefully crafted to accelerate execution will break down into incremental little fragments of tactics that gridlock your people and squander your resources.

This is a very difficult discipline to follow for leaders. Picking just three initiatives and sticking with them takes some risk and courage up front. If, on the other hand, you challenge your team to do anything and everything to hit the numbers, you will be taking no personal accountability for focus. As a leader and leadership team, you need to provide clarity on the most high-impact ways for people to contribute to executing the strategy you are committed to achieving.

Larry Mondry, a seasoned CEO and operating executive, describes the focusing process like this, "In a large organization, we can say we have five things to do at the top. At the next level, each of those translates into ten tasks, and then ten more tasks on those ten, and so on. By the time it goes all the way down the organization, the time spent becomes enormous and spread out all over. You need to find just a few things that really matter, top to bottom, and focus on those."[1] This fragmentation is greatly underestimated and is one of the main causes of gridlock and undermines powerful execution.

Although every situation is different, when given the challenge of focusing on three things, most organizations typically end up with a similar set of general categories for transformational initiatives. One is typically focused on customers and specific customer needs. A second is focused on people and talent management. The third is typically focused on shareholders or financial performance. In some situations, there is a fourth initiative that is a critical problem for the business that needs a short-term focus, such as technology time-to-market, energy efficiency, globalization, and so forth. Often, the fourth idiosyncratic initiative helps complete the definition of the strategic vision in the transformation of an organization.

In addition, although the core three are categorically very similar across successful companies, they become unique for each company in terms of the two to three areas of focus that are selected for each one of them to guide attention and allocate resources to drive them. For example, one company might focus on margins and pricing to drive their financial growth initiative, whereas another might select an acquisition strategy and new product development to achieve its growth initiative.

After selecting the initiatives, each one needs to be run through a rigorous gap analysis and then shaped in terms of clarity of scope, targets, milestones, and action plans. These initiatives become the critical link to translate between the market-oriented strategic vision and the operations-oriented tactical plans, which every person in the organization will translate into individual commitments. Every employee cannot engage directly in the setting of the vision and business success model. However, it is possible, indeed critical, for every employee to fully engage in how they will personally drive each of the key initiatives at their job level and within their sphere of influence.

There is a process for getting everyone in the company—not just the top few levels of executives—to set personal commitments to action that are relevant for their job level and scope for each company-wide initiative. It is a rapid, high-engagement approach that you will explore in Chapter 7, "Rapidly Engaging the Full Organization." The result of this final step in focused alignment is the creation of a clear and compelling line-of-sight accountability from top to bottom in an organization.

The set of templates in Figure 6.1 illustrates a framework to operationalize the transformation initiatives at the company or department level. After this part of the shaft in the transformation arrow is clearly articulated, the next step is to achieve alignment among all the subunits—that is, have them complete their versions of the templates and submit them for approval. Then, you need to use a rapid, high-engagement, all-employee cascading process to help managers and employees at all levels develop corresponding individual commitments to action.

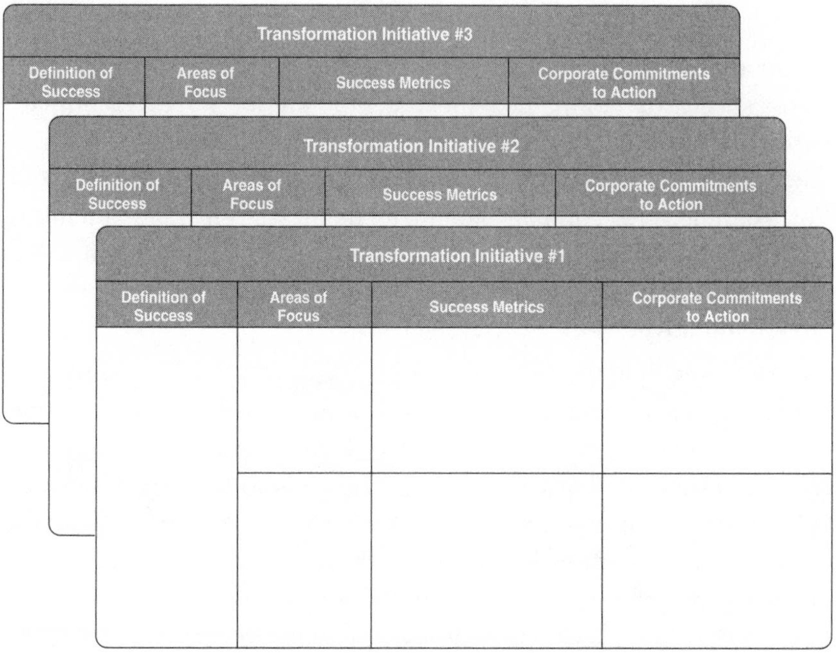

Transformation Initiative #1			
Definition of Success	Areas of Focus	Success Metrics	Corporate Commitments to Action

Figure 6.1   Transformation initiative templates

Have You Lost Your Marbles?

If you decide to not focus on a simple set of three aligned transformation initiatives, what can happen? Well, according to the following story, nothing will happen. And that is the most damaging outcome of all.

An executive of one company described the mishaps due to lack of focus that occurred prior to their launching the ACT process. A consultant was brought in to help facilitate a process for rapidly identifying improvement areas and driving actions. The management team gathered at an off-site meeting and immediately began identifying as many potential improvements as possible across the business. Many flip charts were filled up with ideas that were created and posted on the walls of the conference room. Next, they began categorizing the ideas by functional area. There were about 40 to 50 items on each list, which seemed like too much to tackle at once. So, each executive leading a functional area was asked to take on the top five items on their list.

The management team was already operating in gridlock, with schedules that were maxed out on existing work. They were all working hard to improve their part of the business. So, in preparing to leave the meeting with their list of improvements, they were already feeling overwhelmed. But, to make sure that there was accountability, the consultant described how there would be a big jar of marbles on the CEO's desk. The number of marbles was equivalent to the number of initiatives for improvement that they had just launched. The idea was that each time you finished implementing one of your improvement projects you could go to the CEO's office and remove one marble. The plan was to empty the jar of marbles.

After some time, there were almost no marbles taken from the jar. And the only way it was emptied was when it was thrown out, along with the consultant. What went wrong with the approach? A simple lack of focus and alignment.

One of the vice presidents who suffered through the marble game said that upon leaving the idea generation meeting, the feeling of the team was that they had just been assigned a whole new set of initiatives while nothing had been taken off the table to allow for implementation of the new ideas. Worse yet, all of them were busy pursuing their own isolated initiatives. So, as they started thinking about implementing all the new ideas, they realized they had no resources available to get things done. Moreover, if anything required cross-functional support, they were on their own because their peers were all focused on different improvements.

Fragmented, under-resourced lists of ideas overlaid on an already overtaxed system are persistent nemeses along the path to transformation. This is what happens when you don't stick to a limited set of initiatives, with full alignment at the top. So, the next time someone comes around saying they want to help you create a new list of improvement ideas without first determining where they stand relative to the existing to-do list, tell them they've lost their marbles. And if they aren't willing to help you and your colleagues focus and align your already stretched resources, take your marbles and go home!

What NOT to Do

So far, you've thought about the critical need for dialogue about confronting reality and for developing a vision and a business success model that are motivating, focusing, and challenging to stretch the organization. You've also thought about the need to articulate only a very few major initiatives, each with a few clear areas of focus to drive attention, resource allocation, and action. The last step in successfully focusing an organization for a major transformation launch or strategy execution effort involves deciding "What Not to Do." This is the step that most executives skip over and pay for dearly later in their transformation and execution efforts. Making the tough trade-offs about what to stop so that resources can be focused on the most important initiatives is not easy. It just has to get done.

Zombie Projects

At a major telecommunications company, now like so many a part of the new AT&T, there was a name for certain projects—zombies. They were long dead, but their spirits somehow kept wandering the halls in a stupor. Sound like a Dilbert comic idea? Well, these zombies walked the same halls of where Scott Adams, the creator of Dilbert, worked before leaving for a career as a cartoonist. Zombie projects had been supposedly killed through inattention or lack of formal funding, but, in fact, they continued to live on as pet projects of key managers who couldn't or wouldn't let go. We joke about these projects, but, in truth, they raise the question of whether a company's leadership is really aligned with its vision. Lack of alignment can derail months of solid progress toward righting a business. To drive home the point, we offer a story about a technology company.

It was a sunny July day in California, not the sort of day you would expect to see zombies. The senior leadership team was gathering one last time before rolling out the new vision and set of transformation initiatives to the full company. The chief executive began by talking about the strategic direction. He discussed the need to diversify beyond hardware and into software, as well as to invest in new technologies to augment the position in what had been the company's traditional markets.

Then, the executive team set to work discussing alignment: How did individual divisional strategies, most of them demanding strong new commitments to change, align with the new corporate vision? How would they need to collaborate across divisional and functional lines? The session assumed a workshop atmosphere. At each of several tables, groups of division colleagues hammered out the top three commitments their division would make to support the vision.

As one division team after another shared its most important commitments, the optimism in the room became almost palpable. For the first time, everything and everyone seemed perfectly in sync. The team from the sales department talked about building capabilities to sell both software and hardware. The human resources staff talked about recruiting employees with software expertise. The finance group talked about specific funding of projects related to the core strategic initiatives—putting the money where the mouth is.

Then, it was the R&D group's turn to present its commitments. The team talked about the need to build a new division to handle software, and it identified the new R&D portfolio set of priorities that was right in line with the strategy. All over the room, heads were bobbing in approval and relief because the R&D group had a reputation for going its own way, regardless of company and customer needs. Then, just as the applause was about to begin, an R&D team member raised his hand. A zombie was about to stagger in.

"Before we move on," he began, "I just need to get some clarification about all of this. I can see how most of our R&D work relates to the strategy—except for Project X [as we will call it]. Now, Project X is going to provide a major breakthrough in price, speed, and reliability in our products—but I don't see how it fits."

Sensing the urgency of squashing this topic immediately, the CEO strode quickly to the front of the room. With that, the R&D manager also stood up, as his teammates waited for the showdown.

"I know this has been a really important project for you," the CEO began, "and that you've spent a lot of time on it. I also think it's a good idea." Hearing those conciliatory words, a lot of people began to worry that much-needed change was about to be sacrificed on the altar of R&D. But the CEO continued, "The problem we've had in the past is that we've gone after way too many 'good' projects. Now, we need to move faster on fewer 'great' projects. Put Project X aside for now and make sure that the strategic priorities get done first."

The R&D manager couldn't, or wouldn't, take the hint. "But I have people working on this," he rebutted. "We're just about ready with the technology."

What was really happening was not a battle over Project X. It was a battle over alignment. Would the leadership line resources up behind its agreed-upon vision? Or would it start chipping away at its support of the top priorities and divert resources to a project that didn't fit the strategic direction—and one with which the company had hardly any experience at all?

The CEO stepped in again, but this time not so gently. "Let me make this perfectly clear," he said in a low but firm voice, "I expect all activities on Project X to stop right now. We have more than enough needs on other R&D teams, so everyone will have something new to do. The team members on Project X are all top notch and we'll get them reassigned into the priority areas. Now, let's move on."

And with that, a bullet pierced the zombie's heart.

Driving true alignment of plans across a complex organization is tough. Any small amount of misalignment at the top gets magnified through the levels of the organization. In the most unlikely places and at the most unlikely times, challenges can beset the senior leadership team's effort to align the company (and sometimes the top leaders themselves) behind the vision that has been forged.

The tough thing is that after a tight focus is called out, projects that might have value, but just aren't the highest priority have to be dropped. If they aren't killed, they will diffuse needed focus and squander scarce resources. And all the zombies will make the organization slow to execute, overload the resources, cause silos to form, and dull execution.

Restack the Whole

In addition to removing the zombies, another challenge after agreeing on a clear focus is determining how deep to reset action plans and priorities. If an organization hopes to execute a strategic shift or transformation, the whole system needs to be addressed. All priorities from top to bottom need to be reset. Playing on the margins with 10% to 15% of incremental spending or pancaked overlays to existing plans is, by definition, only going to produce incremental changes in results.

There are several games people play when attempting to avoid a big reset. For instance, even relatively skeptical team members are willing to participate in the early stages involving the development of a new vision and business success model. Given a very strong commitment by the leader, these savvy managers will understand that they cannot avoid participating in the development of the new direction. But although they may play well on the front end of this creative process, they often avoid putting all their cards on the table. Instead, they play a game of poker—watching others turn over their cards to ensure they can win in the end when resource allocation decisions and commitments to organization changes are made. These incrementalists typically come up with many "small adjustment" ideas in hopes that the transformation process won't really impact what they do on a daily basis.

One of the most common ways to avoid full commitment to transformation and strategy execution is to argue for a continuation of "baseline funding" while making new incremental investments on the "strategic initiatives." Incrementalists often argue that because a majority of revenue is derived from the current business, disruption needs to be minimized. Unfortunately, the perpetuation of baseline funding and tactics in the face of major transformational challenges simply ensures the continued pursuit of the status quo. Although it is true that much of the funding will still be necessary for the base business, it is the process of questioning the importance of each activity that is valuable.

The critical few transformation initiatives, by contrast, are targeted for quantum improvements in a relatively short period of time. The initiatives are not intended to be new incremental projects. By both definition and the way they are created, if they don't cause priorities up and down the full organization to shift, dramatic performance improvement won't unfold through the whole system.

Another common "head-fake" in execution is the idea of a pilot test. This is not to be confused with the useful practice of launching innovative start-ups within larger companies. In those cases, a skunk works approach can be quite valuable. However, when a full transformation of the core business is being launched, a toe in the water approach won't work.

The argument goes something like this. "These strategic ideas sound like real breakthroughs in thinking. Very different from what we do today. To make sure we get it right, why don't we set up a pilot in one small area of the business. We'll see how things go there and really perfect the model. Then, after we've got that done we can roll it out across all the divisions." Again, this sounds supportive and logical. However, pilots also allow the majority of the organization to sit tight and avoid change for a considerable period of time. And such pilots often founder for lack of support from the complete executive team. Even if they eventually work, critical time has been lost and often they are tagged as being limited to only the immediate setting of the pilot and the incrementalists will find other reasons to avoid the transformation.

The reason many executive teams allow these symptoms of misalignment to build and ultimately undermine the success of a strategy or transformation effort is often due to a lack of clarity and incomplete communications up front. Bill Barnes, a seasoned executive of Fortune 500 companies and private equity investor, understands what it takes to get full alignment. He points out, "The step many people skip is having a full dialogue about differences in opinion and taking the time to really dig down to find the underlying reasons for lack of alignment."[2] People can tend to jump to the cliché of agreeing to disagree too early. The result is having a team of executives in slight disagreement where priorities don't match up and half-hearted execution extends across the organization. Bill continues, "Before closing on the final plans, you need to have lots of different points of view represented, optimists and pessimists, engineers and marketers, and corporate and operations perspectives. Let there be heated discussions, explore options openly, and then come to closure with full understanding of the different perspectives. You can still call a time when you have to agree to disagree, but it will be disagreements about the underlying assumptions and not disagreements about the final direction and priorities across the full organization." In fact, as Bill and his team built global operations around the world at one of the fastest growing computer companies in the world, he would often recall a saying that he had heard while working in Bolivia, "We're in a hurry, so we'd better go slow."

"Restacking the whole" does not mean that you need to take on reckless or overwhelming amounts of change all at once. What often is required is the achievement of focus and execution on an initial set of transformational initiatives: a harvesting of key things learned and then a recommitment to and alignment with a refreshed set of initiatives after the first major performance year. At one company, for example, the first wave of the transformation was targeted at improving their core operations. Initially, they weren't extremely clear about a longer-term strategy, but they knew they had to immediately address a host of operational issues. So they focused and aligned the entire organization around three initiatives to make rapid, breakthrough improvements in their core operations. The result was a more engaged workforce, a reduction in silo behavior, a great jump in operational results and customer satisfaction, and the preparation of the organization for the bigger strategic shift that was coming.

This set up a second year push, with a more thorough strategic planning cycle completed, where they could leverage the same ACT process to align the full organization around a bigger stretch in strategy that took the company into entirely new markets and product areas.

Individual Commitments to Action

The first step in transitioning from planning to doing is setting individual Commitments to Action (CTAs) throughout the organization. The entire organization needs to engage in the process of developing and committing to act on a limited set of individual commitments that are in alignment to the transformation initiatives.

The end goal of engaging the full organization in the process is to generate a situation where all people are able to set specific commitments to action that are aligned to drive the overall results. These commitments need to be relevant for their level of contribution, are aligned to support the top objectives, and are things that they were able to help design. The commitments need to be "their" commitments to support the transformation. The odds of a person following through with excellence on commitments that they helped develop are much higher than just completing tasks merely assigned by others.

This step is often nonexistent in strategy communications sessions and that is why they become one-time events and not launching pads for driving results.

In performance management and goal-setting processes at companies, the step of understanding what the team needs from each person and the context of the strategic direction is typically missing as well. It is more usual that the goals are set only between an employee and his or her direct manager, usually with no specific understanding or dialogue about the company strategy and without any dialogue with the rest of the peer team on what is needed from that individual. The only documents discussed at an individual goal-setting session might be a copy of last year's performance review and a draft of the new year's performance review document for the individual. Then, the session becomes an administrative task of filling in blanks rather than having a real dialogue about priorities, personal commitments, and job design for the coming year.

In the transformation at one of the largest technology companies that shifted its business model from being just a products company to being one of the largest IT services companies, the company leaders felt they had everything under control. When managers were asked how goal setting and performance management worked in the company, they almost uniformly reported that each employee at the company set his or her individual commitments at the beginning of each new calendar performance year. Furthermore, they believed that these commitments were reviewed as part of the performance management process semiannually. But, what really happened is that most commitments weren't set until June, just prior to the time of the semiannual performance appraisal! The problem was fixed by hooking the goal-setting and appraisal process to the annual cascade kick off. In one rapid sweep from top to bottom, all employees nationally set their commitments, which had to be reviewed by their supervisors within three days prior to being recorded in the company's electronic tracking system. It was fast and drove complete alignment of individual commitments from top to bottom.

Alignment of Commitments— Reducing Silos

It takes a commitment of time working with the team to effectively confront reality, set the direction, and create transformation initiatives. At that point, many managers feel like the commitment to action part of the process is a break from the teamwork and a chance to take the team's plan and run to daylight with just their piece of the transformation. To some extent, they are correct. Personal commitments to action have to be set by every person in the organization by themselves. However, even with all leaders looking at the same strategy, it is very easy for the commitments to get out of alignment across functional groups. One company was working on its second round of the process. The first year had reenergized the company and had turned a declining revenue trend around. However, despite this focus, they realized that even with just three initiatives guiding their plans, the execution was still too diffused. During the first year, they had all taken the corporate direction and run cascades through each department in alignment with the overall direction. However, they had not spent time as a VP team to align and check off their commitments to action "with each other" adequately enough.

In going through the process the second year, they all agreed that there was a need to not only align on the top-level direction and initiatives, but also to spend the extra cycles to align their individual commitments to action at the functional/department level. With a simple exercise of writing each vice president's goals on index cards and posting them on a wall, they quickly saw how the goals were diffused. There were dependencies that were out of sync. There were differing opinions on what was meant and different ways of delivering on the same initiatives. So, they took the time to sort through the inconsistencies, prioritize actions across departments to support the overall goals, and then lock in their individual commitments. Now the department and functional goals were puzzle pieces that neatly knitted together the whole set of initiatives and the strategy. Execution was set to be more focused with fewer interdepartmental conflicts throughout the entire organization.

Len Rodman, the chairman and CEO of Black & Veatch, who used ACT to complete the transformation of his partnership to a private, $3 billion global engineering services company, had this to say about the impact of the process on the dramatic cultural shift required to make the fundamental change in corporate governance and management process:

"We had traditionally been a company best described as a loose confederation of states or a company that played smaller than we are. There was significant autonomy in the various parts of the organization, which manifested itself in unhealthy internal competition. Today, we see it to be more beneficial to be ONE Black & Veatch worldwide and to leverage the strengths of the entire company. While this is not entirely universal, we are seeing good things happen from improved financial performance to more well-rounded managers."[3]

As the top three initiatives are set, it is very common for there to be, for example, one that focuses on employee development and engagement. Given that people are such an important factor in strategy execution, it is no wonder that engagement shows up as a top priority. However, management teams often mistakenly identify the "people" initiative as one that the human resources department (HR) should own and execute. The reasoning is that HR will need to launch programs, deliver training, and conduct recruiting to support the people initiative. However, if the VPs of all staff departments and business units in a company do not take on an individual commitment to improve the quality of people on their team, the people initiative targeted for quantum improvements in a short time period will be doomed to disappoint.

Successful people strategies cannot be owned only by HR—they need to have full commitment and active involvement from the full leadership team, and every leader on that team should have a reasonable set of personal commitments to action to support that type of initiative. A general manager can make a commitment to deliver the key programs HR will develop, such as 360 reviews or improved recruiting and interviewing processes. This way, when the general manager's team is asked to get involved in the initiatives, it is to support their boss and their team's goals, not just to respond to being told to do something by another department. This holds true for all other types of initiatives as well. Responsibility for growth, quality, or product development, as further examples, must be broadly borne by all members of the leadership team, not just by the department that specializes in the initiative.

Working on the alignment of the initiatives up front and across the organization will ensure that team members in different work groups will all be working under aligned priorities and tactics. Silo conflicts are reduced and greater execution results.

Alignment of Values

One indispensable element in generating and keeping alignment is the living of shared values. Every day, people in the organization will be faced with making decisions that will either move the organization forward or not. Living by a core set of values allows individuals to make decisions on situations that haven't been addressed before and to stay in alignment with the team as they make those decisions.

Don't Try to Replicate the Scout Oath

There are many reasons why culture and values often fail to receive the status they deserve in the workplace. Rather than go through all of that detail here, it is critical to know how to help your team members make good decisions when they are faced with a tough choice and when you or others peers aren't around to help them think it through. One CEO put it very well when challenged by his team to create a set of values, which ended up being 15 items strong after long discussion with his team. Now he couldn't argue that anything of importance was left out. But how was an employee to take guidance from all of them at once?

The problem was that many of the values were of the kind that could be found in any scout oath, including trust, respect, truthfulness, honesty, and so forth. The CEO pointed out that all of these values make up a set of rules to live by that just define being a good person. He described that the people we hire need to have learned these basic values at home, school, and religious groups before coming into the workforce. If they don't, we haven't hired the right people. What we need to develop are just the really important behavioral changes that are required to drive our business forward.

Bedrock values like those just mentioned begin to be developed in employees, not when they arrive in a company, but when they start out their lives. They are the result of the confluence of parental supervision, role modeling by respected peers and adults, trial and error in the real world, and so forth. These are the kinds of things we hope and definitely ought to screen for when we select people for employment in our company. Without such traits, which are part and parcel of being a good person and a good citizen, no organization can sustain itself and flourish. What is critical to develop is a set of specific values that are uniquely required to help the company achieve the highest priority initiatives.

When you think about developing your corporate values, make sure the company is bringing aboard the kinds of people who already have good basic values: trustworthiness, integrity, a good sense of humor, a team player, and the like. You shouldn't have to teach anyone those basics. Rather, focus on creating no more than three values that are strategically aligned with the major initiatives upon which the transformation will be borne.[4]

To illustrate, during the turnaround of Office Depot, the new CEO and executive team eventually selected three primary initiatives to launch the revitalization of their company.[5] They said to all constituencies that they wanted the company to become the "most compelling place in the industry to *invest, shop,* and *work*." Underlying these catchy initiative titles, they developed ways of specifically measuring each:

- *Invest*—Shareholder value creation
- *Shop*—Customer satisfaction
- *Work*—Employee retention and reengagement

When they turned to select the values that made the most sense to emphasize during the transformation effort, they had a long list that had been posted in all the conference rooms by the previous regime. After some focused dialogue, the team relatively quickly and painlessly decided that an emphasis on three particular values made the most sense and could probably make the greatest contribution given the selected initiatives. The values they singled out for special attention were

1. *Respect for the individual*—The company's employee base was quite diverse, so this value was believed to be a critical factor in achieving the best place to work initiative.
2. *Fanatical customer service*—During the long wait for approval of the merger with Staples, which was ultimately denied by the Department of Justice, the company had lost its focus on the

customer. Driving a value in customer service was viewed as critical to creating the best place to shop.

3. *Excellence in execution*—During all the turmoil, the company and its employees had also lost their focus on execution. This value was designed to help encourage the restoration of excellence in execution, which, in turn, would contribute to becoming the best place to invest.

Figure 6.2 shows how the transformation initiatives, outcome metrics, and values were clearly aligned, making the business drivers and values mutually reinforcing. This alignment greatly simplifies and focuses both operational and personnel or cultural efforts on the same initiatives. It is easier for people at all levels to understand, remember, and execute.

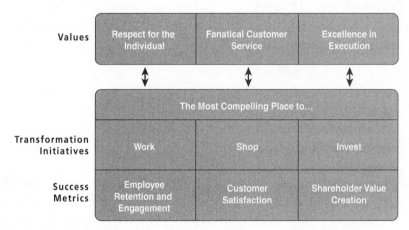

Figure 6.2   Relationship between transformation initiatives and company values

After the core values are identified, they need to be anchored in individual commitments to behavioral changes, initially at the top, starting with the CEO and his or her direct reports, and then throughout the entire enterprise. Alignment and engagement on these happens simultaneously with the business transformation initiatives.

Put Your Money Where Your Mouth Is

This shouldn't have to be said, but, unfortunately, it needs to be said: When the three initiatives are developed, they must impact the way that investment decisions are made and cause a realignment of budgets to reflect the new priorities. Too often, the stated strategy is not aligned with individual goals, and neither of those are aligned with the operating budgets. In some companies, the strategic planning process is done by the top executive team, budgeting is run separately by finance, and performance goals and management are programs run by human resources in a vacuum. These elements need to be coordinated in the right sequence and reinforce each other to get full alignment. In addition, it is not good enough to create an "incremental" budget for the transformation initiatives where a small percent of the total operating budget is set aside to fund the initiatives. That creates overlay initiatives that add to the gridlock and don't force a full alignment to the initiative priorities. With alignment of the strategy, business model, values, budgets, and individual commitments, the full system will be pointed in the same direction. That's what is needed to break gridlock and get on with producing BIG results.

The Bottom Line on Alignment

To drive home the importance of alignment from top to bottom in an organization, consider the reflections of two very successful transformation leaders. Both CEOs, one led the dramatic turnaround of a high-tech company, whereas the other steered his basic materials company "from good to great." The high-tech leader had this to say five years after the launch of his successful turnaround: "So, what's the most valuable lesson I learned from the ACT process: #1 is alignment at the top. #2, through the cascade process, is alignment at all levels." It might surprise you that the other CEO, after successfully taking on a very different transformation challenge, one of taking a company that was doing very well on all accounts to a much higher level of performance, revealed something very similar in terms of the major lesson he learned. He concluded that, "I think the business challenge that the ACT process handles beautifully is the congealing of the top leadership team on what you want done and then cascading it down so it is communicated to every employee." When asked the same question, the CFO during that "good to great" challenge, observed that,

"A by-product of this process is that when you require a business leader—whether at the senior leadership team or quarry manager level—to make presentations to their own people about their goals and commitments, they are really publicly stating what 'we are going to accomplish.' It makes those people realize they have to act as mentors or leaders. It's not just a selfish game anymore. These people to whom they've made the speeches are now watching to see if they are going to walk the talk."

If your objective is to generate strategic alignment quickly, which is what is required to transform a company or a major component of it, you need absolute alignment starting at the top. If you have any misalignment at the top, it will only become magnified as it goes down through the organization. Big leaders cast large shadows! And, if you encourage one department to try to "change the world" while permitting another to focus on the "same old, same old," you will be setting up both departments—as well as the transformation you hope to achieve—for failure. So, be very careful about considering "pilots" or phased rollouts that get parts of the organization out of sync with each other.

Instead, plan for the engagement of the complete organization, with each group fully focused on the few initiatives and corresponding values and behavioral changes that can contribute the most to success. If all of the executive leaders are aligned, and their goals and performance measurements are complementary, your odds of reaching success and full implementation go up dramatically. George Coll, SVP at one of the world's largest retailers, points out, "If you're not uncomfortable with how tight the initiatives are, they're not tight enough. The more tight and narrow the initiatives, the bigger impact they can have because people and resources will be leveraged to their best."[6]

Then, clear the decks of all misaligned projects. There is no room for exceptions. Shoot the zombie projects, remove nonteam players from the team, and align to a single and simple one-page view of the complete future direction. Resist the idea of having staffers or consultants run "overlay" transformational initiatives over the top of what the business operators are doing in hopes that your people can absorb the changes later. This creates lack of accountability for the programs and ultimately overloads the system when the initiatives are brought back into operations for execution. Finally, align and focus the few values and associated behavioral changes that are most likely to help your organization surmount the specific transformation challenge with which you and your people are confronted.

Tips for Absolute Alignment

- **Three transformation initiatives:**
  - Set three transformation initiatives and specify areas of focus and success metrics for each initiative.

- **Absolute alignment from top to bottom:**
  - Quickly address even small deviations from the focus at the top as these get magnified going down—senior executives cast big shadows.
  - Drive accountability throughout the entire organization through setting individual Commitments to Action at all levels.
  - Restack all priorities top to bottom or you will, by definition, only be playing on the margins with incremental changes. This will make many people uncomfortable, but it is necessary.
  - Reset investment and operating budget levels to align with the initiative priorities.
  - Establish clear guidelines for resource allocation that will enable you to quickly identify and kill the zombies before they kill your transformation.

- **Align values and behaviors:**
  - Select a few values that strategically align with the initiatives.
  - Anchor the values in behavioral change commitments at all levels in the organization.
  - Quickly address and handle any situations where leaders will not align fully.

Endnotes

[1] Based on an interview conducted by Michael Kanazawa on March 27, 2007 with Larry Mondry, prior CEO of a $4 billion retailer. Reprinted by permission.

[2] Based on an interview conducted on October 26, 2007 with William Barnes, VP of private equity investments at one of the largest Swiss banks, who formerly developed the Asia market for a $30 billion computer manufacturing company. Reprinted by permission.

[3] Based on an interview conducted by Robert H. Miles on December 13, 2007, with Len Rodman, chairman, CEO, and president of Black & Veatch, a global engineering services firm.

[4] For a more complete treatment of values, refer to an earlier work of Robert H. Miles: *Leading Corporate Transformation: A Blueprint for Business Renewal* (San Francisco: Jossey-Bass, 1997), 51–53.

[5] Based on direct support of Bruce Nelson's transformation project while CEO at Office Depot.

[6] Based on an interview conducted by Michael Kanazawa on March 8, 2007 with George Coll, SVP at one of the world's largest global retailers. Reprinted by permission.

7

Rapidly Engaging the Full Organization

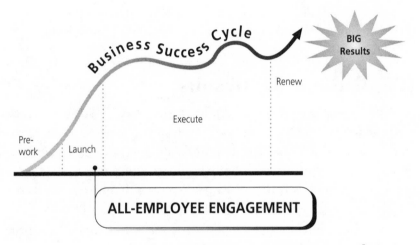

ALL-EMPLOYEE ENGAGEMENT

"Compliance breeds mediocrity, engagement drives excellence."

How can you engage thousands of employees within a matter of weeks?

Leaders don't generally ask that question because they are not aware that such a feat can be accomplished in a rapid, reliable manner. But it's one of the major questions they should be asking when challenged with taking charge of a new organization, setting out on a strategic shift, or launching major growth plans for their business. This is especially important given the fact that many transformation efforts stall at this specific point because the great ideas and strategies at the top never make it far enough down in the company to have a true impact on customers—which is where it really matters.

Past efforts, they recall, can take months—if not years—to roll out from top to bottom. More often than not, these efforts were implemented as one-off programs, not integrated into normal business operations, conducted by consultants or special "train-the-trainer" facilitators. Those other types of programs end up as overlays to the business and don't leverage the natural chain of command. They ultimately get replaced or just run out of energy before they generate any big results.

The problem with these approaches is that by the time the message reaches the full organization, the top has already moved on to new challenges and strategies, putting the system out of alignment. And, as you'll see, a message delivered by anyone other than the direct manager will not drive execution down at the next level.

It's All about the Results

The largest immediate boost in performance that companies often get in following the ACT process is a dramatic increase in employee engagement, which translates to immediate jumps in results across all dimensions of the business. Sometimes, the improvements start to build even before new initiatives have been fully implemented from the top. Does that surprise you? It's surprising to many leaders.

Creating a fully engaged workforce, one where individuals bring their best every day, is a necessary element to generating great results. An engaged workforce is one in which people have passion for their role in the organization and continually look for ways to contribute to their organization's performance. As you look to hire new employees, wouldn't it be great if the HR department would let you cut loose an ad like the following?

Now Hiring Leaders

...for <u>all levels</u> in our organization!

*We want a few high-impact people looking to make a
big difference at work!*

Are you a self-motivated, innovative thinker and risk taker?

Can you work well with others, yet not blindly follow the crowd?

We clearly all hope to be able to attract people like this. Indeed, if we do only a halfway decent job of hiring, our organizations should be filled with high-energy, creative-thinking people, who make up high-performance teams that are driving big results. Right? Not exactly.

Many of the great employees we hire begin to feel underutilized, marginalized, and disengaged all too soon. A study of 840,000 employees of U.S.– and U.K.–based multinational companies showed that employee engagement begins dropping at about six months into the job and by the end of Year Two, 57% are disengaged. The levels of engagement do begin to improve for those who stay beyond two years, but this is not a strong start.[1] This means that those in leadership positions are not on balance, engaging teams effectively.

Sometimes, it feels like if we were really truthful, our job ads should read more like this:

Now Hiring Followers!

We want people who will sit down, shut up, and do their work to meet the metrics on a daily basis.

Are you willing to take orders without questioning the boss?

Can you hammer through your own tasks to hit your own targets regardless of the impact on others?

We all have up and down times at work. There are periods of time when you are supercharged with energy, optimistic, full of ideas, and can't say anything wrong. Aren't there also some days when you can barely drag yourself into work, your mind drifting to questions like, "What am I really doing here?" as you slog through what feels like drudgery? Have you watched athletes on a team change their attitude and the whole game momentum shifts their way? None of that is different from the collective engagement of an entire workforce. You can, as a leader, change the collective attitude and energy of your team by truly engaging individuals in the business and that will translate directly and immediately into better across-the-board results. Over time, it will also translate into a high-powered team that has momentum on its side for continued innovation and growth.

Quantum Jumps

For several years, a large, public utility company facing impending deregulation struggled to generate a more competitive and high-performing workforce. The spider chart in Figure 7.1 clearly shows that during the three years prior to the ACT-based intervention, very little overall movement occurred on various dimensions of employee satisfaction and engagement. The year immediately following the launch of a high-engagement transformation, quantum improvements were achieved across all dimensions of measured employee satisfaction and engagement throughout the 92 highly unionized plants in the company's portfolio.[2] That shift in attitude resulted in $400 million in cost savings, a major reduction in grievances, and huge improvements in safety.

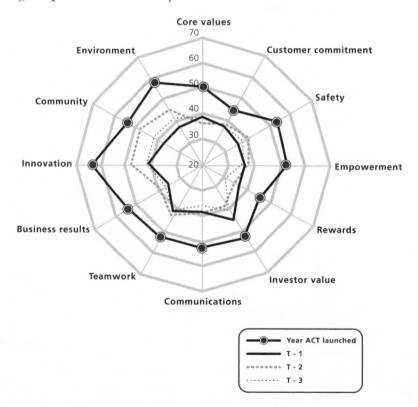

Figure 7.1 ACT-based employee engagement shift[3]

This is a clear picture of what can happen when attitudes shift based on high engagement. This jump in performance was driven by a shift in engagement. The employees just needed to be engaged in thinking through how to operate their area of responsibility differently, not be told what to do and how to do it.

"Back in Black" Friday

What does a quantum jump in employee engagement look like and what does it do for you in leading a transformation effort?

At a national retail company, sales had been on a constant downward slide for five years. In fact, the company believed that perhaps its brand had been totally forgotten and it might need to change its name. There were also big challenges coming from new competitors and business model shifts that needed to be made.

It was about halfway through the performance year when the new CEO and COO decided to apply the ACT process to accelerate a transformation they had called for at the beginning of the year. For retailers, Black Friday refers to the Friday after Thanksgiving, the day that many retailers finally go beyond break-even profitability and go from being in the "red" (losing money) to being in the "black" (making money). It is typically the single day of the year that has the highest sales. It is a huge indicator for retailers each year on how they are performing overall. After engaging the full organization from the top executives through to the cashiers and warehouse staffs in early August, the company experienced a large jump in employee engagement taking them from the competitive bottom quartile to the top half compared to similar companies.

That jump in engagement felt good to the executives, but would it translate to results? By the time Black Friday results were being tallied, they knew the answer was yes. With no major increase in mass market advertising spending, the company had generated the largest sales day in the entire company history (including the heydays that had long since passed). It put them on track to have the first profitable full year and full year of positive year-over-year growth in same-store sales in the recent past. What had changed? The marketing and merchandising teams had been engaged by the new executives for weekly creative thinking sessions, store employees were allowed to prioritize serving customers over taking inventory, and everyone felt like they had some say in how to do their job better every day. At that point, there had been no rebranding and no massive ad spending to bring customers back—there had just been a simple reengagement and focusing of the entire team.

Following the close of the year, the executive team was discussing the great results and one executive asked what the team thought was the key, "What have we actually implemented or done differently?" One of the operations staff managers put it best, "Maybe that's just what happens when you get 14,000 people engaged and excited again."

Employee Engagement Is Not Barbeque

But not all engagement attempts bear such bountiful fruit. One ill-fated attempt to increase rank-and-file employee engagement involved a planned "evangelical" event. It was conducted by a high-tech company in Silicon Valley during the height of the 1990s boom. The company had well-branded products, but more standard alternatives had virtually devoured its business. Barely clinging to a 3% domestic market share, executives at the company decided to make a major push to reengage their workforce.

Plans were carefully laid to transport all employees to a local fairground where company leaders would hold forth with a big-screen, multimedia appeal to all hands. It was designed to outline the company's new vision; it sketched the broad outlines of some new initiatives; and it called for a return to the values and behaviors that had once made the company great. Ranging somewhere between a religious tent revival and a Big Ten pep rally, the event amounted to a great exhortation by executive leaders for all employees to perform differently and better on the job, all reinforced by lots of pyrotechnics and scheduled applause.

A week later, a key team member who attended the event said that all he could recall with clarity was the quality of the barbeque!

Clearly, this is not the pathway to employee understanding, commitment, and engagement. But generating engagement is essential to achieving breakthrough results.

Observing failed attempts like this one led to the design of a comprehensive, but streamlined vehicle for rapidly creating "leaders at all levels" in a transforming enterprise. We call it the *high-engagement, all-employee cascade*. It is simple, streamlined, and fast—an intervention that combines the benefits of employee training and communication with performance management in one sitting.

The following section points out very specific design elements of this proven process architecture for creating rapid and effective engagement. Some of what you will explore here will sound trivial, but it is not. There is no panacea; there is no catch phrase to lead you through this. Success with employee engagement comes from the cumulative impact of a few, very deliberate choices.

High-Engagement

Imagine that an executive team has been working collaboratively to confront reality, create a strategy, and determine focus for the organization. What do you need to do after all the planning? How do you get the rest of the organization engaged? Surprisingly, it is the exact same method for how the top team was engaged. It's that simple.

- Generate dialogue and feedback.
- Allow people to hear the message from their direct boss with a localized interpretation ("What does it mean for us?").
- Challenge and expect individuals to translate the plans into personal actions ("What does it mean for me?").

Critical Importance of Dialogue

As we discussed before, dialogue is a critical element of success. Yet there is a natural tendency among executives and staffers when pressed for time to cut dialogue out of important meetings and other forums. Perhaps these executives think that if they just concentrate enough on communicating clearly, that employees will "get it" and get on with it. Nothing could be further from the truth.

Hear It from My Boss

There is an old saying that employees join companies but leave bosses. This saying points to the fact that people at each level experience "reality" at work as the one that their direct boss creates. To accentuate this point, a recent employee survey at a global company asked employees how they would like to receive important corporate communications. By a huge margin, they preferred direct verbal communication with their direct manager.

It is not that people don't want to hear from the top executives or receive corporate update e-mails; it is just that what they really want to know about strategic shifts or new initiatives is, "How will it impact our daily work, and me, specifically." In the hallways after a company-wide broadcast by the top chief, you often hear, "OK, so what does this really mean?" And sometimes you'll hear bosses say to their direct reports, "Don't worry, just keep doing what we're doing, this one will blow over pretty soon…" That "blow-off" statement is reflective of why people want to hear things from their direct boss because often senior teams that lack dialogue are out of alignment.

There is also a critical point to leveraging the full leadership chain of command to communicate. If the top leaders keep everything to themselves and then communicate directly to the entire employee group at once, they are cutting off the power of their team. As pointed out by Robert Luse, SVP of HR at a company with over 300,000 people, "If leaders are finding everything out with the rest of the pack, then it sets up a real 'us-versus-them' mentality of the top leaders versus all the rest. So, if a handful of people—for example, five to seven—at the top make all of the plans and then roll out everything all at once to the full organization, pretty soon, even the vice presidents start to view themselves as the 'general population.' Giving information to leaders at every level and making them accountable for communicating it with their teams puts them in a position of power."[4]

Unbounded, But Grounded in Reality

There is a balance in generating a strategic dialogue that is often not in place. First, there needs to be a ground rule that there are no topics that are out-of-bounds to be raised as questions or challenges. At the same time, the dialogue needs to be firmly grounded in reality and facts.

There is a common concern that an open dialogue simply opens up the ability for anyone and everyone to take potshots at a plan and nit-pick the ideas until they finally give way to the old way of doing things. This certainly is the strategy of some people. So, sometimes leaders protect from this by saying, "Don't ever bring me a problem without a solution as well." The only issue with that statement is that sometimes employees hit new problems and need to tap the experience of others to find a solution. And dialogue is really about asking the right questions rather than just coming up with answers. Effective dialogue is rooted in asking questions to reach deeper levels of understanding and clarity, not holding "bitch sessions." Proper structure of the dialogue handles the balance between full candor and simply complaining.

Another commonly missing element is follow-through on the dialogue that keeps it grounded over time—a translation of the ideas and feedback into personal commitments and actions. Too often, people leave an "idea session" with a thousand ideas written on flip charts on the wall. It is invigorating to come up with all of the ideas, but nothing is ever done with them. And that is demoralizing over time. It also allows people to throw out ideas that are not well thought out or are just more ideas for the sake of sounding good to their boss and peers because they are participating. To drive a productive dialogue about jump-starting your business or shifting its strategy, there must be an expectation that all prioritized ideas will be driven into action. Even early dialogues on strategy need to be translated into implications for action to ensure that a dose of execution reality will be infused into the plans—rather than ending up with a strategy analysis binder that reads great but can never be implemented.

One CEO puts it in terms of three levels of thinking, "Vision is where the rubber meets the sky, strategy is where the rubber meets the road, and tactics are where the rubber meets the back of your head. We need to be doing all three!"

Putting It All Together

Following countless applications across different industries, organization types, and global cultures, a seemingly simple and mundane, but very powerful vehicle for consistently generating high-quality dialogue has emerged. For simplicity, let's just call it *tablework*.

Here's how tablework works. First, a larger group is broken down into smaller groups of no more than six to seven people seated at round tables. The reason for this number is that if you have more people per dialogue group, there will not be enough airtime for everyone to participate in a reasonable time frame. You might have a room full of round tables each buzzing in dialogue on the same question, so the gathering can be as large as hundreds of people, which is broken down into small tablework groups.

The second rule is to have very clear instructions and a fixed time frame to address each specific question. The time needs to be fixed and relatively constrained for each question to drive for clarity and the appropriate level of analysis and decision making within the group. Every tablework group that experiences successful dialogue always mentions that it would be nice to have had more time. But every work group that tries to leave the time open-ended only generates an over-thinking of the issues and gets further into the details and generates longer lists than is required. Dialogue by its nature is intended to create expansive conversations about a topic, so if you start without a tight structure of scope, timing, and specific answer formats, the conversation will drift all over the place and generate no useful conclusions. So, keep it focused and time-bound.

With clear instructions in hand, the tablework starts with each person taking a few minutes to think of his or her own response. This quiet time at the beginning is essential in that it allows the internal thinkers a chance to process the questions before the extroverted talkers start generating active conversation. During this initial quiet time, each person writes his or her answers down on a worksheet. This simple, initial task forces each group member to come to some conclusion with their own ideas before the conversation starts. This helps clarify peoples' thoughts before active dialogue begins. It helps to avoid rambling speeches, and encourages everyone—not just the most vocal—to become more emboldened to share answers that might appear to be too controversial or unrealistic before real dialogue begins in earnest.

Next, each person is invited to share his or her best answer or two with the people at their table. At this point, there are only questions for clarification from others. This is a time to get ideas out in the open, not to edit or judge them. The step allows people of lower organizational standing or less forceful personalities to be fully heard. Oftentimes, the best new ideas come from unexpected people.

To make sure the tablework group follows this routine, three roles are assigned before the process begins. One of the tablework participants serves as a Recorder, who is responsible for capturing all the ideas and ultimately prioritizing them on a structured worksheet. This structure also keeps tablework "bullies" from shutting down other points of view before they are fully shared, often with comments like, "You know, in the field it really isn't like that…" or "Technically, you're right, but it will never work because…".

In addition, a Facilitator and a Presenter are identified by the group members. The appointed Facilitator leads the discussion at the table to select the best answers to share with the larger meeting group and keeps the process on track and on time. When the task is completed, the Recorder notes the final answers on a worksheet, and the Presenter, who has been organizing his or her thoughts during the group's deliberations, will stand up and share the opinions and recommendations which have been summarized on the group's worksheet.

Each tablework group will have generated dialogue and then captured, weeded, and prioritized the best ideas. Multiply that by every tablework group assembled in a large meeting forum. As readouts are done to the larger audience, typically very common threads appear. It is clear to see where convergence exists and where there is disagreement. This structure of readouts also protects individuals from worry about putting forth controversial topics, as they are reporting on their team's work, not just voicing their own opinions. A majority of people, despite what individuals tell you as a leader, have difficulty telling the leaders in a constructive way that they do not agree with them. The readouts allow that to happen in a nonthreatening and predictable way. This is an element of what we often refer to as "creating safe passage."

What can arguably sound simplistic is actually a very powerful method for rapidly engaging an entire organization with a leader-led approach. Bill Maddox, an executive who has led both business sales and human resources departments in back-to-back appointments at a multibillion dollar company, points out a critical aspect of the table-work process: "Simplicity has to be a part of this. The agendas, meeting designs, and even the questions asked need to be simple. This lets the people focus on doing the thinking rather than running through a complex program. The value is in the discussions with each other. And when it is simple enough, people all the way down to the front lines can use the same tools and meeting designs to lead their teams."[5]

The only remaining step in the tablework process is to close the loop on how leaders will accept the input from the group. This is a critically important step. Participants in a tablework dialogue will want to know that their feedback was heard and is being honestly considered. There is a temptation for leaders to want to process the feedback immediately and come to conclusions and answers, but that can undermine the idea that full consideration will be made of the ideas. So, to close well, the process requires that the leader share his or her observations about the quality of the dialogue and the ideas that have been presented. The structured worksheets from each tablework group should be collected for further analysis. Note that there is no need to collect every individual's worksheet; that just creates an overload of items that the group has already weeded out, and it defeats the purpose of providing "safe passage" for participants for some of their important but controversial ideas. Finally, a commitment needs to be made by the leader that the feedback received will shape the thinking in the revised plans and commitments. Indeed, before the group breaks up, the leader should announce the future milestone in the process when people can expect to hear the final outcomes.

To create authentic interactions with the tablework, the areas in which you are requesting help and feedback can't be set in stone already. If you have already come to a full conclusion and don't want to change your mind on a particular topic, don't open a dialogue about it. Everyone knows when a forgone conclusion is rolled out for supposed feedback. That will certainly be received worse than not asking for feedback at all. And, to be clear, not every decision needs to be opened for dialogue at all levels. Top strategy development is handled primarily by the senior executives, but it should be opened for dialogue with the middle management team for a reality check and input. So, when you design your timeline for engaging the organization in a strategy execution or transformation effort, be sure to build in the appropriate cycle for dialogue that you need before the final decisions must be made.

This method of tablework—which gets everyone's ideas out on the table before requiring everyone to narrow the choices down to those that can have the greatest potential for impact— puts power in the hands of leaders at every level in the organization to engage their direct team in dialogue, idea generation, and decision making. By simplifying the method for doing this, leaders at all levels are able to transfer active championing of the required breakthrough thinking, passion, and performance to their own teams.

In many traditional approaches, as illustrated in Figure 7.2, lower level leaders are only expected to play passive roles: they are simply asked to communicate messages from above and make the changes they are told to follow in their workgroup. Passive participation, such as simply "allowing" or "enabling" changes results in compliance to demands from above at best. By contrast, if what you really want is to generate excellence in execution throughout your organization, you can establish and model by example the expectation that leaders at all levels below you take an active role. By establishing the simple process of tablework for engaging teams at all levels, you enable people throughout the organization to serve as leaders of your process.

The Role Leaders at All Levels

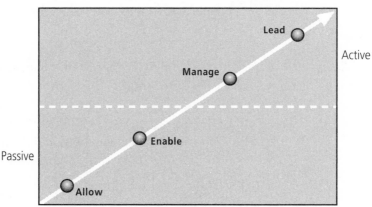

Figure 7.2 The role of leaders at all levels[6]

There is tremendous power each of us has to step up as a leader to dramatically impact an entire organization, no matter what our standing or rank. Joe Montana, Hall of Fame quarterback of the San Francisco 49ers, stressed the importance of this idea in a story he told us about a rookie player's impact that was also captured in his book, *The Winning Spirit*.[7] "The first day of practice I threw him passes, and he kept dropping them. It was kind of embarrassing as the ball bounced off him and slipped through his hands." Not the kind of performance you would expect in this highly competitive situation. But Joe continued, "But finally, he caught his first pass. Normally, in practice a receiver would run about ten yards after catching a pass, jog back, throw the ball in, and wait in line to do the drill again. Not this kid. The rookie tucked the ball away, turned upfield, and sprinted full-speed to the goal line sixty yards away." And he kept sprinting for touchdowns every time he caught the ball in practice, even as veteran players ribbed him about having to wait and joked about what he was doing." The rookie Joe was describing was Jerry Rice, currently the only player to score over 200 touchdowns in a career in the National Football League.

Jerry's odd rookie behavior became a challenge to other veteran receivers on the team to step up and to the defensive players to try to stop him in practice. As Joe describes it, the rookie changed the way the whole team practiced and played. The impact of one person willing to step out from the crowd and risk going beyond "normal" behavior is how entire cultures get changed. It takes a willingness to challenge the rest of your team to rise to a new level of excellence— even those veterans or people with higher standing. In too many cases, managers at all levels are kept in place as followers by self-imposed limits. They merely allow or enable changes to occur by simply following what they are told. In ACT, these same managers are called into action to actively lead execution of the transformation initiatives in their part of the organization, no matter what level or standing they have. And to do this right, each person in a leadership position needs to be willing to create the expectations and the setting in which even rookie receivers who initially drop the ball can have a big impact. And such leaders need to do this by first stepping up and out on to the limb on their own.

Reaching Scale and Speed

Tablework activity, when employed with senior executives on the front end, starts the dialogue snowball rolling. Without full consciousness about it, as they use the tablework process to develop and agree upon the high-level strategic plans, initiatives, and values, executives begin to appreciate the importance of the structured dialogue that immediately begins to break down discussion barriers and structural silos. A new level of candor quickly emerges with the leadership team, and they find themselves getting much more done in far less time that can be immediately put into action.

Then when the senior team engages the middle managers, they use the same tablework process. In this way, the executives are now teaching middle managers how to use the process as well—teaching by doing. Then, given the simplicity of the approach, middle managers can easily turn around and leverage the exact same tablework process and tools with their teams, on their own.

Using the simple tablework structure and process, teams all across the organization can self-facilitate their dialogues. In fact, one reason why leaders don't encourage dialogue throughout the organization is that they have trouble conducting it with their own teams and aren't sure how it would ever happen throughout the full organization. Sometimes efforts are made to send all managers to training classes to become facilitators or to send consultant facilitators around the organization to do the job. Both of those techniques are too slow to implement and not really effective. The training can be a good reinforcement for depth of understanding, but not as the primary method to quickly drive an open dialogue at all levels of the organization.

When consultants or "train-the-trainer" internal resources are leveraged to actively facilitate the dialogue itself (that is, standing at the front of the room and controlling the conversation), the authentic and critical direct link between the leader and his or her direct reports is broken. Organizations that have effectively learned the tablework process have the ability to have dialogues that cascade through organizations as large as 100,000 employees around the globe in a matter of weeks, not months. This is possible because they are leveraging the existing organizational structure rather than bolting on an overlay team of people who become a choke point of resources to moving more quickly. So for efficacy and speed, experts can be leveraged to help architect the process and tools and give a little help with the first round or two of use, but the critical conversations within the dialogue across the full team need to be run by the work groups themselves. Consultants can communicate some outside perspective, staff members can provide training, but true engagement has to be done by direct reporting managers directly with their teams. The relationship is shown in Figure 7.3.

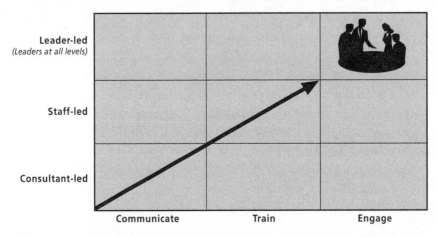

Figure 7.3 Pathway to high engagement and high accountability

Lighting 1,000 Fires Only Gets You Burned

A word of caution on going overboard with sparking innovation across a large system is to be careful about maintaining focus. Some people have misinterpreted and misapplied the concepts around full-system change. Their concept is to "light 1,000 fires" all around the lower levels of the organization and let all of that energy boil up to the top. In their eyes, isn't that "real" full engagement? Actually, it is just anarchy. Like a wildfire, this process is out of control, lacks direction, and ultimately just creates havoc. So, part of the idea is correct, that you need to learn how to fully leverage and release energy in your full team. But, it has to be done in a directed manner.

At Office Depot, Bruce Nelson was faced with a challenge as he took charge as the chief executive officer. The company's plan to merge with the number two competitor in the market had just been blocked by the Department of Justice, creating a critical need to gear up for organic growth again.[8] In response, and prior to Bruce's appointment as CEO, management had launched a massive "whole-systems change" effort that had spawned over 1,000 initiative teams all at once, each with a mission to crack and drive its own assigned initiative. There was quite a bit of running around, creating plans, and excitement at the beginning. However, when it came time to execute, you can guess how effective it was. There was just way too much chaos to track progress, align resources, or make any meaningful strategic changes to the business. This was the out-of-control wildfire effect. People were busy, but not having material impact on turning the revenue growth and business fundamentals around. It was frustrating to management and it was frustrating to the teams. By the time the new CEO was on the scene, the organization was hopelessly gridlocked in a matrix of action plans and resource requests that were all going nowhere.

The first order of business of the new CEO was thankfully to disband the 1000 teams and work with the largely inherited leadership team to distill the three initiatives that, if everyone in the company focused their time, attention, and resources, would add the greatest value to the company's turnaround. From there, the engagement of the team was pointed and aligned. Innovations and business improvement ideas all added up to delivering on the top objectives for the company, to be the best place to work, shop, and invest. And with the right focus, the full team was able to take Office Depot from one of the worst performing to number two in shareholder value creation on the S&P 500 within a year.[9]

The collective loss in creativity, passion, and determination across organizations has created one of the most underleveraged resources in business today, our human capital. It is due to a lack of engagement. If you choose not to attend to this critical step of engagement in your transformation, you'll have disinterested employees, great strategy binders gathering dust on the shelf, and mediocre results from your efforts. By planning for a high-engagement, leader-led cascade process, you can quickly drive breakthrough results by tapping a resource that is bounded only by the limits of human ingenuity and passion—in other words, limitless.

Tips for Engagement

■ Build the capability to engage in dialogue through a tightly structured, high-engagement, all-employee process that is leader-led.

■ Expect top-to-bottom engagement in a matter of weeks, even for teams of 100,000 or more employees, by leveraging the natural management structure.

■ Keep each level of management in direct dialogue with their team—don't just rely on communicating broadly to the masses to get the message across.

■ Keep engagement focused on the top corporate priorities (for example, strategy, business model, transformation initiatives, supporting areas of focus, and values).

Endnotes

1 Kenexa Research Institute, "Kenexa Research Institute Uncovers the Two-Year Itch—The Importance of Driving Employee Engagement: Satisfaction Increases with Tenure," *Kenexa Research Institute Press Release*, February 5, 2007. www.kenexa.com/en/AboutUs/Press/2007/07FEB05.aspx, accessed Oct 2, 2007.

2 Robert H. Miles, *Leading Corporate Transformation: A Blueprint for Business Renewal* (San Francisco: Jossey-Bass, 1997).

3 See note 2 above.

4 Based on an interview conducted by Michael Kanazawa on May 17, 2007 with Robert Luse, senior VP of HR at one of the world's largest global retailers. Reprinted by permission.

5 Based on an interview conducted by Michael Kanazawa on April 23, 2007 with Bill Maddox, previously VP of business services and VP of human resources at a $4 billion retailer. Reprinted by permission.

6 Robert H. Miles, *Corporate Comeback: The Story of Renewal and Transformation of National Semiconductor* (San Francisco: Jossey-Bass, 1997). Reprinted by permission of the author.

7 Joe Montana, *The Winning Spirit: 16 Timeless Principles That Drive Performance Excellence* (New York: Random House, Inc., 2005).

8 Based on direct support of Bruce Nelson's transformation project while CEO at Office Depot.

9 See note 8 above.

8

Productive Speed

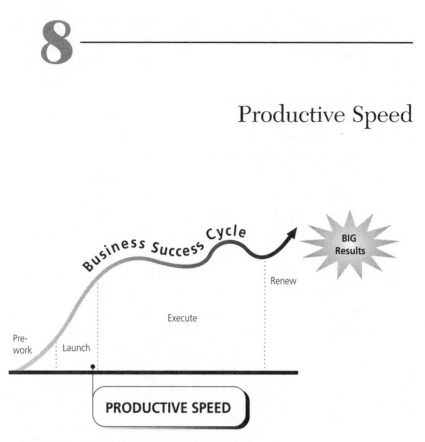

"Speed is the new management discipline."

Get the Train Moving, Now

On any business day in Japan, roughly half the country's 123 million people hurtle to work at 100 miles per hour on the world's fastest trains. That's a distinction envied by other countries, but not necessarily by the 63 million Japanese riding the rails. Efficiently loading the crush of passengers is so imperative to the nation's 300,000 railway workers that white-gloved "enforcers" rush along every platform, shoving and squeezing laggards aboard packed cars.

Let's be glad no such enforced mania is needed or even effective for success in business transformation or strategy execution. To put a large organization in motion, what matters is to get the train moving the right way, down the right set of tracks, right away. When that happens, you will be truly surprised to see how many people climb aboard before it leaves the station! The right people will get on immediately. Those who want to make the trip but were thinking they might be able to postpone it until a more convenient time will step on as well. Those who are uncertain about whether they want to go in the new direction will have to make up their minds. At some of the next few stops, some will get off because, after a closer look, they've changed their minds!

Forward motion gets both intellectual and emotional attention. In one sweep, it signals intention, purpose, and commitment, as well as the direction in which the organization is laying its new tracks.

Wait two years and then return to the scene of a corporate transformation launch and ask the CEO what could have been done differently that would have had the greatest impact on the success of the effort. You will get the same answer, every time. All of them wish they had moved more rapidly and all of them now believe they could have.

They wish that they had gotten off to a faster start. They wish they had launched more quickly into execution what was obvious at the time needed to be done. They wish they had dealt with nonaligned members of their leadership team sooner. They are kicking themselves for not reengaging employees faster behind their new vision and key initiatives. They wish they hadn't waited so long before beginning the learning process to test their initial business assumptions and refine their key initiatives. And they wish they had gotten more quickly to some visible early returns to be able to reinforce the commitments and expectations of employees, customers, suppliers and investors. Bottom line, they wish they had been better equipped to master the new management discipline of Speed.

Speed is a key enabler of success in transformations and strategic shifts. But it has to be the right kind and dosage of speed. *Productive* speed reinforces decisive action, which helps generate interest and energy and accelerates the realization of early returns and, ultimately, breakthrough results. But, unfortunately, as many executives try to apply more speed, they often feel that, "The faster I go, the 'behinder' I get!" Unproductive speed shows up as frantic flailing that produces a lot of activity, but no breakthrough results.

If you watch Olympic speed skiers, the fastest athletes make it look effortless. They are relaxed, yet focused. They carve deep, wide turns that are perfectly timed to put their shoulder just at the edge of the gate where they turn. By the time they start their run, they have already visualized their entire journey to the finish line multiple times so that when on the race course they can anticipate almost every twist and turn. That is how they achieve speed. Amateur skiers can be seen bombing down the hill with rooster tails of snow flying up around them, waving their arms, and seeming to be going fast, but, in reality, it is mostly wasted energy.

The same principles apply in business, but are not well understood. In fact, the key elements that create real speed, such as planning your route, developing a routine, staying calm, and thinking through the challenge before taking it on, are often believed to slow down the business. As a result, leaders shortcut these steps and don't take time to do strategic planning, focus and align the team, and engage employees. They think those kinds of processes are all bureaucratic and plodding—that it is better to just start doing something. There is a balancing point in all of this. But the average leadership team spends far too little time in preparing to run at top speed, and, hence, they operate handicapped, running at a frantic pace with a lot of wasted energy. George Coll, challenged with running his team like a start-up within a global multibillion-dollar company, explains speed this way, "Speed is a choice and it is a competitive advantage. A transformation process provides a vehicle to accelerate change. It can be a ritual like a pre-shot routine, not a rut."[1]

People make excuses that that there is no time for strategic planning or for having a dialogue with the team to prepare. As a result, they leave the starting line of strategy execution without having a plan—without a visualization of what they will encounter when they try to execute. Others throughout the organization don't understand what they need to do and, therefore, can't anticipate the right actions. Instead, they have to sit and wait for a succession of orders to come from the top. The system slows down as a result. The leaders get impatient and start demanding more of a "sense of urgency," which only serves to intimidate the team and make them second-guess their decisions even more. The team tenses up and becomes unable to solve problems for the obstacles they encounter. That causes the system to slow down even further. Then, the leaders start to micromanage everything, the top performers get frustrated and leave, and you are left with an organization of "yes-people" who wait for each new tactical change order from above. This doesn't work.

At the other extreme lie traps of analysis-paralysis—studies and projects that never end. Data are never quite enough or sufficient for some management teams. They just can't seem to put a fork in it. The results, ironically, are just about the same as in the opposite extreme. As leaders stay far removed from the operations, up in their offices in deep contemplation over what to do, forward movement grinds to a crawl, talent exits the scene, and those who remain drag themselves to work day after endless day waiting for some change for the better.

In between these extremes lies the *productive* kind of speed that has invigorated the transformation and strategy execution efforts that succeed.

The Benefits of Productive Speed

Getting to effective business results faster is, of course, the goal of applying speed. And as it turns out, it's not just about getting the same results faster; it is getting to better results faster. That is the payoff of *productive* speed. In our experience, as you increase the pace, shorten the decision cycles, and accelerate the alignment and engagement processes, the greater your results will be. Now, we're willing to concede that eventually there might be some natural limits to these effects of increased speed. It's just that we haven't encountered them yet!

The reason results get better is that speed reduces unproductive dithering; it doesn't allow time for dysfunctional political positions to crystallize. It avoids overanalyzing and, more important, overengineering solutions. It shifts the emphasis to a learning-from-doing mode, which enables leaders to achieve results and continue building on that success to reach even further goals.

In the early 1980s, it was believed that strategic plans should be ten years long (about the span of a typical CEO's tenure during those days), and that it would take multiple years to launch a transformation and turn an organization. But over the ensuing quarter century, many forces have conspired to dramatically accelerate the cycle times within organizations and the markets in which they compete. Perhaps the most profound and prolific influence on speed—the cycle time of execution—has been technology. As companies began to use the ACT methodology on the West Coast during the 1990s, the executives in these companies were quite appreciative of the tools for focused alignment and rigorous execution. But, what was new was that they all wanted to do these things in much less time. As they explained, the cycle time associated with their product development as well as the changing needs of their customers were a fraction of the big metal-bending and paper-pushing enterprises of the past. As time has progressed, another derivative phenomenon has unfolded. The ultimate diffusion of high technology across all sectors has caused companies in all sectors and of all shapes and sizes to become more capable of operating on a faster cycle. The "need for speed" has become ubiquitous across industries. The upgrades in the ACT methodology spawned by the high-tech sector have become useful to all industries, with fewer and lighter steps involving a more rapid launch pace to execution.

Other pervasive forces have also been at work reinforcing the need for speed. Not the least of which at the corporate level has been the increasingly heavy push for takeovers. To put it bluntly, if you take too long to improve your business, somebody else will get the job done for you! Rapidly expanding global competition, increasingly fickle customers, just-in-time supply chain management, and impatient activist shareholders are all colluding to drive the pace even faster today. To thrive and even survive today, executives need to be able to drive rapid cycles of improvement in their company strategies, business models, and operations.

When getting launched with speed, the objective is figuratively to get everyone in the pool and headed in the same direction, and only then to teach the finer points of the basic strokes to very motivated swimmers. Rather than the other way around, which typically involves trying to teach unmotivated employees to make changes they're not sure are warranted or have the skills to pull off.

All Aboard at Internet Speed

This brings us to the CEO of a successful technology company that hit a much unexpected problem during the Internet boom. The CEO had transformed the company from a niche software player in the 1980s to the second-largest retail software vendor behind Microsoft in the mid-1990s. It was an exciting time.

Given all its success, it was hard to believe that the company was experiencing difficulties. But revenue growth had flattened and several attempts to identify fast-growing businesses for acquisition had come up empty. As a result, the stock price had lost more than half its value. Worse yet, all this was happening at the beginning of the Internet boom. A war for talent had start-ups enticing star players with huge stock-option deals. At the company, talented people were jumping off the train in growing numbers. Many literally jumped into new BMW convertibles supplied by their new employers. Something had to be done—fast.

The CEO and his senior executives had an impressive track record. They had built companies from scratch, created breakthrough products, and led teams with a passion for new technologies. But the company now felt slow, plodding, and not very inventive. Every day, the *San Jose Mercury News* profiled the latest wunderkinds. Fresh-faced engineering geniuses like Marc Andreesen, the young brain behind Netscape, were making millions almost overnight. The CEO and his executives had no intention of sitting idly by, watching their company flounder.

They began by confronting their current reality. The company had grown by acquiring software makers with strong products but poor distribution. Its solid relationship with retailers helped give a quick boost to the lagging sales of companies it acquired. By the middle 1990s, though, few companies were left for the company to buy. It was still the dominant player in its market, but it lacked the means to jump-start growth. New markets had to be identified and a capability had to be created to internally innovate and develop new products.

A separate problem revolved around the company's structure. It had developed into a fairly loose collection of eight business units representing previously independent companies, each with its own product line. Little collaboration took place; in fact, the eight units often sniped at one another. Then, in the late 1990s, the company reorganized, coalescing into three highly focused, customer-centric business units—Security and Assistance Business Unit, Remote Products and Solutions, and Internet Tools. The three executives selected to run these units were chosen for their presumed ability to lead large, complex teams, generate growth, and boost new product development. Most important, they were viewed as both individual leaders and team players.

Obviously, the new arrangement left several of the old business-unit heads out of key leadership positions. Some of them—former chief executives of acquired businesses—were more comfortable leading small teams with no corporate oversight. In short, they weren't the kind of general managers the company now needed. They soon left the company. To use the train analogy, the company was positioned on a specific track and was starting to move in the right direction. The "wrong people" knew it and got off the train, just in time to allow for a smooth departure.

It was after that, in the summer of 1997, that the CEO assembled his senior management team. They agreed on a strategic transformation for the company: It would no longer focus on silo products; it would be a customer-driven company with the spotlight on solutions. To kick off the first year of the new company, they vowed that customer research would get as much attention as technology research. By understanding customer needs, the company would begin to create its own innovative products rather than just look for ways to acquire them. And while the market for retail software would remain a core piece of the business, growth would also come from moving into corporate markets. Above all, the leaders were brutally honest about the challenges their organization faced. In the end, they embraced a plan to take the company train down the track they had laid out together. With growing enthusiasm, they urged managers to step forward and speed the train to the next destination. They named their corporate transformation process "Taking Charge."

Rolling forward, this strategy put the company on a new path that kept gifted people in the company, eased out those who didn't fit into the new strategic plan, and attracted newcomers with exactly the right talents. By 1999, the shift toward corporate customers had become a significant part of the company's business.

Some people counsel that everything must be perfectly prepared for any kind of launch, with the strategy aligned and all the right people in the right positions. But many leaders who follow that advice find themselves shunted onto the side tracks, still waiting to fire up the engine as the market roars by and employees leave to find better vehicles to build their careers.

Preparation is important, but not at the expense of motion. As the example shows, being in motion has value in itself because you begin immediately to accrue small victories that entice the undecided to make a commitment to jump on board. Conversely, if you're going nowhere, you can't keep the right people who are ready to get things rolling and attract the right recruits. Also, you can never predict who might have to leave or who among the seeming laggards will be inspired to improve their game. Then, too, when things aren't going well, everyone's theory of action seems to be as good as any other; forward motion ends the theoretical debate.

Perhaps the most important reason to get moving is that every day of action accelerates the cycle of organizational learning and adaptation. Movement starts the learning process that must precede any necessary adjustments and refinements, which, in turn, increases your chances of besting your competitors. Cultures that are focused on execution aren't likely to let problems fester for years. In these cultures, the moment a solution is envisioned, it is put into play. If it proves to be faulty, it is just as quickly jettisoned and harvested for things learned to apply to the ongoing business.

In reflecting on the transformation experience of a global retailer, the president and COO recalled that one of the most important benefits was being able to see new leaders emerge from the ranks. Most of the executive team had tenures of 10 to 15 years, long by today's standards. The organization had struggled in recruiting outside talent and in making decisions about top team members who might not have been in the right roles for the new market requirements. But, continued waiting to get the right people on board was not getting the team anywhere. They had to get the organization in motion—no more waiting.

As the train began to move from a pure operations focus to a market-centric approach, it became clearly uncomfortable for many of the leaders to make the shift. At the same time, natural leaders who had before not been exposed to the senior team in terms of their strategic thinking and leadership had the chance to interact more directly with the executives. Within the top three layers of management, individuals with talents in strategic planning, process design, and customer research began to shine. These were skills the company did not think it had and it was a talent resource that was completely overlooked. By getting things in motion, these individuals were able to jump on board quickly, take leadership roles in helping the organization make the shift, and took the seats that others, by title, should have taken. For the president, the ability to get the train moving first and then use that motion to sort out the right people to keep was invaluable.

Designing the Process for Speed

The best way to drive the productive speed you need is to architect the process, checkpoints, and governance correctly so that people can handle productive speed. Without a specifically planned process to drive the pace, procrastination or distraction will set in. And delays that could have been anticipated and avoided will come up as surprises to derail the effort.

The way to avoid this procrastination is to develop a process architecture up front that lays out the important waypoints where there will be analysis, input, decisions, plans, and then execution. This architecture has to include all of the critical transformation principles of confronting reality, focus, alignment, engagement, and follow-through. In addition, it must clearly articulate when and where each person in the organization will have a chance to learn, provide input, and then make decisions that impact their area of responsibility—this includes all key governing bodies as well. The generic ACT process is shown in Figure 8.1.

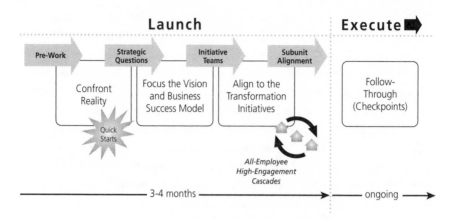

Figure 8.1 Accelerated Transformation launch road map

Typically, you should compress the first three steps into no more than a three- to four-month cycle, leaving only two to four weeks between major checkpoints and working sessions. If more time is allowed into the planning process up front, it will begin to weaken the launch by undermining the sense of urgency and won't add any more quality to what is required to get launched and to begin learning from execution.

The corporate finance team of a major energy company was facing the need to transform their organization. They had spent several months preparing to launch the next phase of transformation and were looking to complete detailed benchmarking to identify the required changes. For some people, there was a lot of pent-up demand for just getting on with the changes. Others were happy to keep asking more and more questions to delay the need to change—of course, they didn't vocalize it that way in the open. At the launch of the process, the CFO laid out a tight timetable for the process with three to four weeks between major decision points. This left a lot less time for overanalyzing, eliminated the dithering, and forced people out in the open to show their real perspectives because decisions were going to be made whether they voiced their opinion or not.

The first rounds of confronting reality and focus came to closure quickly and with just the appropriate amount of due diligence to support the pent-up decisions they already knew they needed to make. They realized that they could address the big "no-brainer" issues right away, get the process started, and then at quarterly checkpoints or the next annual cycle, ratchet up expectations. No need for perfection, which would postpone the engagement of the organization.

Just on the verge of engaging the full team, the delayers began to make their case again, this time louder. In the end, they won out for various reasons and were able to take the transformation process off of the timeline. They argued that there needed to be more bench-marking and best-practice analysis conducted before involving more people. Several extra months elapsed and you know what it got them? A large bill for a lot of benchmarking and best-practice work, a lot of frustration among the people who wanted to just get on with the changes, and a list of initiatives that was almost identical to what they had crafted on their own with some quick due diligence and dialogue within the leadership team. The delay didn't add anything to the improvement of the solution; instead, it wasted time, money, and momentum and caused needless second-guessing of the team's views.

On the front end of transformation and strategy execution projects, a concern is often raised. It goes something like this: "How can we get anything done in three to four weeks between the working sessions of the senior leadership team? If we are supposed to be making big decisions, we need more time for analysis." But when organizations have introduced more time, the same thing always happens. Nothing gets done for the first three to four weeks and then all the work tends to get jammed into the last two weeks, or even two days, before the next gathering of the senior team anyway. Despite this truism, the executive teams in most organizations find it uncomfortable to agree up front to get behind a shorter-cycle launch. This is where you as a leader have to help them understand and step up.

The No-Slack Launch

As the process is launched and the train begins to move, any slack that emerges in the speed and pace can quickly cause a decline in momentum. If too many stretch-outs and reschedules are introduced, forward momentum for the transformation or strategy execution effort can grind to a halt so that all you have left to work with is stale rhetoric. Be sure to set the proper pace to move your team and organization through the launch road map you have established to guide the effort.

Like so many things in life, there is never really a "perfect time" to launch into something new. It used to be that for convenience, companies would wait until the beginning of a full fiscal or calendar year to launch their efforts. But as the cycle time of everything has decreased and the pace of change has sped up, waiting two or three quarters to get launched is often not an option. If you have a hunch that the organization is stuck in a rut, now is the time to launch.

A typical launch can take anywhere from three to four months, depending on the willingness of the leadership team to apply the necessary focus to get it done. There are two important aspects of this approach to a launch: make it streamlined (that is, simple, with few major steps) and fast-paced.

Enrique Salem, who has served as CEO and executive business leader at several companies, reflects on the fast launch. "I've had very few opportunities other than with this process when we've gotten everybody from the CEO all the way through the last person in the organization involved in hearing the same message, aligning goals, and making commitments in such a short time. I think a lot of people completely underestimate the power of getting the entire organization hearing the same simple message and getting behind a single focus from top to bottom. It was really amazing how much energy was created at one time."[2]

Figure 8.2 reveals the streamlined process architecture you will find useful to launch a transformation. It shows the road map that was adapted to support the transformation launch of a $4 billion global company of about 14,000 employees. Here's how the road map works. First, its streamlined aspect means that all of the planning, launching, and engaging of the three top levels of leaders takes place in just five 1-day events: three for the Senior Leadership Team (SLT) and two for the Extended Leadership Team (ELT), which includes the senior leaders and their direct reports (essentially the leadership teams of the major components of the organization).

Launch Roadmap

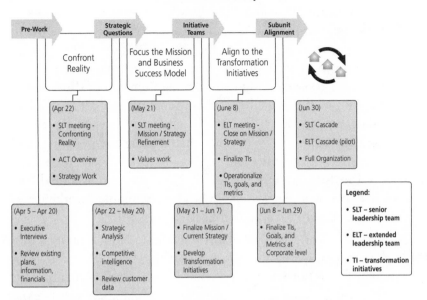

Figure 8.2 Expanded launch road map

The top row of boxes shows the major steps that take place as events in the ACT process. The middle row of boxes indicates working sessions for either the SLT or ELT. The bottom row shows the time spans for analysis and planning work. Again, notice that the time spans for this work are only three to four weeks in duration. This company was a fast mover, but even for them there was some concern up front about their ability to keep up with the pace outlined in the road map. As they got into it, they proved to be up to the task.

As discussed, one of the biggest causes of delay in these launch efforts is the time allotted for getting work done between the meetings. We've all been to big brainstorming meetings where there are long lists of ideas generated and the closing comment is a bold statement about, "OK, now we'll need to get on with doing something about these right away!" But in the end, it usually takes a week to get the meeting notes published (if they ever come out). In the background a team of administrative support people have considerable labor for days to translate scrawlings from numerous flip chart sheets into readable meeting notes. Leaders struggling to push on with all this information typically have to review the long lists of more or less random ideas before breaking them into categories and assigning them to work teams. This step typically adds at least another week or so of phone calls and lots of prodding and cajoling to get people to open up their schedules to take on the new project work. The project leaders then have to schedule the first meeting to talk about scope and purpose for their working team. So another two to three weeks can elapse before the first project team meeting can get scheduled. At this point, we are four to five weeks out from the working session and nothing has happened to advance the thinking and planning. And it will take another three to four weeks of work to get the analysis done and the team report prepared. Now you've consumed two months between working sessions. With four scheduled working sessions, you are at eight to nine months for a launch!

How can you effectively collapse the whole launch process into three to four months? Without losing anything? In fact, gaining not only precious time but also energy, commitment, and momentum?

First, set the complete timeline with prescheduled dates at the onset of the launch. That way, everyone knows exactly what needs to be done in terms of decision points at the key working sessions and the analytical grunt work that needs to take place between each main event. This enables your team to envision the full path, much like the speed skier. Now they know when the turns are coming and how and when their effort will need to be applied. Second, schedule the timing to either avoid or encompass other major corporate events so that you don't swamp peoples' calendars. Then, make sure to end each working session with a 30- to 60-minute working session to kick off the first meeting of any working teams that have been tasked to complete work before the next leadership session. This will feel like tactical work that could get done outside of the meeting, and it is. However, if you let up on this, you will add weeks to the overall timing to get the same work done.

In these working sessions, have the leaders identify the project leads, talk about who from each of their divisions needs to be assigned to work with the project leaders, and hammer out the objectives and scope, including interim reviews by the commissioning executive. Meeting notes are kept to a minimum, and they are captured in real time during the meeting by relying on simple, well-designed working templates on which just the highest-priority points from each working group are recorded, not their entire lists of ideas.

By the time such a working session is completed, the meeting notes are already done, the working teams have been assigned, they've scrubbed their objectives with peers and leaders, and the full project leadership and staffing have been worked out. At this juncture, it will take a day or so for the team leads to invite the right division representatives to the first meeting and the work can begin within days, not over months, following the conclusion of the senior leadership team working session. By using this approach, you will be able to drive more analytical rigor than you have been able to coax and cajole out of previous strategic decision-making efforts, while achieving tremendous engagement and input from working-level team members assigned to the work blocks between the leadership sessions. In a real crunch, some organizations have been able to work through the four key steps of the transformation launch with as little as two weeks between the management sessions.

By not allowing the normal amount of slack to enter the system, you not only speed the cycle time to engage the full organization and shorten the time to generate results, but also engineer a very significant shift in the operating rhythm of the company. There will be more of a sense of the value of speed generated through real-time feedback and dialogues, tight frameworks to prioritize discussions and actions, and expedited (or eliminated) administrative tasks.

That should give you an idea of how less is more in the game of transformation and strategy planning. As Jim Nassikas, the founding president of the Stanford Park Hotel on Nob Hill in San Francisco, once replied when asked why his employees seemed so effortless when performing consistently well, "It just comes down to a lot of 'monumental trivialities'!"

Quick Starts

Nothing builds momentum and a sense of urgency like clear progress and early wins. When staring at even the compressed launch timeline of three to four months, many businesspeople will look at that like an eternity today. And it is a long time. If the organization is not used to following processes and simplified templates, people will also mistake these as items that will slow the organization down. To clearly demonstrate the bias for action, *Quick Starts* are a critical element.

Just three weeks or so into the transformation of Anadigics, Inc., a high-flying semiconductor chip company that had lost its shine, the new CEO, Dr. Bami Bastani, gathered his senior team for the first confronting reality work session.[3] They met to review market realities, customer opinions, and the results of confidential interviews with the key leaders of the company. All of those fact sets indicated that there were big problems to fix to get the company back into a high-growth mode.

To distill the most important focus areas, the group worked on an exercise to quickly identify the "really bold ideas" for moving the company forward and the "really stupid things to be avoided." That simple exercise, as is typical, netted out some urgent issues that had long been avoided but that deserved immediate attention. They ranged from the need to launch an entirely new generation of products, to reorganizing into profit and loss oriented divisions, to fixing morale.

During a break in the session, Bami pulled a small circle of advisors together to contemplate the short lists of dos and don'ts the tablework groups had developed. After the larger group reconvened, most of the executives were expecting him to make some supportive comments about the quality of dialogue and thinking he observed during the previous session before introducing the next work session. In the back of their minds was the multiweek launch road map they had seen in his initial explanation of the process. This led them to expect that the process would take that long to unfold before real decisions would be made to cause action to take place. Not the case for this new CEO.

Bami opened the session by stating that the company might have put itself in a position of being a generation and a half behind on technology. This would require potentially 18 months to two years to resolve. He went on to say that over the next couple of months, many tough decisions about current R&D spending would require more analysis and refinement of the strategy to guide those decisions. On the subject of the morale issue, he explained that the leadership team would work through a process over some period of time, first setting values and then living them and gradually restoring confidence in winning throughout the company. Making people feel better on the inside, on the other hand, he reasoned was something that every individual would need to address on his or her own. Raising morale would not be a focus of the transformation effort, but would certainly be an expected outcome.

Finally, Bami addressed the organization design issues, agreeing with the team that the current design was not allowing leaders to make important decisions about their businesses. As a start-up, the original functional design had worked fine. As a growing public company, however, this structure had become too centrally focused and needed to be changed. He felt that if not addressed right away, the antiquated structure would stifle progress on the transformation itself and the initiatives that would follow. He targeted restructuring as a "Quick Start." In his mind, there was no need to have more dialogue or analysis about this obstacle and no reason to wait for the full process to unfold to take action. At that moment, he decided to change the structure and immediately tasked the vice president of human resources with initiating the design of the new divisional organization to be implemented immediately.

Decentralizing decision-making was the cornerstone of this bold move. Prior to the new CEO, Anadigics was organized in a centralized manner where the three cofounders had assumed financial, operational, and technology roles. Two factors had resulted in a decision-making gridlock, the new CEO observed: the retirement of the cofounder who had successfully led operations and the lack of sufficient systems and infrastructure to succeed as a public company for its size.

This decisive action, or Quick Start, was a clear signal to the team that issues they brought up would be seriously considered for immediate action if warranted. That even the streamlined launch process would be interrupted and accelerated for cause. It signaled to the team that this was not some overly bureaucratic process that was being followed. When the time was right to make a call and move on, there would be no waiting.

After being established by the executive leader, the Quick Start convention kept members of the leadership team on the edge of their seats for the remainder of the launch process. As a result, the team moved into the next exercises and next days and weeks of work sessions with an acute sense that what they were working on would absolutely have an impact. By the time the group reconvened several weeks later, a long-standing obstacle bound up in a legacy organization design that had left too much direct power and control in too few hands had been removed. Whereas at the time of the arrival of the new CEO, many of the VPs confided that they didn't think that anything could be done to shift the traditional power base that had been put in place to maximize the control of the founders. Seeing the CEO address this persistent impediment as a Quick Start was inspiring and it made them want to take on even more. In their minds, anything was now possible.

As Bami reflected, some time following this intervention, "Quick Starts established confidence in the organization that we could win. They were very powerful, and that sent a signal to the team that this was going to be an action-oriented process." Quick Starts addressed the organization structure issue and the need to move to decentralized market-focused business segments; they also created 90-day wins that could energize the organization. By the end of the second day of the two-day "Recognize Reality" workshop, executive teams were formed to address the low-hanging fruit that would have significant impact in the company and its operations. These were tracked weekly in results meetings and reported on at the next quarterly leadership checkpoint meeting. The streamlined organization and the 90-day wins that were produced as a result of the Quick Starts were turning points for Anadigics. Bami reflects, "We knew then that we could overcome the obstacles and effect a turnaround. So, Quick Starts established the kind of positive atmosphere we were hoping to create to propel Anadigics forward. As we took on the task of articulating the company's core values, I was not surprised when "Responsive and Decisive" was overwhelmingly chosen by the management team as one of the core values."

As you refine the architecture of your transformation process and get the effort launched, look for those major no-brainer issues that are getting in the way of progress, the ones that don't require a lot more analysis to address, and take them on immediately as Quick Starts. People will appreciate your decisiveness and honesty, knowing that their time won't be wasted on a process that might not address the really important issues facing the company. The boost in energy and momentum you will experience will be palpable.

How Do You Keep Time?

Having established a strong drumbeat that builds momentum through the full organization, you need to add one more element to be able to successfully lead with *productive* speed. It is less tangible than the development of the road map or the declaration of Quick Starts, but it is a critical element nonetheless. It is how you as a leader manage the *sense* of time for the rest of the organization.

In English, there is one word for time. In ancient languages, there were more. Specifically, there were words that meant how time passes in sequence, the ticking of the clock, the passing of years. A different reference was to what we might call today a "moment in time" in which something significant happens. This second type of time does not have a sense of duration—only of depth and purpose. Although there is no equivalent word in English today, we do speak of getting "lost in time" when visiting with a dear friend or having a real "moment" with someone where you unexpectedly connect very deeply with them.

One of the most difficult balances for a leader to strike is between wanting to move with speed and taking the "time" to have deeper dialogue and engage a broader group to enrich the thinking and generate ownership of the decisions. When staring at an e-mail Inbox that continues to grow like a weed if unattended and struggling to cope with a constant barrage of ringing phones, buzzing text messages, and "one-quick-thing" interruptions after another, it is easy to feel like there is no time for anything but to keep up on the tactical treadmill. But leaders might choose to respond to the ticking clock in very different ways. One way intensifies the pressure on people around you and the other way allows people to catch their breath and quickly drop into deep conversations.

Let's examine the two styles in action. One president of a division of a large telecommunications company used to come rushing through the door consistently four to five minutes late, breathing hard, with a big stack of papers under her arm, saying something like, "Another crazy day. Sorry about the late start for this meeting!" She would look over the agenda for the meeting and quickly add, "OK, we don't have a lot of time for all of the things on the agenda, so let's hit the top points and then I need to leave a few minutes early to prep for my next meeting." This setup for the meeting invariably caused any presenters to feel extreme pressure to click rapidly through their presentations, talk quickly, and respond to questions if and only if asked. Conditions like these don't really give attendees a chance to grasp the full gist of the presentation or to feel comfortable asking questions for fear of slowing things down. So, in the end, everyone nods and says, "No real questions here, the presentation was good. Thanks. We'll think about what you've said and get back to you." Then, the presenter cuts out early with no call to action to lock in the major takeaways or actions. This leaves the topic to recycle over and over again, creating even more of a feeling that there aren't enough hours in the day to do everything.

Another division president in the same company had a much different style. Even if he was a little late for meetings, he would walk deliberately into the room, very composed, and say something like, "I hope you were able to get started and that my schedule didn't hold you up too much. Now, can someone give me a brief on what's happened so far? I want to understand where we are on each of the projects on the agenda." He would then fit into the flow of the meeting and make an effort to hear out each presenter and then ask very pointed questions, sometimes at an astonishingly deep level of detail. He was prepared. Others would join in the dialogue and then the answers would start to become fairly clear about the decisions to be made or next steps based on the presentation. His willingness to "make time" for the deeper dialogue allowed the team to get into the real issues and make decisions. They could then move on to the next set of issues to move the business forward. These moments of dialogue-based decision making are that second type of "time" that leaders must produce out of the hectic and fast-paced schedules we all lead.

Neither president had any more hours in the day than the other. However, the leadership presence and approach by the first president made the team run in frantic cycles in which no depth was reached in their conversations and no actions were taken as a result. The second president kept the team feeling relaxed and in control so that even when pressured to make decisions, they could drop into a zone where they could have an open dialogue, debate issues, and then take decisive action quickly.

One of the best nonbusiness examples can be found in the way that Joe Montana, former quarterback of the San Francisco 49ers, would run the last-minute, come-from-behind wins that made him famous and earned the team four Super Bowl titles. This has only been accomplished by one other quarterback in history. Others would see 1 minute, 58 seconds on the clock and begin to really fear that time was running out. To hear Joe talk about those experiences today, he makes it sound like two minutes was all the time in the world. He explains that it takes eight or nine seconds to run a play, so, to him, a couple of minutes left in a game was a lot of time. And, his perception of abundant time would rub off on the whole team. The 49ers would drop into a zone under his leadership in which they were in control, focused, and accurate. The result was fantastic execution when it really counted, with little time to waste.[4]

In business, there is no end to the game, so no literal two-minute drill. However, when you gather your team for regular staff meetings or off-site sessions, what tone do you set about the sense of time? Do you amplify the pressure of time and rush through everything in a whirlwind or do you allow for the team to drop into deep dialogue and get to the real issues? As in the example of Joe Montana, that ability to drop into the zone will actually speed up decision making and execution. This critical element of leadership has not typically been explored by observers of business leaders today, but it turns out to be a real key in achieving true productive speed in transformations and strategy execution.

By creating a well-structured game plan and deliberately managing the sense of "time" with your team, you will actually accelerate your overall effort.

Speed as a Leadership Discipline

Organizational speed is something that absolutely can and should be managed better. The keys to creating speed are counterintuitive to many leaders. *Productive* speed is achieved when the right kind and amount of process architecture is put in place to stimulate rapid, but deep, decision cycles in management working sessions and ongoing performance checkpoints that drive true progress, not simplistic tactical reactions.

Taking time to enter into meaningful dialogue with your team can also seem like a luxury that your limited schedule won't allow. However, leaders eventually discover that shortcutting dialogue to get to faster action only leads to confusion in execution, where debates are repeatedly revisited, problems are dealt with too late, and, hence, big decisions that could create profound breakthroughs are avoided. Leaders who have mastered the ability to drop in the zone with their teams and get deeply into issues quickly have discovered new levels of clarity, focus, and speed in taking decisive action, which, in turn, gets them to bigger breakthrough results faster—and isn't that what we really want from *productive* speed?

Tips for Productive Speed

- Get the train moving quickly.

- Get a grip on the meaning of "productive" speed and how to facilitate it.

- Identify Quick Start initiatives and generate early wins even before the full transformation process plays out.

- Preschedule all working sessions through the launch and all quarterly checkpoints for at least one full performance year following launch.

- Create "time" to get your team deep in the zone to address the real issues.

Endnotes

[1] Based on an interview conducted by Michael Kanazawa on March 8, 2007 with George Coll, SVP at one of the world's largest global retailers. Reprinted by permission.

[2] Based on an interview conducted by Michael Kanazawa on April 20, 2007 with Enrique Salem, SVP at a $5 billion global software company and prior CEO of a successful technology start-up. Reprinted by permission.

[3] Based on an interview conducted by Robert H. Miles with Dr. Bami Bastani, CEO of Anadigics, Inc and former president of National Semiconductor, on April 9, 2007. Reprinted by permission.

[4] Joe Montana, *The Winning Spirit: 16 Timeless Principles That Drive Performance Excellence* (New York: Random House, Inc., 2005).

Creating Leadership Power at All Levels

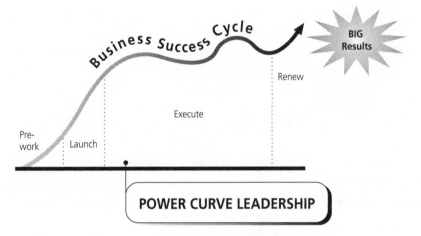

"Power given away comes back in multiples."

One of the underlying drivers and benefits of the ACT process is that it creates leaders at all levels. The process overall, and especially the high-engagement cascades, provide a structure and set of expectations for leadership that can fundamentally shift the organization and produce innovation and stronger results. There has been much written describing the dynamics of leadership power, engagement, and empowerment. This chapter does not intend to provide the depth or theory on this topic that can be found in prior works, but rather to describe through a simple framework how leaders have been able to generate organizational power by shifting the approach to leadership at each level in their organization.

The Power Curve

How do you measure the success of a leader? The common answer from leaders who have achieved great results is that the success of a leader is measured by looking at the success of their team members. One CEO, who took his company from being a hundreds-of-millions-of-dollars company to being a multibillion-dollar *Fortune 500* company, puts it this way, "I've always judged my personal success not by how far I have come, but by how many people I've brought with me." The more power individuals at all levels bring to their work, the more powerful the organization.

To put this idea in context, let's look at the Power Curve chart in Figure 9.1. The Power Curve is a concept that represents how you build power in an organization. It highlights for leaders the shifts that need to take place as one moves from being an individual contributor to a top-level executive. The High-Powered curve shows a healthy organization where the power to make decisions, innovate, and run the business is broadly shared throughout all levels of the organization. Too often, however, leaders operate in a way that looks more like the Under-Powered curve. In this case, all significant decisions are made at the very top; middle managers have minimal control over operating budgets or decisions; and employees simply follow the rules made by others above them.

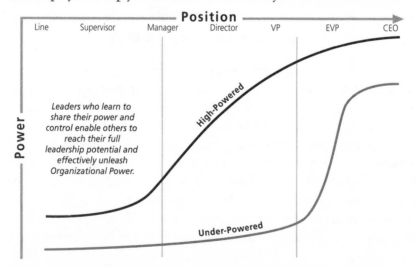

Figure 9.1   The Power Curve: High-Powered versus Under-Powered Organizations

© Dissero Partners, May 6, 2005

The Under-Powered Organization

An under-powered organization is one where the top leaders tell their underlings what to do and make all of the decisions. In this type of organization, the strategy is often set at the top and then quite literally rolled down to the organization. Managers, directors, and even vice presidents feel powerless to change anything significant and just wait to follow orders.

If your curve looks like this under-powered example, ask yourself if you or your team is choosing to hire people with less experience, skills, and intellect than those currently holding power at the top. If so, you will spend all of your time "teaching" your young management team, keeping up their energy, and cheerleading from the front. This is exhausting, limiting, and doesn't enable you to harness the full power of the organization. And although making every call can feel deceptively powerful at the top, doing so really limits the influence and full potential of the top leaders as well.

Leaders in this situation are often frustrated by the lack of initiative and innovative thinking by their team. But, any objective observer in the room can spot how leaders holding on to power monopolize decision making and shut down any creativity that might otherwise emerge from their teams. Why should anyone else attempt to contribute while under the control of an all-powerful, know-it-all leader?

The unfortunate result in the typical under-powered case is that while leaders create strategies, the rest of the organization lacks understanding of the strategy, lacks passion and commitment to drive results, and has no vested interest in making the strategy work. Missing valuable inputs from below, such leader-spawned strategies lack the commitment, clarity, and specificity required for robust implementation.

Shifting Up the Power Curve

If the organization is under-powered, the challenge is then to shift the Power Curve "up" to look more like the High-Powered curve. In this case, the senior executives engage the full organization by releasing accountability of day-to-day tactics to middle managers to create time for strategic thinking at the top, and structure time and forums to effectively vet their strategic ideas with lower levels in the organization. This results in a cascading of power to all levels, which leads to breakthrough results. Let's look at what takes place at each level to move towards the high-powered organization.

Executive Management

The top band in the Power Curve includes executives at the EVP and CEO levels. Organizations are always a reflection of their top leaders, including both the positive and negative things that are done as well as what is left undone. If the top leader is interested in the well-being of people and leads by asking questions, leaders down below will become imprinted to help others find solutions on their own, from midlevel managers down to salespeople practicing consultative selling with their customers. If the top leader always has to be the "smartest person in the room with all the answers," so will every person in the organization, all the way down to the customer-facing employee who tells the customer in overly technical terms why their product isn't working because of user errors. In this way, everything a top executive does gets magnified throughout the organization; so it is critical to get this part right.

As executives reach the top levels, they are faced with a tough balance between serving as the top leader and allowing others to lead as well. The new executive knows he or she was hired based on experience, skills, and knowledge and wants to demonstrate that clearly to the team to build confidence. Hopeful employees want to know that their new boss has a vision and clear sense of how to win and, therefore, they have a tendency to look to their leader for answers. However, at the same time, the newly promoted leader likely does not have the depth of experience or knowledge of the new team and organization to definitely know what to do. And the middle managers below them are leaders themselves who don't really appreciate simply being told what to do.

As a result, the interaction that the VPs below the executive desperately want and need is to engage with their leader in an open dialogue about the business strategy and have a deeper conversation about the organization. They want to question the logic of "conventional wisdoms" without being shot as nonbelievers or tagged as trying to dodge their next round of quarterly numbers. They want to be able to interact with the full team to debate issues that exist across organizational silos without being accused of political posturing. If as a top leader you take this desire for open dialogue as a questioning of your authority, you will shut it down immediately, which will disengage your subordinate leaders. So the balance point you must strike is to engage and facilitate open dialogue for input while being ready to make the tough calls when necessary. In the end, the final calls do rest on the shoulders of the top leaders. The question is: Do you want full information and support from your team when you make such calls?

This Is Your Day Job

It was the end of an all-day working session with senior executives in the company boardroom. These men and women had spent nearly ten hours in the room, reviewing plans and renewing commitments to each other and to the company's chief executive. The air was stale, the trash cans were overflowing, and notepads were covered with scribbles.

As they prepared to leave, one senior vice president stood up and said, "Okay, now I need to get back to my day job."

He was the tireless leader of a fast-moving business unit in one of the hottest areas of Internet software development. Chances are, he was just wisecracking about going from this exhausting meeting to another with his own team. Or maybe he was simply trying to lift a worn-down group. But the CEO was still there, and he was in no laughing mood.

The company's executives had lately felt overloaded by the transformation, working hard to launch new initiatives while also carrying on their day-to-day responsibilities. The CEO and most of the senior team spoke repeatedly about setting a new baseline, but many were hard put to change their work habits. People were taking on more and more and excelling at less and less. As a result, resources were stretched thinner, people ran faster, but the transformation slowed down. The whole day had been about resetting the whole baseline to clear priorities.

The vice president's comment about his "day job" drew the CEO's immediate attention. With a sense of disbelief, the CEO growled, "What do you think we were just doing today? We were setting strategic priorities for the company. And if you don't think that's a part of your real job as a senior vice president and officer of this company, you're mistaken. I want everyone to understand that setting priorities for our teams is one of the most important things we can do as a leadership team. If you're not spending time on this, you're not doing your job."

If the CEO's expectations hadn't been clear before, that was no longer the case. The VP quietly explained that his comment was meant as a joke. The tension in the room slowly began to abate. The time pressures will be great as the senior executives create time in their overloaded schedules for working on the strategic direction and focus. The only way for them to create time is to call upon their teams of vice presidents and directors to take on more daily responsibilities. In other words, let go of a bit of control.

Everyone Takes a Half Step Up

The middle managers of the company should be fully capable of running the operations on a day-to-day basis, at the very least for a few days at a time. To increase the power of the organization, executives need to release more of the day-to-day tactics to the control of the middle managers, at least by a half step up, which opens the time to think strategically about the business. Tony Weiss, who worked his way through almost every functional role on his way to president and CEO of a major corporation, points out, "Even if you did have the ability to do each job below you best, you just can't do that. You cut off the personal commitment of everyone else. The senior executives really need to set direction, provide support, hold people accountable, and help course correct when necessary."[1]

If this happens at the executive levels, it creates room and a challenge at every level for people to take a half step up. With the expanded responsibilities of directors, managers will have to release some of their control to their supervisors to cover the work they took on to de-load their directors. Capabilities are expanded at all levels and time for broader thinking frees up at the top so that better and more timely strategic decisions can be made. What does this look like in middle management?

Middle Management

In the middle of the Power Curve chart, from the director level and on to VP, there are large spans of control, multiple layers of management, and greater complexity with which to deal.

A common trap for managers and supervisors is that they often get promoted to director or VP based on their ability to meet the numbers or for technical expertise. Many hard-charging people will deliver results by doing things on their own. If their team has trouble delivering on a piece of analysis, the boss will just do it over the weekend. When a critical sale hangs in the balance, the boss will go in for the close. And when too many customer calls come in for their people, to keep service ratings high, a frustrated supervisor will start fielding them himself. You can hit the numbers for a while by doing this, but you are not building the capabilities of your team, and this approach is neither sustainable nor scalable.

Your team members, in turn, carry this approach into their next-level job, believing that it is more important to make the numbers and look good than to build a fully capable team.

The hero approach can work when the team is 10–15 people, but it breaks down when the team becomes large and includes other leaders who each have their own teams to lead. If you micromanage at the middle management level, you will stunt the growth of the team leaders below you and eventually drive them out of the business. You will end up with a junior team of followers that all key off of you. There is no scale in that; there is no power. Your job in middle management is to pick the right people as your team leaders, set a clear direction and priorities, and then help your team to build the capabilities and skills of their own teams. There is a sharing of power with your direct reports that can create scale and drive a high-powered organization.

A Real High Flyer

Years ago, the airline industry was just starting to work through consolidation and very challenging profit pressures. Walt Torgersen, a midlevel manager at the time, was handed an organization. It was all ground operations for a major carrier at the Detroit Metropolitan Airport, a full team of about 350 people. The real challenge was that it had been run previously by three managers, five crew chiefs, and 34 supervisors. Through two rounds of job cuts, Walt's new management team had been pared back to just him and the 18 supervisors. It was a massive 24/7, time-critical operation. Although there were cutbacks in management, there were no cutbacks in performance expectations.

For a few months, he tried valiantly to manage in the same command-and-control model that he had learned through his experience in the company and industry. Late one night while staring at a stack of papers so large that even another all-nighter couldn't clear it, his mind broke free from the old model. He set a personal objective to completely change the model of how things were done as a leader. It was mainly out of necessity due to complete task overload and a desire not to lose his sanity and his marriage over the incredible workload and stress.

His airport operations team had been having difficulty meeting the standards for turnaround time with baggage handling and many other performance indicators. With the larger span of control, even with his experience in the various work groups, he could not get his hands in and solve the issues in every area. The job was way too big. He also only had supervisors in each work area who held no overall management authority outside of their specific job area. So, he took the problem to his team of supervisors who each ran various pieces of the operation.

He started by telling the supervisor team that the job was too big for him alone and that he needed their help. He described the standards, shared a few ideas, and gave each of them authority to run their area. In addition, he asked several of the stronger supervisors to pick up key functional roles to help consolidate communications and decisions. These functional areas were things like budgeting and scheduling. Each group started to own their own results, and as supervisors became busy with higher-level tasks, their union teams began to step up as well and pitch in to help. At each level, people were stepping up to do more. As Walt describes it, "People just came alive. There was no way you could ever have mandated that people do the things they were doing. In fact, in some cases, the workers were even stretching safety standards to push performance higher and that had to be reined in a bit."[2] Walt did have considerable experience and had ideas to share on how to do things better as well. In those cases, his approach was to plant ideas, to casually brainstorm with people at quiet times during the day, when the time was right, to get them thinking.

Within a few months, the paperwork was being handled in the work groups and not only were the performance indicators moving up to standards, but up to the top of the company across all airports. At the end of the year, the baggage handling crew, for example, had set historical performance records. Executives at headquarters called to invite Walt to speak at an executive function as recognition for a job well done and to share how he was able to drive the team to deliver such great results. Most people aspiring to reach the next level of executive management would have jumped at the chanced to get "face time" with the executives and to receive the accolades. He didn't go.

He explained to the executives that he really didn't know the details of how the team did so well, that it was his team leads who really made the changes. So instead, he asked his team leads if some of them would like to go instead. Two went to represent the group, one baggage supervisor and one union-represented bag room lead, not exactly what the executives had expected. It also wasn't what his team had expected. The proud looks on the faces of his team as he asked them to go to the headquarters meeting were all the accolades Walt needed. He went on to become a top executive at the airlines later, leveraging the full engagement of his teams that grew to over 3,700 employees. That is how middle managers can release personal power and control to create a high-powered organization.

Front-Line Managers

The left side of the Power Curve chart in Figure 9.1, shows that the role of supervisors or front-line managers. While at these levels, the basics are learning to give clear orders, judging the work of others, providing constructive feedback, and confronting difficult people and situations while staying in control. However, there are also clear differences in leading through sharing of power at these lower organizational levels as well as huge benefits if done right. In fact, this level of leadership is incredibly important because they head the teams that directly interact with customers.

Consider two examples: Southwest Airlines has an extremely unique customer experience that is capped off by very friendly flight attendants who greet you with jokes, sing songs over the PA system, and generally make life a little more enjoyable. Their high-powered organization is so well established that it constitutes a competitive advantage today. Contrast this with the call center employees at many organizations who seem ambivalent to get your call at best, if not annoyed that you've disrupted their day. Supervisors in the call centers would love for their representatives to have the same positive spirit as Southwest's flight attendants.

Because it seems so out of the ordinary, Herb Kelleher, the former CEO of Southwest, was asked how it was that Southwest got their flight attendants to sing. Here was his response:

> *"Southwest flight attendants sing because they want to. We don't program our flight-attendant training to teach people to sing or tell jokes. What we say is, 'If that is your basic personality, feel free to go ahead and do it.' We're not trying to train you to be anything different from what you really are. If singing buoys up your heart, makes you feel good, go ahead and do it. We have tried to say to our people, 'You don't have to put on a mask, you don't have to be an automaton when you come to work. You can just be yourself.' Wasn't it Robert Frost who said, 'Isn't it a shame that people's minds work furiously until they get to work?' Well, that's because they feel that they become artificial and constrained by the workplace."*[3]

It is not a rule, it is not command and control, and it is not just holding people accountable that makes excellence emerge from people in front-line jobs. People, regardless of rank, want to be valued for what they do well, to be put into a position where they can excel, make a difference, and then be allowed the power and freedom to be their best. In many call-center environments, supervisors and service representatives interact only over how to follow minimal standards. In contrast, Southwest Airlines is an example of what is possible in a high-powered organization; one in which an engaged workforce brings extra creativity to continue improving the customer experience every day.

Big Ideas from within the Team

After you start leveraging the full organization's power through the shifting of the Power Curve, you will immediately benefit from big and practical ideas that boil up from the organization. And that is how innovation and breakthrough performance are achieved.

To many executives, the quality of strategic thinking is surprising when they open it up to their teams. Mike Benjamin, head of marketing for a nearly billion-dollar software division, reflected on the quality of the strategic thinking throughout his company. The top managers of the division were gathering in Athens, Greece to provide input and help shape the division's emerging strategic initiatives. Mike had worked to generate a practical focus on one of the three initiatives called Marketing Excellence. He wanted the initiative to be understandable and relevant to the field sales and operations teams that were coming in from their tactical roles around the world.

Some executives had been especially worried that the field groups might not connect well with a more strategic view of the initiatives and wanted to make the initiatives more tactical. Mike described the feedback he received, "I was really surprised at what a broad and strategic view the team had. The quality of strategic thinking was great. It caused me to broaden the scope of the initiative to something with much more impact to the overall business. And it was great knowing that it was really what the company and the field specifically wanted. It wasn't viewed at that point as 'the marketing team's push for more funding,' but rather what we all needed to do to accomplish the strategy."[4]

In addition to generating a strong strategic view, many of the recommendations senior executives receive when they sincerely encourage involvement and solicit feedback from below are powerfully simple and carry important practical operational insights as well. At a recent tablework session at a multi-billion dollar global concrete and rock business, this became very clear. The work group consisted of a number of field operations teams, including truck drivers. One of the top corporate initiatives was to manage energy costs better. A company-wide target was set and each part of the company had developed commitments to deliver their part in creating an overall fuel cost reduction. As the assembled truck driver group began to work the issue, there was the typical silence as people thought about how they could help the company manage energy costs better. Slowly, as people began to share ideas, the room erupted into lively dialogues at each table.

Before the readouts began, the leaders weren't quite sure what to expect or if there would be any real breakthroughs. They were genuinely surprised when some real nuggets were revealed. One group of drivers came up with the idea that at major construction sites, there is typically a long line of trucks that forms early in the mornings in which many trucks sit idling while waiting to receive permission to enter the construction site. The presenter at one group stated, "After a specified period of time, we should shut down the engines and wait to restart when the line begins to move. That would definitely save gas."

Another idea came up, "You know, I don't think we really check tire pressure very often on our trucks. We think that the maintenance crews should keep the tire pressure up in the tires. That would create real savings across a fleet of thousands of trucks." Some quick mental calculations made it clear that these could actually create very large savings across this multi-billion dollar company. And, not only would these ideas likely have been overlooked in a more top-down exercise on energy savings, but now the people who brought up these ideas really wanted to prove to the company that the savings would be real. Implementing these actions that had been identified by the front-line workers added up to significant savings for the company. That's how you jump-start a fundamental transformation process at the grass roots level while releasing power into the organization.

Those ideas and the related savings did not require months of benchmarking, reengineering, and new IT systems. It was just generating a high-powered organization that included the people closest to the real work in talking about how to get an initiative accomplished with practical, simple ideas that were quick to implement.

Sharing Power Creates Power

One of the hardest things to do in creating a full shift toward a high-powered organization is to trust your team enough to give some of your power away to them. Typically, the top leader must create the initial drive for action. However, after that is done, it is imperative at all levels of management rise to the occasion and take ownership of their piece of the effort. Too often, micromanaging and overly tight controls at the top limit the power of the next level down, and this style of leadership gets magnified to a point that people are marginalized throughout the organization.

The most powerful thing any manager can tell one of his or her team members in confronting a business problem or decision is, "What do you think we should do about that?" And then hearing their idea, build on it, ensure it's aligned to the strategy, and, most important, give them the latitude and resources to do something about it.

Tips for Power Curve Leadership

- Starting with the top of the organization, create a high-powered organization by sharing power at each level.

- Make strategic planning and priority setting an expectation of the management "day-job" in addition to tactical operations and day-to-day results.

- Releasing accountability for day-to-day tactics to your team creates the necessary time to engage in the thinking and strategic planning necessary for setting up breakthrough results.

- Assigning team-wide accountabilities for individuals creates greater ownership for the overall team results and better leverages the leader's time.

- Generating a high-powered organization creates greater innovation that will come from the bottom up.

Endnotes

1   Based on an interview conducted by Michael Kanazawa on March 29, 2007 with Tony Weiss, prior president and CEO of a $4 billion retail company. Reprinted by permission.

2   Based on an interview conducted by Michael Kanazawa on May 21, 2007 with Walt Torgersen, prior VP of maintenance operations at a global airline. Reprinted by permission.

3   C. Lucier, "An Interview with Herb Kelleher," *Strategy and Business* 35 (2004): 119–126.

4   Based on an interview conducted by Michael Kanazawa on May 9, 2007 with Mike Benjamin, VP of marketing at a nearly $1 billion software division of a global oilfield services company. Reprinted by permission.

10

Building Operational Traction

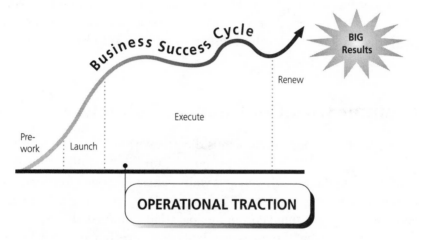

"Traction is where strategies meet breakthrough results."

We all know it; the Achilles' heel of any effort to shift direction is the ability to build traction by following through. The critical path to achieving breakthrough results is always encumbered by diversions and distractions that have the potential to cause the initially committed to wander off the path. The basic mechanics to follow through are well understood. Set goals and use metrics to track progress, keep your priorities in check, follow up on progress, make timely adjustments, and so forth. It is all so simple, but how many of your New Year's resolutions do you keep? How often do you think of them after declaring them at the beginning of the year?

It's unnatural for many of us to doggedly follow through on things we say we will do. In fact, it is so difficult that Dr. Edward Miller,

CEO of the hospital at Johns Hopkins University, pointed out, "If you look at people after coronary-artery bypass grafting two years later, 90% of them have not changed their lifestyle."[1] So, even when our lives are on the line, it is tough to follow through with changes to which we know we need to stay committed.

How can you break that cycle of setting goals and ignoring them until setting new ones again when you realize you haven't followed through? You tell others what you intend to do and, therefore, publicly commit, you put a plan in place to get into a routine, and you get a workout partner or personal trainer (aka a professional nudge). Not surprisingly, the same things we use for making personal changes can hold true for leading your business from BIG ideas to BIG results.

Commit with Confidence, Publicly

Following through on a plan is directly correlated to the amount of investment and commitment you make up front to build your own confidence in the plan. If you and your team spend one afternoon, or maybe just a long flight on a business trip, developing a strategic vision and creating some corporate goals that sound good, how confident will you be that the plans are right? Not very. In fact, you'll know in your gut that the ideas were quickly put together off the top of your head and are not rooted in any real analysis and strategic thinking. So now, what will happen when results are not building as quickly as you hoped and a new "silver bullet" idea is pitched up for growth? You'll likely jump at that new idea and scrap the old plan. There will be no confidence and conviction in the existing plan to see it through.

Some flexibility is fine and many midcourse adjustments will be necessary, but it is the constant switching, layering on, and dropping of initiatives that causes confusion, gridlock, and lack of accountability. With any long-term plan, there will be ups and downs in the results and you need to have a strong enough conviction in your plan to stick through the small cycles. Of course, there are also the larger cycles when full-course corrections might be necessary. You will address those with regular doses of confronting reality, which are best done on an annual basis or when major industry events occur. But it is the daily, weekly, and quarterly shifts and pressures that can cause organizations to blow too much with the shifting winds.

What do you need to do to boost your confidence in your strategic plans? The steps of engaging your team to confront reality and then setting a strategic direction that is rooted in customer and non-customer input, field perspectives, and a sound business success model are great starts to building confidence in your plan. Conducting a rapid due diligence assessment up front puts external validation and depth of thinking into your plans. Announcing to the full organization the full "safe passage" process road map that shows all of the launch efforts and quarterly checkpoints up front bolsters the plan with public commitment as well. In fact, prescheduling the dates of all major checkpoint meetings for the year really helps set a drumbeat that gets everyone's attention and won't be easily forgotten. Finally, setting, documenting, and communicating your personal commitments to action, which should include a commitment to lead the transformation process through the full cycle, will help seal your commitment and, therefore, the commitments of others.

Building Traction

In addition to the conviction and commitment to the plan, there is a need, especially in the early stages, to make sure that the transformation initiatives are fully sponsored and driven from the top. Building traction takes muscle and drive; it is not an automatic part of the process and is why it takes senior leadership up front. The key to building traction with the initiatives is to make sure that they become a part of the normal daily running of the business rather than being treated as a special program or overlay.

One company had created a set of three initiatives, one of which was on Customer Focus. Within customer focus, there were two main areas of focus, one relating to customer perceptions (for example, value or service) and the other on building the company brand. Co-champions on the executive team were named to lead the effort. One was a line manager running merchandising and the other a functional manager running marketing. The selection was intentional to make sure that what had been a disconnect between the two silos in the past would be bridged. It worked well to get the two departments in sync at the beginning stages.

Over time, the merchandising VP began to run weekly sessions with his part of the initiative team focused on customer perceptions. The VP used the initiative team as a platform for bringing merchandising, marketing, and store operations/salespeople together weekly to tackle the problem as a team. They tackled the biggest problem first, customer perception of value. Customers thought the company did not have very competitive prices. The team worked these meetings into their normal planning cycle for merchandising decisions that fed into the weekly marketing plans and also directly into the store operations. In short order, customer perceptions began to change.

The marketing VP was early in the stages of building brand positioning and worked more directly with the ad agency and marketing team on defining the brand. This was good to get things started, but a by-product was that when it came time to launch the new brand and for the store employees to "live the brand," they were not easily moved. The sphere of influence of that part of the initiative team had stayed too narrowly focused and ownership didn't move beyond marketing. The field organization had not been a part of that transformation team. They saw the normal executive reviews you would expect in a campaign development process, but hadn't been engaged in the process. As a result, it was very difficult to get the company fully committed to the new brand positioning.

The merchandising VP forced traction on his initiative across the business by making it a part of "daily life" for people in the normal operating roles for them. It wasn't a special program or overlay to doing their jobs. It became a part of doing their job. And that is the most powerful way to build traction on the initiatives.

The structure for doing this starts with the creation of initiative teams. These are cross-functional groups that are responsible for *oversight* of the progress on initiatives, sharing best practices across the organization, and keeping an eye out for the needed midcourse corrections. The company-wide initiative teams are responsible for tracking progress, reporting at the quarterly performance checkpoints, and leading a team of people across the company who serve as critical communications links and reality checks between their operating groups and the company-wide initiative team overall.

Often, executives are initially confused about what the term "oversight" actually means as applied to their role as co-champions. What works is to have each set of initiative co-champions and their company-wide team share primary responsibility for overseeing progress on and learning about their assigned initiative during the Execution Phase. This role is quite different from the particular line management responsibility that each manager has for driving all of the initiatives in his or her area of authority. Quite simply, the burden of driving the execution of all the initiatives should not fall on the co-champions. The achievement of the initiatives unambiguously remains the responsibility of line and functional managers who each own a part of the resources and actions required for success. Figure 10.1 shows the relationship of these dual responsibilities to be carried out by senior executive team members.

Figure 10.1 Execution and oversight roles of executives

So, the oversight duties of a co-champion are assumed in addition to whatever line or functional management responsibilities he or she might have for achieving the initiatives based on personal commitments to action. And, none of the other executives and managers is off the hook from having accountability to execute on their part of the initiative.

Another somewhat different aspect of this approach is that these initiative teams are led by co-champions. Typically, it is said that if more than one person is in charge, then no one is in charge. But, in this case it is different. There are two reasons to go with co-champions. First, it is too easy to ascribe initiatives focused on the market and customers to only the marketing vice president to lead. Similarly, talent or people engagement initiatives are often given just to the human resources vice president to run as some special new program. That leads to business-as-usual programs being launched by functional groups that the operations and field groups might or might not participate in or help drive. That does not create real traction in execution.

For example, consider two ways that a talent initiative can be implemented throughout a field organization. In one example, the field operations managers partner with human resources' staffers to develop better hiring practices and make training more practical to day-to-day operations. These changes are spearheaded by field executives with the support of programs from human resources. The team generates quick results as managers at all levels realized that this initiative is impacting the accountabilities they had themselves as line managers.

Contrast this with an example where field executives completely count on human resources to do the work for them, in a "silo" approach to management where each group is on their own to succeed or fail. Field executives periodically review and approve programs that human resources design. However, it becomes tough for the human resources teams to get the time for the reviews, much less create time in the field operations to get their programs implemented. Managers in the field fail to view talent management as a part of their "real" job and don't spend much time on it. The new hiring practices come off as just more administrative policy guidelines, and the development programs become optional, not required, courses to which employees are sent only when there is a lot of slack time on their hands. As you can imagine, the poor implementation results would certainly reflect the lack of accountability and ownership created among line managers to develop and support the talent initiative.

This "silo" approach to leadership is one in which different organizations are not set up to collaborate for success, but rather their accountabilities are compartmentalized to such a degree that success is severely handicapped. In most cases, line and functional organizations cannot reach excellence on their own. Contrast this situation with one in which functional departments each have their own commitments to support an initiative. Marketing produces more effective campaigns when sales offers input on how customers will respond. Engineering designs better products when marketing provides customer and competitive analysis to guide the design process. Human resources is more effective when local managers actively participate in recruiting top talent. And, manufacturing has higher quality when partnering early with engineering so that products are designed to be easy to build from the start. The co-champion design initially helps to ensure that the typical gaps due to silos are bridged in the process of operationalizing each company-wide transformation initiative and encouraging each functional organization to contribute whatever they can to the achievement of it in an accelerated manner.

Strong leaders as co-champions create the foundation for breaking down silos, driving the initiatives into daily routines, and generating the initial push and transfer of ownership across the full organization at one to two levels below the top leaders. This is what creates traction and gets things in motion.

The best choices for co-champions, therefore, are pairings of functional staff leaders with their counterparts in operations or field groups who are responsible for carrying out the plans for a particular initiative.

After the co-champions are selected, they then need to develop a *cross-functional* team that should include a representative from every major group that is needed to deliver on the initiative. There might be some functions where this doesn't apply, but typically there are more dependencies between groups than it might appear on the surface.

As an example, sometimes the legal department will lobby for being excused from the whole effort and initiatives. However, they are typically pulled back in strongly to support and help create breakthroughs on sales initiatives that require more flexible and faster reviews on contracts, or on better intellectual property management, or establishing hiring and firing capabilities that are more strongly performance driven. And truly, if a group has no connection at all to any of the top initiatives for the organization, you wonder why you have that department at all. Perhaps it would be a good candidate for outsourcing if it truly has nothing to do with accomplishing the mission.

Accountability

Having a tight vision and focus, absolute alignment of the organization, and high engagement of the full team are critical foundations for success. But, these requirements are not enough. Without individuals throughout the organization staying committed to doing something different tomorrow than they were doing yesterday, the organization as a whole won't move forward.

Accountability in execution always starts at the top of the organization. Everyone needs a nudge now and then to keep focused and on track. A tight process can help keep you in the groove, but even that is not sufficient support for the leader. Serving as a nudge to the top leader can be a problematic role. For one thing, if your doctor keeps nagging you about lifestyle changes, it is really easy to just stop going to the doctor.

One CEO pointed out that following the transformation Launch Phase of the process, the need for continually driving the process forward was very tough and very much like going to regular checkups with the doctor. After the process was rolling and everyone was on track, he actually found it somewhat difficult to be the source of constant challenge and accountability. Indeed, it had actually crossed his mind several times to just let go of the process rather than feel the constant drumbeat on focus, follow-through, and accountability. The internal executive team members driving the process felt the heat as well. But being able to fulfill the role of a designated nudge is critical to keeping the focus and engagement of the organization high and the results moving forward.

Establish up front an unambiguous agreement that provides clear jurisdiction for your direct reports to call you out if your leadership of the transformation wanders. Between the integrity of the process and the open invitation to be nudged, your odds of following through go way up.

Simple Closed-Loop Accountability

Without simple systems in place to track accountability, follow-through will elude the organization. However, these systems often evolve into administrative burdens that are so complex and time-consuming that managers simply don't use them. At a very basic level, the fact that numbers are tracked in a system doesn't provide any accountability. It is the closed-loop nature of returning to the objectives and goals repeatedly that matters most and that doesn't have to be all that fancy to work well.

To drive west from Newark Airport on Interstate 78 is to take a trip in a time machine. You pass from the industrial purposefulness of Newark to rolling hills splashed with dense stands of maples and birches, a world that seems almost colonial, with a ribbon of expressway surreally running through it. But as you exit the interstate on to Mt. Bethel Road, you first have to pass what had been the sprawling, high-tech campus of Lucent. A bit farther on is a warehouse-like structure with an elaborate exoskeleton, reminiscent of the cheeky Pompidou Center in Paris. That's where Anadigics, Inc., produces the gallium arsenide chips that are vital to wireless communication, cable access, set-top boxes and infrastructure, and fiber-optics solutions.

From Dr. Bami Bastani's first day as the Anadigics chief executive, he knew that the company needed the kind of business revolution he had helped generate at National Semiconductor earlier in his career, as a general manager. Anadigics had launched on the NASDAQ exchange as a highflier in the mid-1990s as an innovative and fast-growing radio frequency (RF) semiconductor company. But after it went public, several competitors turned up with disruptive, next-generation processes for making chips. Anadigics had lost several key customers to smaller competitors that had outgrown it. The innovative technology that had propelled Anadigics to the forefront was becoming obsolete. With Anadigics having exhausted the impetus of its founders, the Board of Directors had successfully concluded a search for an experienced candidate to fill the role of president and CEO from Silicon Valley. The new CEO knew he had to energize the senior executive team and leverage their capabilities to turn the company around.

The agenda Bami was first and foremost concerned about was the experience of the senior management team he had inherited. The company possessed tremendous focus through the leadership of its three founders, which was a key reason for its early success. The centralized decision-making approach of its founders was still very much in place. Consequently, while the next level down in the organization was populated with brilliant engineers, both creative and accomplished, it was not strong on operational discipline. Instead of staying focused as a team and working efficiently to make timely decisions, they tended to spin unpredictably in their meetings, Bami said, bringing more and different data to successive working sessions and constantly reopening old decisions rather than closing on new ones. Bami recalls, "We had too many open 'decision folders' and not many were getting closed by the management team."[2]

In the executive conference room a week later, eight members of senior management were gathering—and commenting, a bit acidly, on the new gadget set up near the lectern. It was a "printing whiteboard," with a scrolling surface and equipment that prints out on paper. "I heard that Bami ordered it himself and it was pretty expensive," said one vice president. It had an imposing presence in the corner of the room, but was soon forgotten as Bami entered and the meeting started.

Bami ran the session with force and skill, making it clear that the work they were about to undertake would be no picnic; new ways would have to be found to get things done. As the team ran through the big issues to be addressed, a few specific, short-term actions were suggested, each of which Bami wrote on the whiteboard. In time, there were five items, ranging from getting direct feedback from key customers on where improvement was needed to exploring new technology processes that could completely change the industry.

It was now late in the day. Energy was draining from the session. A few executives were stacking their papers and beginning to look at the clock. One floated a trial balloon: "Well, that was really a good session. There's clearly a lot for us to think about." Others inched toward the front of their chairs and looked at Bami. But instead of signaling the end of the working session, he stood up and walked over to the printing whiteboard.

"You know," he said, "I've been in a few meetings here where great ideas are talked about, but nothing ever gets closed. Let's not let that happen with the things we've talked about today." Then, he went through the five action items, assigning each one to a different member of the team and asking each executive to say what he could do with that issue in the two weeks before the team's next session. Bami wrote the assignments and commitments in a free-form grid on the whiteboard.

The room buzzed a little as people realized, with some dismay, that this wasn't just feel-good talk about returning the company to its winning status. Bami clearly expected them to be accountable for important initial steps in the process—and in real, short-term time.

"Good," he said. "Now it looks like we have a plan. Is everyone clear?" Agreeing quickly, they began to rise from their seats.

"Wait," Bami said, "One more thing." He walked to the whiteboard, punched some buttons, and produced nine copies of the points and assignments that had been captured on the whiteboard. As each executive filed out, they received their copy of the action agenda and he kept one for himself.

Two weeks later, when Bami began the next session, he pulled out his copy of the whiteboard plan and began to ask for progress reports on each of the five action items. The message couldn't have been clearer: Discussion and dialogue were useful, but working sessions were intended to actually accomplish something. What is more, people were responsible for following through and would be called on it in follow-up sessions.

From then on, working sessions at Anadigics took on a new tone and rhythm. The team was far more focused and purposeful; each member was better prepared, knowing that real work was being done in the meetings and that records were being kept. Inevitably, the new discipline percolated through the whole organization as senior executives transmitted the new expectations down the line: "Be responsive, decisive, and always close the loop" had become part of the management vocabulary.

In another example, the CEO of Florida Rock Industries, John Baker, was driving a "good to great" transformation to double the market value of the company. He pointed out that building traction came down to "…two really nuts-and-bolts things. One is you need to create an ability to communicate from top to bottom. Then, there are the little things…as far as writing things down and following back up with what we're going to do. We all know that the greatest trick to avoid any responsibility for your actions is to just be quiet and never say anything. If you are forced to get down on paper that this is what I'm going to do about this particular initiative, then you take responsibility for it and go do it."[3]

Promises Versus Declarations

What does accountability really mean? For some, it is a *promise*. Do what you say you are going to do. That means setting sales goals, customer service goals, product launch dates, or other project delivery dates. Hit your goals and you keep your job, exceed your goals and you get some extra pay, but miss your goals too many times and you are let go. This sounds pretty straightforward on the surface.

However, the critical missing ingredient is an incentive for the individual performer to stretch beyond what seems imminently "doable." If the system under which your performance is judged is based on a firm promise, why would you ever sign up for a goal that you didn't already know you could reach? Under such a basis of accountability, it is in your best interest as a performer to set purposefully low goals or at least keep them in a range where no major risk or need for major breakthroughs or innovations is implied to win.

In many real work situations, goals are things that simply need to be met, absolutely. For example, when we set a sales goal—a "promise"—it needs to be met at 100% or at least hit within a very narrow performance band. That is a world of accountability in which we normally operate. But the call for a shift in strategy, a major boost in growth or business performance, is not routine in its expectations. This is the domain of human activity, which is focused on getting from BIG ideas to BIG results.

An important distinction that is usually overlooked needs to be made, and explicitly built in to accountability systems to unlock innovation and breakthrough thinking, which are the prerequisites to breakthrough success.[4] In contrast to a promise, a commitment might be called for, about which it is not completely clear how to achieve, even if it is fully attainable. This might sound like heresy to you in the context of the normal performance management approaches used today.

Think of this other dimension of accountability as making a *declaration—for a breakthrough*. For this discussion, consider a declaration as a commitment to shoot for an objective whose ultimate goal might at first be neither completely clear nor fully attainable. Although others have split much finer definitions of the words promise and declaration, to keep things simple and useable, consider a "promise" an absolute goal and "declaration" a statement of intent when the means to get there are unknown. The most notable declaration historically might be the one President Kennedy announced when he challenged Congress and the American people with landing a man on the moon and returning him safely to the Earth before the close of the decade. To bring the declaration idea into focus, let's look at its dynamics in a real work situation.

Shoot for the Moon—Drive Innovation

Sam Araki, one of the members of a team that accomplished a massive innovation effort understands the power unleashed by making declarations. On May 1, 1960, a U2, a U.S. spy plane, was shot down over the USSR. At the time, it was the only method for taking aerial photographs without the risk of being shot down, but that had just been proven wrong. Today, of course, we can all log onto Google Earth and have a look ourselves from the sky, but back then we were far from what we have today. With that event with the U2, President Eisenhower immediately accelerated a long-term project to develop satellite photography capabilities and demanded a working solution in just nine months. Of course, when the team of specialists, including Sam, was assembled, they had no idea if any of this was possible and certainly no idea of how to get it all done in nine months, but they took on the task anyway. They made a declaration for the "impossible."

A team of the best and brightest from multiple large corporations and government institutions was pulled together into what became project Corona. And it was definitely not a cold beer, feet in the sand type of alcoholic beverage you might be thinking of today. This rapidly assembled group was told to do the impossible (at the time)—get a satellite up in space that is able to take pictures of the Earth with enough detail to be useful for reconnaissance and return the film to Earth—all of this without computers. As Sam describes it today, "We had 12 failures and missed the nine-month window."[5] In the end, they had an explosion on the launch pad, many hurdles, and delivered two months late on the nine-month target. But they achieved the end goals. By statistical performance evaluation, you would say that they were 22% past the delivery date. It would be a failure in terms of meeting the promised date. But, of course, it was not a failure at all.

The Corona team generated technology breakthroughs that otherwise would have taken years, if not decades to be worked out, and brought from the labs into reality. After finally being declassified over 30 years later, Sam received the prestigious Draper Award for the tremendous breakthroughs and innovations he contributed to that program. Obviously, the program was a success. If it had been handled in the traditional manner of "accountability" where the contractors had to promise a delivery date by signing a performance contract that would penalize late delivery and potentially set people up to be fired for not meeting the dates, do you think they would have shot for a nine-month delivery date—and delivered results in 11 months? Not a chance. That is the power of working in the realm of *declaration*. Sam's advice to large companies trying to drive innovation today, "You need to give people the freedom to innovate, let them set what seem like impossible goals for targeted breakthrough teams."

In a more recent example, Bruce Diamond, the CEO of a chip company in Silicon Valley, was reflecting on a declaration-type challenge he put forth to his team when he arrived. The challenge was to take the cycle time from order to ship from 17 weeks down to 3 weeks. Customers needed the cycle time to be faster. His people said it could not happen. They explained how this company was a special case compared to companies Bruce had worked at before. He explained to the team, "Let's just give it a try and see how far we get."[6] As they chipped away and built momentum, they got further than they thought they could. After several months of work, they had taken it from 17 weeks down to 3.5 weeks. Customers, of course, were delighted. Bruce chuckles, "Hey they didn't really hit the goal of a three-week cycle time, but not bad, huh?"

During the process of shortening the cycle time, the team would gather for reviews with Bruce weekly. As they hit problems and delays, Bruce jumped in with the team to solve the problems and come up with creative ideas to try. Some worked; some didn't. Working together under a clear declaration type of mandate to accomplish the "impossible"—as contrasted with a "promise" style—was a huge motivator for the team to strive for breakthrough performance. Bruce understands the breakthrough in possibilities when you shift from managing promises to working declarations.

Bruce had played it out before, leading a company that manufactured microchips from below 70% product yields to over 90%, another so-called impossible goal by his team and peers. When asked how he came up with the idea for declaring for breakthroughs in this way, he explained. "Way back at National Semiconductor, I was working for a leader, Kirk Pond, who later became the CEO of Fairchild. When I joined his group, he told me the goal was to hit 100% product yields. Now that goal was for sure impossible. But Kirk was relentless in the declaration. And in the end, he would measure us on how close we came and what ideas we could come up with for pursuing perfection. We always ended up with great yields and we were rewarded for that. It was uncomfortable at first seeing a goal written down that was such an obvious stretch, but it made us create some real breakthroughs."

The bottom line on accountability is that when leading a transformation and driving for innovations and performance breakthroughs, it is important to understand when you should be driving and supporting the team to make *declarations* and when to be making *promises*. Make a clear distinction or people will avoid taking risks with their plans and goals.

People wonder why the rate and magnitude of innovation is so low in companies. It is not because people have lost their creative edge or innovative thinking capabilities. It is that people are afraid to take the risks necessary to achieve breakthroughs. So, you don't need wild off-sites to break out of the box, you need leaders to learn how to manage in a mode of declaration where sometimes projects will never achieve the goals set for them. People need to be able to fail, sometimes. Promise-laden accountability systems and approaches can inadvertently squash innovation. You need both promises and declarations, just be explicit about when you are in each mode.

Above and Below the Waterline

Clearly, there are some cases where you need to have an absolute commitment, a promise from your team, and others where you want the team to take risks. One of the good ways to determine when to apply declarations and when to apply promises is to categorize the type of issue you are facing. In some cases, there will be business-critical and time-critical issues that cannot slip. In those cases, ask for a promise. In other words, if you think about a boat on the water, if a hole was punched in the hull below the waterline, the boat will sink. These below-the-waterline issues need to be solved with promises. Set the goal with the team and then expect delivery. That's it. Shipment dates to customers, accuracy of financial statements, base revenues on core products—these often need to be treated as promises.

In contrast, when you are driving new growth, looking for new opportunities, looking to create competitive advantage by delivering breakthroughs in service or performance standards, you would be better served to make a declaration. Set the goal high, some might think it is impossible, and then work with the team to push it as far as possible.[7] As George Coll, an executive leading a new business-line initiative at one of the largest global retailers, points out, "Just the attempt at building a new business can generate huge breakthroughs that can be applied to our core business. This program is going to pay for itself just based on what we're going to learn and be able to apply across the company. We already know we'll end up with tools to better manage our field organization's efficiency and quality that can be used in the core business. If the new business itself plays out like we think it will, that will make it a home run."[8]

If George had been told that the goal was to build a business that had $X in revenue by Y date, and that his success or failure just rode on those two goals, he would have been forced to negotiate goals that were promises and work within the safety of known solutions and safe objectives. But with a declaration to launch a new, meaningful business for the company—one that had the potential for spinning off lots of innovations—his team has been able to play full out in a creative way to push the edges of innovation. They certainly need to deliver outputs, but there is no reason to limit them to known solutions; that's not the point and that wouldn't drive innovations. As a result, they are playing above the waterline where if they fail, the boat won't sink.

Don't Get Overly Fixated on the Dashboard

Today there is an ability to control and manage almost every business processes with software, and as a result, there are huge databases of information available to use in setting up scorecards and dash-boards. In general, the statement that, "What gets measured gets done" is true. However, if what gets measured turns into a complex system of data warehouses or massive spreadsheets with PivotTable reports or online tracking systems with thousands of different metrics to track, the realities of the business and of how everyone is perform-ing can become hopelessly obscured.

If the complexity of the reports allows too many things to be measured and there is a long production lag, the metrics are useless. In driving breakthrough performance on a few major initiatives, what is needed is a simple scorecard of top-level metrics that externally val-idate if the stated strategies for executing the initiatives are working. Certainly, there is a good reason to have detailed internal metrics and scorecards to track tactical business processes across different func-tions: Many things need to be targeted for continuous incremental improvements or monitoring. That's just good management. But when those same principles are applied to transformations and strat-egy execution, they break down. You need to select just a few impor-tant things that are targeted for quantum improvement in a short period of time. These things need to rise above the din of incremen-tal change to focus everyone on the major drivers of quantum change. Otherwise, you will lose sight of what has the highest impact and leverage in achieving breakthrough results.

In addition, the scorecards can only tell you so much...and not always the full picture of reality. You've probably heard about one of the most famous but tragic incidents in aircraft disaster history, the crash of Eastern Airlines Flight 401 near Miami, Florida, on December 29, 1972. The pilot, copilot, and flight engineer had become fixated on a faulty landing gear light and had failed to realize that the autopilot had been switched off. Watching only their dash-board, they didn't see that the plane was headed toward the ground. The investigation concluded that the cause of the crash was pilot error. The distracted flight crew did not recognize the plane's slow descent and the aircraft eventually struck the ground in the Ever-glades, killing 101 out of 176 passengers and crew. All the crew had to do was look out the windows and they would have seen their reality and been able to adjust. This is, of course, an extreme example, but the lesson learned is still clear today. Keep an eye on the dials, but don't lose sight of what is happening in the real world around you.

Ground Truth: The Real Results

There is a term in cartography and especially aerial and satellite photography that is called ground truth. Ground truth refers to information that is collected "on location" and "in reality" to validate what is being interpreted through high-level images or remote sensing systems. It calibrates what your systems are telling you to what is really going on. In other words, all the reporting systems in the world have flaws and are no substitute for true observations of reality—ground truth. More than just management by walking around in order to be seen as a leader of the people, it is a tool to keep honest assessment of the front-line operations that are the reality that customers see. The CEO of a several-hundred-million-dollar start-up that grew to over $14 billion in revenues explained his process for gaining ground truth. It was simple and effective. Each morning, he would come to the office and review results (sometimes actually starting the night before). He would take note of which areas were underperforming. However, he would not look at just the level of results right below him, he would look down into the details. That's why he sometimes started the night before. Then, when it came time to check on what was going wrong, he would not call in his direct report who owned the overall area. The CEO would call the lowest-level manager he could who owned the area that was having trouble. Needless to say, nobody was thrilled to get a call.

However, when the CEO called the manager, he would put him at ease and clearly stated that he was just calling to help troubleshoot and see if there was anything he could do to help. He had an agreement with his direct reports and middle management that he would never tell somebody what to do, that was their job. On these calls, the CEO would simply question, challenge, and brainstorm with the manager of the underperforming area. Usually, they knew what to do and some had recommendations for more systemwide changes that were good ideas. If they had difficulty, he might help or suggest other peers or resources in the company to turn to as well. This process gave the CEO two things simultaneously. First, it was a clear message that the CEO cared about daily results and, therefore, so should everyone else. Second, it gave him a constant ground truth checkpoint on what was really happening in the organization.

Gwen Edwards, a veteran executive of large companies and past CEO of a start-up, shared a highlight of her career relating to ground truth. Unlike operating a start-up, executives in a large company can easily get far out of touch with what people are doing on the front lines to drive results on a daily basis. She points out that, "One of the most valuable things you can do as an executive is to find out what is really going on out in the field with customers."[9] At one of the largest telecommunications companies in the world, Gwen was serving as a VP of sales, and the organization was having a very tough time with order accuracy, which was negatively impacting customers on a daily basis.

Gwen tells of an amazingly simple, fast, and powerful approach the president of her group used to generate ground truth. There had been an ongoing debate and finger-pointing about the problem of order accuracy within the staff management team. The president was fed up. His request to get the ground truth was simple. He requested that 25 sales support people, responsible for processing orders, keep a journal for a few weeks on everything they do on a daily basis. Then, he wanted to gather the group together for a day, without all of the middle management, and go through their journals with them. That was it. Gwen helped launch the effort and was invited to join the meeting. The sales support team members flew to corporate headquarters a few weeks after the project had been launched and the president sat and listened carefully as every person read highlights from their journal and reported on what they had to go through every day. When they finished, the president looked around the table and declared, "Your jobs are impossible. What I don't get is how you can do them every day!" People laughed, but explained their pride in the company and desire to help customers get what they needed. This quick exercise pointed out exactly where the hot spots were that needed to be solved and the president committed to making the changes quickly.

The president could have launched a task force of managers to look at the problem; he could have commissioned a months-long, time-and-motion and best-practices benchmarking study. Both of these would have taken more time and resulted in executive-level presentations for the president to review and approve. Instead, in this case, he chose to go for the ground truth. And, as often is the case, the answers are not that tough to find and not that complex when viewed in the real world.

Finding ground truth is not just simply management by walking around and glad-handing the troops. It is about an authentic engagement between the leader and people who are closest to the customer in working-level jobs. Formalized field visits with the chief that are preplanned and scheduled are not views of reality. Those are artificial visits where everything has been shined and perfected for show. At one retailer, compliance to store audits was high, claims of progress to serve customers better were positive, and sales were improving. It all looked really good on the executives' balanced scorecards. However, a drive past the stores in person revealed sparsely populated parking lots compared to the competition, and employees on smoking breaks out in front of the stores. Entering the stores revealed a messy and less-than-welcoming atmosphere. The real progress was far behind what the reporting systems were showing. Not surprisingly, as executives in the company made more of a practice of casual drop-ins on the business, the initial pattern was confirmed—ground truth.

Any system you put in place is prone to having blind spots or to being manipulated by those who can't and won't work to truly perform. That is the nature of monitoring systems. The only way to avoid running blind is to put ground truth reality checks in place for yourself and for leaders on your team to keep in touch.

Misguided Incentives

In addition to performance management, incentive systems need to be aligned as well. In a larger organization, it usually takes some time to plan how the performance management and incentive systems will be aligned to support the new commitments to action. Planning for this shift needs to begin as a parallel activity when the transformation effort is launched.

Often, there are conflicts between the strategic goals and the existing panoply of incentives. This inconsistency will always cause execution that is aligned with the priorities set by the incentive system and not with the new strategic goals. Natural self-interest is a primal driver. People follow what they are paid to do. At times, leaders will allow incentives to be tied to an outdated success model while professing that people should "do the right thing" and follow the strategy. Even worse, some leaders make a distinction that "strategic" goals are those things that are tough to quantify and might not have a defined set of return-on-investment performance indicators. If your strategic initiatives can't be operationalized and tied directly to the financial success of the organization, don't take them on. They'll just become more money-losing executive pet projects.

The strategic initiatives that guide all of the organization's commitments to action need to be the most important and high-impact initiatives for the company. Being transformational in nature, they will need to be viewed as a restacking of priorities, which establishes a new baseline for daily operations. That doesn't mean you stop doing all of the normal daily tasks such as paying payroll, selling to new customers, and managing expense budgets. It just means that those need to be done in the right priority, alignment, and context within the new overall direction. If not, the initiatives become only ineffectual overlays to the way employees "really get things done around here!"

In short, when it comes to launching a fundamental transformation or new strategic initiative, virtually everyone's performance management objectives and incentive (bonus and salary) expectations need to be reset to achieve full alignment between the transformation initiatives and individuals' specific commitments. If the performance system also deals with values and behaviors (which it should), those need to be fully anchored in behavior change commitments as well. This alignment needs to start at the top of the organization with its executive leaders and then cascade in full alignment down through all managers and employees at all levels of the organization.

When challenging a business to generate breakthrough results, business as usual in all parts of the organization needs to be questioned. An executive vice president at a large corporation, who had also served as CEO of a successful start-up company, put it this way: "In this corporate environment, we aren't able to reward excellence. It's a given that different people make very different levels of contributions. But, what does it boil down to at the end of the year? The

average raise percentage is set for the group at, say, 4%. The super-
stars get maybe 6% and everyone else gets 3% to 4%. At the start-up,
we would pay people special bonuses and other compensation for
making big contributions and everyone was driving for the same
wealth creation in the value of the stock. It was much more of a direct
relationship. Why can't we put this flexibility and alignment in place
inside a bigger company? We need to do that." He is right; there is so
much formality and complexity that managers have lost the ability to
truly reward great performance and easily terminate nonperformers.

The strongest performance-oriented systems have two clear components. Performance-based pay is rooted primarily in external business performance indicators, not task accomplishment. You don't
want a situation where everyone does well because they checked
their task boxes while the real indicators of performance, such as
earnings growth, market share, and stock price, are falling. Any
upside potential should be large for accomplishing the real-world
gains—and this is the basis for compensation treatment.

On the other side, people ask, "How do we get people to do their
daily tasks, then?" Simple. If people can't or won't do their daily tasks,
they are let go. The opposite of good pay for a job well done should
not be slightly lower pay for a poorly done job. However, that is the
outcome of many systems today. The consequence of poor work over
time should simply be to let the person go.

The requirement of a tight linkage between performance plans,
incentive structures, and strategy necessitates a much more direct
link between the human resources organization and those responsible for architecting the process and leading a transformation. It is
common for this link to be made late in the process, but it needs to be
put right up in the design and launch phase and kept in place
throughout execution. One way to manage this is to formally develop
a transformation support team that will ensure that all of the process
disciplines (for example, human resources, employee communications, performance management, training and development, strategic
planning, organization development, quality assurance, and so forth)
are among the first to reallocate their resources and align their plans
to the priority initiatives of the overall effort. To support the line managers who are leading the effort, the process functions must first be

aligned to be able to ensure proper executive attention and visibility of these critical functions.

Performance Coaching

Frank and open conversations about performance are rare in companies today. These conversations end up confined to very structured and usually brief reviews of the official documents that tie to raises, bonuses, career potential, and sometimes employment decisions. To make matters worse, because performance isn't really discussed frequently enough, the conversations become very superficial and the final "scoring" of performance for an individual feels (and often is) too perfunctory and arbitrary. If the managers aren't consistently reviewing performance, they honestly won't have much depth to share as the basis of their evaluations. With all of the legal headaches and documentation requirements associated with performance management, managers tend to rate all of their people within a highly undifferentiated band. The great performers don't get rewarded enough and the poor performers slide by, which breeds mediocrity.

This can happen not only at the individual level, but at the organizational level, where quarterly performance reviews on lines of business become missed opportunities to drive for excellence. As put by Enrique Salem, a seasoned executive, "There is way too much 'happy talk' at the typical quarterly operations reviews. A company might be ahead of its own growth plan at 10%, for example, but if the market grew at 15%, it is actually losing ground. People spend too much time talking about all of the great things their organization did rather than focusing on what more could have been done. Everyone can always focus on improving, whether you are ahead or behind your numbers."[10] His perspective of needing to keep your performance in the context of the external market and maintaining a tough edge on always looking for improvement is what drives breakthrough performance.

Starting at the top, if the "happy talk" is allowed to permeate the quarterly checkpoints and performance reviews, there will be no compelling reason for any of the midlevel managers to engage their teams. They'll simply pass on the message, "Let's just keep going and everything is fine." People down the line feel relieved and business-as-usual creeps in. If instead, each quarterly checkpoint is about recommitting to the overall speed and intent of the transformation, pushing progress further if milestones are achieved early, or course correcting where plans didn't unfold as anticipated, that will drive continual learning, commitment, and true performance breakthroughs.

Tips for Building Operational Traction

- Don't start anything unless you are fully committed to follow through.
- On the issues of accountability, know when to establish promises versus declarations.
- Create a transparent follow-through process that keeps everything under public scrutiny.
- Look for creative ways to add to the "traction" in your Execution Phase.
  - Charter a company-wide initiative team for each of your three to four transformation initiatives.
  - End all meetings with clear accountabilities to get things done.
  - Don't switch horses (that is, initiatives) in midstream, unless major changes in the environment force the change.
  - Take quarterly performance checkpoint discussions through the full organization.
- Don't try to measure everything!
- Use scorecard reporting systems as one tool, but don't fixate on those and lose touch with reality.
- Keep a method for ground truth in place to augment your scorecard systems and make it a daily routine.
- Align performance and incentive systems up front.

Endnotes

1 Alan Deutschman, "Change or Die," *Fast Company Magazine* 95 (2005): 53.

2 Based on an interview conducted by Robert H. Miles with Dr. Bami Bastani, CEO of Anadigics, Inc. and former vice president and general manager of the Memory Products Division at National Semiconductor, on April 9, 2007. Reprinted by permission.

3 Based on an interview conducted by Robert H. Miles with John Baker, CEO, at Florida Rock Industries, on March 30, 2007. Reprinted by permission.

4 Distinctions of types of declarations and risk-taking distilled from work with Chris Thorsen's on breakthrough teams 2002–2007.

5 Based on an interview conducted by Michael Kanazawa on April 24, 2007 with Minoru S. "Sam" Araki, prior president of a major aerospace company. Reprinted by permission.

6 Based on an interview conducted by Michael Kanazawa on April 17, 2007 with Bruce Diamond, CEO of a publicly-traded, technology company. Reprinted by permission.

7 See note 4 above.

8 Based on an interview conducted by Michael Kanazawa on March 8, 2007 with George Coll, SVP at one of the world's largest global retailers. Reprinted by permission.

9 Based on an interview conducted by Michael Kanazawa on May 9, 2007 with Gwen Edwards, VP of a $50 billion telecommunications company and CEO of a technology start-up. Reprinted by permission.

10 Based on an interview conducted by Michael Kanazawa on April 20, 2007 with Enrique Salem, SVP at a $5 billion global software company and prior CEO of a successful technology start-up. Reprinted by permission.

11

Over the Hump and Into the Slump

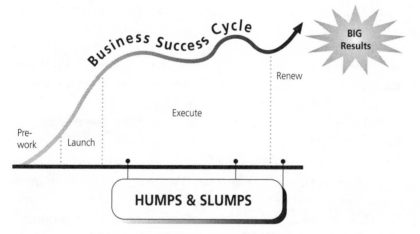

"A successful launch only puts a leader at the starting gate of success."

Jubilation was in the air shortly after the transformation effort at one telecommunications giant began. The CEO was so thrilled with the problem-plagued company's early-stage success in confronting reality and getting people thinking and acting differently that he began to talk about it in public appearances and in interviews with *Forbes* and *The Wall Street Journal*. There's nothing wrong with savoring little victories, but this leader also began to disengage ever so slightly from his involvement with the transformation process.

Soon, an attitude of "Hey, we're over the hump" crept through the entire company; the intensity and sense of urgency that marked the beginning of the transformation process began to wane. Here was a company entering one of the most competitive periods in its history, and people were lapsing back into a business-as-usual state. The old-guard political structures came to life again, and agents of change lost the support and protection they needed to shepherd the transformation through the remaining minefields of resistance. The company might have been over the hump, but now it was into the slump. The transformation never got back on track and, eventually, the company was taken over by a larger, more aggressive competitor.

Or, consider how another company slid into the slump from what seemed like a safe perch. A couple of years into the transformation process, this organization had broken out of a flat-to-shrinking growth trend. They had successfully shifted from being a company that grew through acquisitions only to one that drove growth internally through innovations from customer-focused business units. The company saw whole new arenas of opportunity on the horizon. With the top leadership and employees at every level fully engaged, the rewards were beginning to flow.

Although they could have doubled up on their bets, they began to hedge and make smaller bets instead. They began to compete by simply putting out new revisions of products with a few more features rather than challenge the market with new categories of products or new business models. It was a time when the team could have stretched even further than was possible the first and second year, but instead, the team fell back into cautious, incremental decision making. The slump was under way, proving the maxim that the better the process goes up front, the bigger the risk for a slump.

Bit by bit, the bold moves that had led to early wins and breakthroughs in performance were replaced by hesitation. Management took the lead delaying difficult decisions. One of the business units was clearly out of alignment with the company's new direction. It needed to be sold and its resources redeployed in the divisions that were sitting on the new critical path. When management got an offer, it fiddled around before rejecting it. Later, when the leaders finally got serious about what needed to be done, they were able to sell the unit for only a fraction of the previous offer.

Following a great performance is tough. How can you wow people again? As the natural tendency to slump takes root, leaders often look for the next "big thing" to bring the energy back up. At times, they have looked at the ACT process as a one-time intervention that was responsible for "last year's boost," but now something new is needed. So, they drift into adding new programs in search of an answer. But by doing this, they put their organizations right back into the clutches of gridlock. So, the system gets overloaded, people see another flavor-of-the-day program coming, and progress grinds to a snail's pace.

ACT is really an ongoing process that is intended to be run in recurrent annual cycles as it becomes the backbone of the management process. There is a natural ebb and flow of energy in a company just as there is in every one of us. It is very difficult to stay right at the top of your game day in, day out. And the more you push for peak performance, the more you need to recuperate and recharge the batteries at some point. So, how can you make this work and manage the humps and slumps in your continual drive for turning BIG ideas into BIG results?

The best way to avoid the slumps, or really just minimize them, is to anticipate where they will come and design specific interventions at these predictable points into your transformation process to handle them.

Figure 11.1 shows three of the highest-risk failure points:

- *Post-Launch*—The first quarterly checkpoint after a full and intensive Launch Phase
- *Mid-Course*—The third quarter going into a final push for year-end results
- *Re-Launch*—The replanning and re-launch of the next performance year

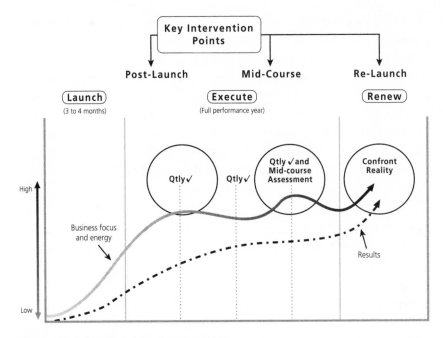

Figure 11.1 Predictable slump points

Post-Launch Blues

Gearing up a full organization for a strategic shift or big boost in growth is absolutely hard work. Doing it in a three to four month cycle is an all-out sprint. If the organization hasn't been used to speed and high engagement, this can be exhausting. The team will really feel a strong urge to sit back for a moment to take a breather. This is especially true if the initial launch is successful and a few of the quick-start initiatives have already shown results. As one executive explained, "It is like you've just run a 400-meter, full-out sprint. As you cross what you think is the finish line, you're told, great first lap, but you're actually running a marathon. So, good start, but keep up the pace."

This reaction is normal and expected. After the cascade work sessions are complete throughout the organization and every person has developed line-of-sight individual commitments to action, people really do need to get down to the business of executing what they said they would do. This requires a more tactical focus and energy. Sometimes, this shift in focus from planning to doing is mistaken as a departure from the ideas of engagement and breakthrough thinking back to the "old way" of doing things. And in some cases, that is what happens. As the day-to-day pressure and grind retake center stage during the first quarter into the Execution Phase, old habits can gradually sneak up on the system. Leaders who were working in a more open and engaging mode can switch back to the command-and-control mode. And priorities set in the Launch Phase will be challenged as immediate expense pressures arise and revenue and other tactical goals have to be met.

Ballast and Keel

At the same time, as the top leader, you might begin to feel like you've done your part in getting the process launched. Because the full process road map, strategic direction, and transformation initiatives have been communicated and launched, it is now time for the team to simply execute.

But delegation cannot be given over to abdication. With delegation, the leader must stay firmly engaged. He or she must actively champion the transformation initiatives and visibly model the new desired behaviors. In their efforts to do this, it will not be sufficient for leaders to simply endorse or preside over these things. There is a saying about the messages of leaders that goes something like, "Just when you are sick of saying it, they are just beginning to hear it."

An extremely smart and creative leader was very much challenged by this dynamic. He had a good ability to converse with people at multiple levels of the organization, he knew the business as deep as any other person, and he had created communications events in the company to get his message out to the troops on a regular basis. These were all the right things to do. The challenge was that each time he addressed the organization, he wanted to say something new, insightful, and creative. And given his sharp mind, he could do that very easily. Unfortunately, the team viewed his new ideas as shifts or changes in the strategy. His efforts to stimulate were confusing and defocusing. His intent was to add more dimensions and depth of understanding to the strategy, but by using different analogies and different frameworks for laying out the key points, it looked to others like he was altering the strategy or the areas of focus every time he got in front of them.

There is an important dimension of leadership that is quite boring to many creative, hard-charging types. It is serving as the ballast and keel for the company. Ballast is the weight that keeps a ship upright when the winds, waves, or other external conditions try to tip it over, and the keel is used to hold the ship on a straight course. This role of holding the course and keeping things grounded is essential for the success of a transformational leader and one of the critical links to generating breakthrough results.

Coming off of a high at which the team is energized, focused, and engaged can be tough for the leader, who needs to switch into the ballast-and-keel role. But that is just what is needed following a strong launch because a real transformation is about execution, where leaders at all levels need to have a consistent message. The top leader has to set the stage for them to do this down below. Starting each staff meeting with a review of the initiatives and progress, individually calling attention to people and plans that have drifted out of alignment, and communicating the same messages over and over is what everyone will see if the leader has effectively shifted into the execution mode. All of the normal communications channels need to feather into this flow as well. A forewarning to creative corporate communications people in the organization: They too will sometimes find it hard to hammer the same message repeatedly rather than put out fresh content at each new opportunity. Therefore, they too need to follow the ballast-and-keel analogy if the organization they serve is going to be able to make the shift from BIG ideas to BIG results.

Assuming the leader is able to stay the course, as the first quarter following the launch rolls around, all eyes will be on the leader again. The half-life for most corporate programs is just about a quarter of a year. So, people will be watching to see if this effort has all just been lip service or a flavor of the month, as opposed to something that will last. Some leaders consider the first checkpoint as too soon to really test results, which for some initiatives is true. But it can't be too soon to test whether leaders and all employees are really executing against their commitments to action and living the behavior changes. Those are the real tests of commitment as execution unfolds throughout the performance year.

With a well-structured quarterly checkpoint that tests progress and accountability and that reengages the team, new life will be driven into the execution of next quarter's performance. This renews the faith that management will follow through, builds confidence that everyone is headed down the right path, and reinforces the sense that accountability to the commitments to action are real. This becomes the fuel that will drive the transformation forward long after the excitement of the launch.

Mid-Course Adjustment

The next high risk point for a major slump typically comes after two quarterly checkpoints or so have passed. Now, at about eight or nine months following the launch, results are starting to build momentum, and the process itself is very well understood and is being used in many parts of the organization. To return to the sailing analogy, land is dropping out of sight over the transom of the launch vehicle and a feeling of smooth sailing without need of course corrections can set in. Folks have survived the new language system of the transformation and have mastered its methodology. They ease back into the captain's chair and begin to relax.

During this part of the transformation process, there will most certainly be unexpected challenges that have come up along the way and things that aren't working perfectly with your process. Such inevitable challenges and issues become opportunities for those who want out from under the accountability and rigor or want to return to the "good old days" to take their shot.

Some time after the second quarterly checkpoint, you'll get a comment or e-mail message that looks something like this:

"Well, this process has really worked well so far overall, but I think we've gotten the best out of it that we can at this point. The work sessions at the last quarterly checkpoint weren't really as creative as before and people just don't need to keep having dialogues and tablework. We were just talking about tactical things anyway. Wasn't this supposed to be about trans-formation? What we really need now to move the business for-ward is a hit of innovation to break out our performance. Next quarter might be the right time to have an off-site on innova-tion using a new break-set thinking method I've been reading about. We can shorten up the tablework activities to make room for this. All that discussion is becoming a waste of time anyway. I'll be happy to coordinate the next quarterly check-point and really kick it up a notch on innovation."

Loud warning bells and red flashing lights should be going off in your head when you get a request like this. If you don't step up right now to affirm the commitments that have been so carefully put in place, others will help you derail all the hard work that initially got everything focused and moving down the right path.

The Process Is Not a One-Time Overlay

Transformations are about launching on a journey of quantum performance improvement—not about incremental nudgings or get-ting to a specific destination and stopping. People in business have been so addicted to considering management interventions as events, that they don't initially see a transformation effort as a permanent shift in the basic management process. Many simply expect that any transformation should have an end point at which the next new thing can then be introduced.

Robert Luse, SVP of human resources at one of the largest retail-ers in the world, closes the door on the old way of thinking when he describes that, "Transformations have to be a 'never-done' approach. People want to see an end to it so they can go back to 'normal.' But really living the process of transforming is what has to become the new normal."[1]

ACT becomes the underlying process of the "new normal" and people can feel that they want out at some point because of the discipline and accountability that it drives. The third to fourth quarter slump is typically triggered by a sense by opportunists that the year is nearing a close and the transformation process seems to be drifting down into routine execution activities and tactical actions. But that is hardly a problem with the process. In fact, that is exactly what the process needs to be driving at that point in time. The middle of the performance year is a time to be heads-down, executing the plans. This is hard tactical work. In response, the quarterly checkpoints should be more about eliminating tactical roadblocks to progress that have been identified and looking for ways to accelerate the initiatives at the operating level.

Because of these predictable patterns, the final quarterly checkpoint of the year—the one at the end of the third quarter—is the perfect point to have a rigorous, multilevel, mid-course assessment of the process itself and transformation progress overall. The idea of the mid-course assessment is to channel any frustrations or shortcomings with the process toward improvements for next year's process. It will always be the case that it doesn't work perfectly the first time through or that it will take some time and practice for it to meld into the way the business is run—the core management process. For that reason, it is important to conduct a deep-dive assessment of the process, with no stones unturned and no levels skipped, to obtain firsthand feedback about what's working and what needs to be changed quickly in all jobs and at all levels.

At one company, there was a lot of frustration toward the end of the first year because the high-engagement start to the process had given way during the year to a more command-and-control style of management as pressures drove some executives back into old behavior patterns. The suggestion came up that maybe the transformation process wasn't working and needed to be switched out for something else. As the senior leaders reflected on this idea, they questioned: How could the simple expectations of having leaders at all levels engage their teams, drive accountability, and follow through be wrong? They realized, of course, that the process was fine, but that some key leadership skills were sorely deficient and needed to be shored up. So, for the next year, they kept with the process, but selectively layered in some leadership training and made some leadership changes when they found those who couldn't or wouldn't make the needed changes.

The key point here is that by the third quarter the process will have substantially shifted into a necessarily tactical execution mode—and that is what it is designed to do. As the "newness" and excitement of the Launch Phase wears off, some people can be expected to start suggesting new methods that are more to their liking and better aligned with their existing skills. Listen for the real process refinements that are needed and act on them without delay. Avoid the temptations to jump to the "next new shiny thing." You don't want your transformation process to ever become "a part of the old way of doing things," so how do you effectively keep it fresh and on the front of peoples' minds throughout the company?

Mini-Cascades

There are many subtle, but powerful sources of traction that are available to help a leader sustain forward momentum and guard against the occurrence of a slump.

Beyond the rigorous mid-course assessment, the quarterly leadership checkpoints, and the active championing by the executive leader, there are other ways to help increase traction during transformation mid-course. One that works particularly well is a complement to the quarterly checkpoint meetings of the extended leadership team. You can think of this intervention as the "mini-cascade," and it takes place at *all* levels of the company on a quarterly basis.

The quarterly mini-cascade, which takes the form of a streamlined version of the initial all-employee, high-engagement cascades, immediately follows each quarterly checkpoint meeting. The cascades and mini-cascades are marked by the same process of sharing a common view of market and business performance realities, restating the direction, and spending time in working sessions to translate the higher-level plans into refined local actions and accountabilities. Before you jump to the conclusion that these steps might be overkill, consider how simple these powerful interventions can actually be. Put another way, mini-cascades are a big deal in maintaining momentum, but they don't have to be treated as expensive, time-consuming, overly produced events. In fact, the more the mini-cascades are simply a part of daily operations, the better. Some of the most successful mini-cascades have been ones that store managers have organized with their sales personnel around a pot of coffee and a box of donuts just before the doors open to customers or those that field supervisors in a rock quarry have set up for their employees on the tailgate of their pickup.

Regardless of how simple the setting you choose for quarterly mini-cascades, the important thing is that they keep everyone, not just the executives at the top, engaged and informed. They bring to everyone in the organization a candid assessment of progress, news about best practices that have been identified during execution, and carefully selected challenges to help accelerate progress at all levels in the company.

By refreshing the entire organization in this simple manner on a continuing basis during the Execution Phase, you also maintain the clear line of sight from top to bottom in the organization that you created with the initial cascade during the Launch Phase. This makes it easy to spot intermediate leaders between you and the rest of the organization who are actively driving and those who are blocking the forward movement of the effort. In essence, by sticking with the mini-cascades each quarter, you continue to reinforce the critical elements of alignment and accountability at all levels. This empowers engaged employees lower in the organization to put upward pressure on alignment, which complements and reinforces what you are exerting from above.

The key to making the mini-cascades work is in keeping them simple and focused on conversations with leaders and their teams at all levels, not on administrative forms and checklists. For example, one company was looking to drive accountability to individual commitments on an ongoing basis. For this, they leveraged technology that would allow managers and employees to use a standard Web-based tool to set and track performance. They believed that would give managers an easy way to have ongoing check-ins on performance. But compliance was considered having 100% of your employees' goals input into the system, not necessarily the quality of the goals. As a result, compliance was above 90%, but the goals were not well thought out and many managers just demanded that people input their goals. They never had an actual conversation with the person either up front or over time. Instead, they relied more on the corporate recording system than on quarterly performance checkpoints at all levels to drive follow-through. Their focus on administrative compliance and focus on tools rather than meaningful conversations diluted the effectiveness of their follow-through efforts.

In another sample company, they embraced the simple concept of declaring their performance commitments as individuals and as teams, starting at the top and going all the way through the organization. During the first quarter after the initial transformation launch, one-page paper forms that showed the individual team members' goals began to be posted in the hallways around the offices. This wasn't by mandate. One team, which was proud of the challenges they had taken on, posted their sheets in the hallway around their work area. Then, the idea of posting caught on throughout the company.

During the quarterly performance checkpoints and mini-cascades, the leaders talked about how to accelerate things that were already working and how to course correct things that were lagging. The leaders each updated their personal commitments to reflect needed changes, often electing not to change the original numerical goals, but to shift their commitments to action in order to accelerate performance of the initiatives. Each leader would work with his or her immediate team and then on down through the full organization until all employees had been through the mini-cascade. These quarterly meetings were not expensive, time-consuming, or overly produced affairs. They were simply the normal staff meetings and tailgate operations meetings that were happening anyway. However, instead of reviewing new policies and discussing other administrative items, they would use one meeting per quarter to focus on performance management at the immediate job level.

Amazingly, employees would update their team and individual commitments and you'd see a refreshed set of commitments in the hallway just a few weeks after the executives reset their priorities and commitments. The resetting at all levels would be in response to challenges and best practices that had been clearly articulated to everyone based on work by the top three levels of leadership at the company's quarterly checkpoint meeting. The role modeling of the executive team, the push to make the commitments real, and the continual drive for improvement is what drove refinements in everyone's on-the-job commitments and performance.

Creating mini-cascades that dovetailed right into the normal operations of the organization is what kept the energy and commitment high enough to avoid any major slumps. When the goals were posted on the walls, they became a constant reminder of the transformation priorities. When each level of management took time to hold a quarterly mini-cascade, it provided an opportunity for everyone at all levels to reengage, recommit, and refocus, which is something that all of us can use at least on a quarterly basis.

Quarterly performance checkpoints and especially the mini-cascades are often a place where leaders start to cut corners on the process. But just like pulling up short on a golf swing, without the follow-through, you rob the full process of power and greatly increase the chances of an off-target hit. It is the same thing with transformations—to enhance traction for execution, they need every bit of creativity that you can muster to keep everyone focused, engaged, and interested.

Launching the New Year

This brings us to the final high-risk slump, the launch of the following year. The biggest challenge in launching the next performance year, which makes it different from the other two slump points, is the need to confront reality again. But how much of a rethinking of the strategy and initiatives do you want to encourage? So much momentum has been built and depth of understanding of the new direction that it would certainly derail progress to scrap everything and start fresh. And it is always hard for the leader and the key executives to work up the energy to go through a full replanning and re-launch cycle all over again. On the other hand, it should also be clear at this point that a lack of regular reality confrontations is exactly what puts most companies behind the eight ball in the first place, so it is always warranted even if difficult.

The key to anticipating and avoiding this slump is to ready the organization for the next full performance year by running it through a complete, though more streamlined set of confronting reality, focus, alignment, and engagement phases. These are the same phases you employed during the initial launch, only in a more streamlined and informed fashion than the first time around. The baseline customer needs, market, and competitive content and process assessments have already been established. But still, take nothing for granted and challenge everything before you finalize the key initiatives for the next year. Moreover, if you did it right the first time, managers and employees will catch you in the hallways and ask you when they are going to receive their playbook for the next year. They'll actually be looking forward to reengaging and recommitting. Don't disappoint these enthusiastic allies.

The ACT process is designed to be repeated on an annual cycle that looks like the ACT process flows in Figure 11.2. Notice that there is some overlap between years where the current year's plans are being executed and the next year's plans are being created. The phases labeled "Re-Launch" indicate where the steps of confronting reality, focus, alignment, and engagement occur for each successive performance year. By repeating these steps on an annual basis, the ACT principles become part of a more rigorous management and business planning process.

Multi-Year ACT View

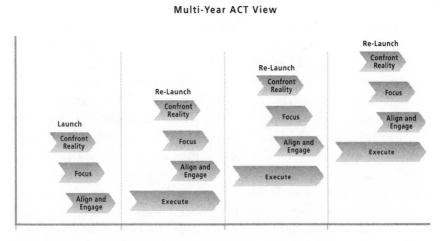

Figure 11.2 Multi-year ACT process view

During each annual re-launch, running through another round of confidential executive interviews, talking with customers and noncustomers, and reviewing major market trends from an outside–in perspective are all useful ways to confront reality again. It is very difficult to know, as an insider, when you have outgrown or overplayed your strategy and positioning. If you shortchange these important steps, you'll miss the shifts in the external environment that need to be factored into your second-year plans. The only way to test for these changes is to be wide open in your confrontation of reality each year.

With all of that said, there is no reason to automatically scrap all of the existing plans and momentum. It is likely that much of a given year's plans will still be valid for the next year. In fact, many initiatives will be, by their nature, multiyear efforts. But inevitably, based on performance and learning the prior year, some of the areas of focus and the metrics that fall within the key initiatives will almost certainly need to be refreshed and refocused.

If a strategic vision is strong enough, it should provide a constant pull forward by creating a tension between today's reality and where the company is going. If it is still serving this purpose, keep it as is. If the business success model is still correct and is proving to be a strong competitive advantage, keep it. The Transformation Initiatives and corresponding values also tend to endure and can be maintained across annual cycles as long as they are still working.

The specific areas of focus for each Transformation Initiative are more typically updated every year. For example, in the case of one retailer, the first year transformation initiatives included Customer Focus, Winning Culture, and Profitable Growth. The initial Customer Focus initiative was aimed at improving the price/value perception customers had of the company, improving customer experience, and establishing the brand. As they entered the second year, there was a lively debate about the most appropriate areas of focus for this initiative for the next year.

The price/value perception had been a surprise as a big impediment to growth for the company. The initial reality confrontation had revealed that customers believed the company had the worst price/value proposition of their competitive set. This meant that in many cases when customers would make up their comparison shopping lists, the company's stores would not be included. For this reason, the merchandising organization hit this issue hard in the first year by putting major programs in place to shift perception and the realities of their pricing strategies. As a result, the company had the competitive gap closed based on external surveys by the end of the first performance year. Revenue growth and higher margins had been achieved and the company had its highest single sales day in history in that year. So, as the transformation initiatives were being reexamined for the next year, price/value perception as an area of focus within the company's Customer Focus initiative was removed. Most agreed with this decision, but some executives were quite concerned that it would signal a relaxation on the pricing issue. In the end, the executive team declared victory on that area of focus and agreed that managing competitive pricing would simply become part of the ongoing operational focus and didn't need special attention.

The other two areas of focus within the Customer Focus initiative now needed more attention. Brand positioning had been firmed up by marketing during the previous year and now needed to be rolled out company-wide. The goal was to focus on all customer-facing employees as living examples of the brand itself, which required a full engagement of the organization and focused execution on specifically designing training and programs. Also, the work on developing the customer experience area of focus in the first year had concentrated almost exclusively on improving the atmosphere of the stores. A more comprehensive approach would be needed for this area of focus in year two that would go deeper into product mix, solution positioning for target segments, and more fundamental changes to the shopping environment.

A sharpening of the strategic vision in year two to focus more on small business customers dictated that the customer experience should also now be more fully targeted across the store and especially with the sales consultants and service technicians to small business customers. So, the two remaining areas of focus under the Customer Focus initiative were tuned up and launched into the second year. They were given extra attention and resources that would otherwise have been diverted to support the former price/value perception area of focus within the Customer Focus initiative. This example shows how the business initiatives can be reset and stretched at the launch of each new performance year, while maintaining the same overall process architecture for the transformation effort.

Oh Right, the Behaviors...

The root cause of many slumps is often based on a regression in the behaviors and mind-sets whose initial changes originally fueled the transformation launch.

In year one, all leaders are specifically called on to generate a new operating model and launch a major transformation of the business. They are also asked to commit to and personally model needed behavioral changes that reinforce the transformation effort. As you get to the front edge of year two, the values and the behaviors that were pointed out at the beginning of the transformation as critical to driving the change can easily fade into the background if you are not vigilant. Things are moving forward, so many wonder why they need to continue to worry about the "soft stuff."

Attitudes categorized as the "soft stuff" often include the sense of urgency, a questioning of everything, tough due diligence on yourself, high-quality dialogue between you and your colleagues, fact-based decision making, and other elements that drive an effective confrontation of reality and driving of accountability. As those behaviors slide backward, so does the energy to challenge assumed business realities and all things sacred to the way the business has been run. When this happens, the whole transformation effort can slide back into the grind of safe (versus bold) bets and incremental (versus quantum) improvement expectations.

As the leader, you will set the tone for the amount of energy, rigor, and competitiveness that goes into the process of confronting reality from year to year. The more energy and focus you drive into that process, the greater the organization will stretch. Given the right process architecture, you will always be in a good position to deftly adjust the amount of stretch you and the members of your team are willing and able to take on each new performance year.

You Don't Get to Relax

The common theme you might notice across the antidotes for the three slumps is that there is a huge responsibility on the shoulders of leaders to set the tone for pressing forward.

Some leaders are often so eager to succeed that they exhaust their energy on the planning and launching stages. They do such a great job of confronting reality, focusing their organizations on the critical areas of transformation, and engaging the executive team in the process that they experience a kind of euphoria that leads them to put the crucial next stage of execution and accountability on cruise control. Many are of the old school in which commanders figure everything out and then toss it all over the fence for the rest to get the job done. They rely on the initial excitement and momentum they created to carry the transformation process through to its conclusion.

It doesn't work that way. As the leader, you need to always be on your game, and particularly alert to the threat of slump and derailment at the three critical points following a transformation launch: the immediate postlaunch slump, the midcourse slump, and the failure to effectively confront reality and relaunch the next performance year.

Plan to Punctuate the Equilibrium Regularly

Without a heavy dose of confronting reality up front every year, a transformation process just becomes a part of the general inertia instead of a way to break away from it. Used correctly, ACT can serve as a process to continuously transform ahead of the market, to reinvent commodity businesses before they lose the ability to generate enough profits to fund the change, to substantially raise the bar and stretch forward continuously, and to become a leader in your business. The idea is to keep loading bigger and bigger challenges for the organization into the front end of each year, building on previous successes with the same transformation process, which over time will become indistinguishable from what everyone in the organization comes to view as "our management process."

By continually taking on larger challenges by using the same, simple, known architecture, your process will become more streamlined and stronger over time. Over time, it should be completely integrated into the normal management process of the company. As a four-year veteran of ACT, Len Rodman, chairman and CEO of Black & Veatch explained, "What started out as ACT is now the process we use for our business focus and communications across the company. Today we are more confident that we have the tools to deal with market and business issues."[2] The strategy will be refined by confronting reality and re-setting the focus each year: Budgets and operating plans will be set through the alignment process, individual performance management targets will be set through the development of commitments to action and behavior commitments, and performance will be monitored through the quarterly checkpoints throughout the year. Therefore, you and your team will be able to spend more quality time on strategic thinking, market innovations, and operational breakthroughs, and you will be able to more routinely turn your BIG ideas into BIG results. At that point, there will be no need to have a special name or "campaign" around the process at all; it will just simply be how business is done.

Tips for Avoiding the Slumps

- Anticipate the natural points where slumps occur and design specific plans into your transformation process to avoid them.

- After a successful launch, make a clear shift to serve as the ballast and keel by continuing to communicate the same messages and holding the focus firm.

- Rigorously assess the initiatives and the process itself at a mid-course point during the performance year to make any required course corrections to accelerate things that are working.

- Be clear that the transformation is a "never-done" process. It is not a one-time intervention, meeting, or event.

- Keep the full team focused on delivering results and accelerating wins through simple and effective, quarterly mini-cascades.

- Each year, go through the same Launch Phase to rigorously confront reality, renew the strategy and business model (as necessary), and realign and recommit the full organization.

- Stay committed to the behavior changes made early in the transformation process to keep the energy and focus up where it needs to be.

- Drive to continuously stimulate and reinforce improvements and breakthrough results.

Endnotes

[1] Based on an interview conducted by Michael Kanazawa on May 17, 2007 with Robert Luse, senior VP of HR at one of the world's largest global retailers. Reprinted by permission.

[2] Based on an interview conducted by Robert H. Miles on December 13, 2007, with Len Rodman, chairman, CEO, and president of Black & Veatch, a global engineering services firm.

12

Are You Up to the Challenge?

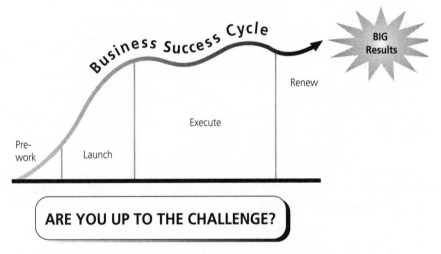

ARE YOU UP TO THE CHALLENGE?

"To a committed leader, the toughest step on a journey is the first."

The best way to end any working session is to launch into the work of the next phase before the meeting breaks up. Similarly, the best way for you to end the book is by launching your next phase of leading breakthrough performance in your organization. But before you do, you have to do a personal gut check. Are you prepared to make a BIG personal commitment to see things through? Are you ready to convert your BIG ideas into BIG results?

White-Hot Commitment of the Leader

Every seasoned executive who drives breakthrough performance always shares one central observation about being a successful leader—that you have to have an unwavering commitment to seeing things through. Any sense of hesitation, lack of confidence, or quick blink during the Execution Phase will result in a massive loss of energy across the organization. You must be willing to personally serve as both the catalyst to get things started and the energy core to keep it going. Not everyone is up to the challenge.

Peter Darbee, a veteran executive of *Fortune 500* public companies, has led transformations for growth, for adaptation to massive regulatory shifts, and even for the survival of a bankrupt corporation. One of the main causes of success or failure is what he calls the "white-hot commitment of the leader." This is a deep, personal commitment to fundamental improvement that the leader needs to make before stepping up front to lead others through a transformation effort. If you are not willing to take personal risks, you won't be able to lead your organization from big ideas to big results. Hedging bets leads at best to incremental change and, more likely, to failure. Peter points out, "It goes beyond the bounds of your current job and into the core of who you are and what you believe."[1]

To take this big step as a leader, you also need strong commitment from those to whom you directly report. If you are the CEO, you need the board behind your efforts. If you are a division president, you need the CEO behind you. You might have to step up initially to make a stronger commitment than you are able to get from above, but to do so successfully, you need at least the support to make the tough decisions, personnel changes, and investments required for success. In fact, all levels of managers will need an appropriate level of latitude to operate and make decisions as well. Realistically, you won't even recognize half of what needs to get done or approved until you actually lead out with your transformation and begin the process of learning from execution. Just take care to keep people above you in the learning loop as you move forward.

But be especially cautious about responding affirmatively to a request from above to lead a transformation when you have been given no latitude. This often happens when reporting to a leader who is not very far up on the Power Curve, but who will nonetheless be expecting breakthrough results from you. If the gap between expectations and latitude is too wide for you to comfortably and effectively operate, consider doing something else. Otherwise, you'll find yourself in a no-win situation and your talents might be better leveraged working for a leader who will both expect great things and support you in taking the risks to achieve them.

Sometimes, the initial idea of launching a transformation does not originate at the top. When John Milton, executive vice president and CFO of Florida Rock Industries, strongly felt a major transformation opportunity at his company was required, he was sensitive to the need for support from above. He worked to secure the alignment and commitment from above that he knew would be necessary. Quickly, the CEO was committed and in the lead. Following the successful transformation of Florida Rock, John reflected that the CEO "constantly amazed me that his commitment was stronger than mine, and that enabled me not to worry about continuing to have a commitment. That makes it work."[2]

Change the People, or Change the People

Often during transformations, the shift in requirements for personal leadership, competencies, and commitment will drive the need to change out team members. How this is done or not done on its own can undermine an otherwise great transformation effort.

The most common challenge is when top leaders begin to expect their teams to behave on the job in new ways, live a new culture, and adopt a high-engagement approach to leading their part of the transformation. Many times, after those expectations are set, various senior leaders can't or won't make the changes in themselves. Often, they can remain out of alignment for quite a long period of time, during which they cast a pall over those in each level below them. If they are permitted to persist in this state of misalignment, the damage to the credibility of the leader and his or her transformation effort will be enormous.

Reflecting back on the defining moment in his transformation several years later, Dr. Bami Bastani, one of the successful high-tech CEOs with whom we have worked, expressed regret at not having acted more quickly on the problem of executive nonalignment.

> *"We had one or two executives who I knew from the get-go were not the right people, and there were two or three others who over time basically came to me and said, 'What the process expects of us is too hard.' So part of the defining moment for me was determining who's going to stay on the team and who's going to go. To me, that is the biggest thing.*
>
> *Of the people who deselected themselves, I would say that at least half of them I had an inkling in the bottom of my heart that I had to change those guys. But you hesitate. Don't hesitate. Give yourself 90 days in total to do all the assessments, evaluations, getting to know people, and getting to know their strengths and weaknesses and what they've contributed. But after 90 days, make those changes. Don't wait two years for some of them to quit on you. I would be more aggressive on that front."*[3]

One of the reasons to use the high-engagement, all-employee cascade process is to create a clear shaft of expectations from top to bottom in the organization that enables misaligned behaviors to be spotted and dealt with before they pollute the whole effort. Also, the speed of the process helps to smoke out the pretenders and foot-draggers right away. However, when the resisters surface or declare themselves, all eyes immediately focus on how the top leader will react. If nothing is done, the whole thing becomes a farce. In contrast, when decisive action is taken either to demand alignment or to remove the head fakers, a reverberation is sent through the organization that reinforces the transformation. This can be most challenging when long-term colleagues and friendships exist between the leader and the wayward manager.

But there is a very positive side to this situation as well. According to the CEO and COO of a national retailer, one of the most surprisingly beneficial aspects of running through the high-engagement cascade process was seeing fantastic talent that otherwise was "below the radar" of the senior team. At the initial confronting reality sessions and cascades with the top 300 or so leaders, they admitted that people they had otherwise pigeonholed or didn't notice before actually stepped up and surprised them in terms of the quality of leadership, strategic thinking, and operational savvy. You don't normally get to see these people and often they get buried under weaker bosses who don't give them the opportunity to be exposed to the senior leadership team. When you create an opportunity for these people to show up, you find new talent in the organization that you can enlist in driving the transformation forward. These people can become the replacement leaders for those who can't or won't make the necessary changes.

The takeaway is that nonaligned personnel changes also have to happen quickly. The damage done by a misaligned leader transcends the impact on the entire effort to shift the business by revealing that the overall leader is unable to make tough but obviously necessary decisions. As a result, people conclude, "Why should I change at my level if they won't take care of business at the top?"

When Bruce Nelson became CEO of Office Depot, he faced the need to very quickly turn around the company's performance. He knew that he needed leaders who could both drive stronger business performance and model the desired culture. He repeatedly encouraged two of his senior executives, who were driving good business results, to align their behaviors with the agreed-upon values. When it was clear they had no intention of following the new values, Bruce fired both of them and announced to the entire organization why he did so. His decisive actions taken early in the postlaunch phase of the transformation at Office Depot sent a shot across the bows of other nonaligned senior executives who likewise were casting negative shadows over thousands of employees below them. Bruce followed and often communicated the idea that in order to generate breakthroughs, "You need to change the people, or change the people." Not surprisingly, a year later Office Depot had achieved dramatic improvements across all three of its transformation initiatives, moving from the bottom to number two in the S&P 500 in terms of shareholder value creation, while reducing customer complaints by 50% and increasing employee retention by 72%.[4]

Jack Welch, who fundamentally transformed General Electric during his long tenure as CEO, was perhaps the first to outline this essential requirement of successful transformation leaders. His basic message was that for transformations to be successful, they must be borne by leaders who can both drive breakthrough results and lead the right way. The two key dimensions of leadership are both required. Jack extended this insight by observing that the most dangerous leaders—the ones who can ultimately bring down a transformation—are those who drive up their results, but do it through a leadership style that is not in alignment with the desired new company culture and values. The real danger is that because for a time they can deliver strong, short-term results, they can be easily ignored until the way they lead causes real damage.

Indeed, this was the situation Bruce Nelson had on his hands. The two leaders in question were achieving results, but clearly not modeling the new culture. Rather than let them undermine the entire transformation process, he let them go, despite their results. At that point, the message was clear. Get in alignment or be prepared to pass the mantel of leadership to someone else. For those who thought their results would always protect them, this came as a thunderclap. To the rest of the executives left standing, it showed that Bruce was serious and that it was time to seriously get on board.

A second problem is the situation in which people are producing mediocre "B" or "C" level results, but are extremely supportive of the new culture. It can be tough to know how to handle this group as well. They are well meaning, hugely optimistic, but just don't come through with the hard business results. They are all heart, but have the wrong skills for the job. These people must also be dealt with quickly, either moving them to jobs where they can be effective in driving results or releasing them if they are not a fit for what is needed.

Gordon Eubanks, a seasoned CEO of large and small technology companies, points out that, "The first goal is to get the 'A' players behind the effort. Then, quickly address those who are behind the transformation but not generating results. If too many 'B' and 'C' players who are enthusiastic to change the culture but aren't driving results line up first, it can be a misleading signal to the 'A' players that the transformation isn't about results and they won't join the effort. And, this challenge needs to play out at multiple levels of the organization."[5]

The key here is that you need to develop a core team of 'A' players who can both drive results and lead the right way. That is a primary and central task of a great transformational leader.

You Don't Have All the Answers (And Nobody Expects You To)

The CEO and COO of a corporation were about to launch their transformation effort to the full organization after having worked through confronting reality, sharpening the strategy, and aligning the executive team. The executive team clearly had ownership and accountability, but still seemed hesitant to move forward. The COO, a no-nonsense business leader, gathered his team and broke the ice by saying, "I think people aren't comfortable that we're really ready to spring this on everybody quite yet." There were lots of nodding heads and a few knowing glances cast about looking for approval. He went on, "Today, we need to get everybody on the same page and ready to go before we kick this off next week." He signaled clearly that he wasn't bugging out, just trying to ease the team's anxiety. Now it became a matter of figuring out how to make people more comfortable.

Each leader was going to be charged with spurring dialogue at a tablework group at the upcoming cascade working session. They would be there to provide clarity when needed—but above all, they were *not* to dominate the conversation. The real sticking point was expressed by a nervous vice president of operations who said it quite plainly: "Well, I don't think we have much to roll out—there's not enough here. I won't stand up in front of everyone and say we don't really have a complete plan yet. It will make us look like we don't know what we're doing. I won't do it."

So there it was, the real reason people were hesitant to move forward. A lot of leaders believe their job is to have all the answers and be able to give specific orders to their teams. But, that's not what people necessarily expect, need, or want. Sure, they want leaders to have a sense of vision, direction, boundary conditions, and measures of success, but they don't want to be told exactly what to do. They want to own their jobs and take pride in their performance, to contribute something, to be valued for their knowledge. Telling everyone what to do squelches job ownership and individual drive, two great assets that every workforce should have.

The CEO and COO reminded the executive team that they together had already gone through such a shift when they had opened up the dialogue about the corporate strategy to the full executive team just a few weeks earlier. They shared that they had personally felt the same dynamic as they opened up themselves to the executive team more for ideas for strategy development rather than telling everyone their answers. As the executive team members reflected on how being included in the dialogue felt and had benefited them, they began to make the connection about why they should be leading their teams in a similar fashion. The CEO and COO had approached their team with challenges and overall direction, but not all of the answers, which is exactly what had motivated the executives to put innovative ideas on the table and address long-standing problems that had been written off as "givens" in the business.

A few days later, the operations VP engaged his full management team. He shared his views on the transformation initiatives, goals, and metrics. A lively dialogue unfolded during the tablework sessions that followed. At the end of the meeting, the VP walked away with some great input to make his plans, making them sharper and more "implementable" in the field. His managers were now engaged; they had ownership over the transformation initiatives and were volunteering to help fine-tune them before cascading them out through all the regions and stores.

For some, it is quite difficult to get over the idea that the boss needs to have all of the answers. One manager, who later became an executive with a 4,000 person round-the-clock global operation, pointed out the key differences very clearly. At one point in his career, he and a coworker held identical jobs. Both were "on call" as managers all of the time. Nights, weekends, holidays—the phone would ring. The coworker had a more autocratic style and everything had to come through him, and when it did he would immediately snap into action, get the right people on the phone, and drive for quick decisions. The other executive would instead ask the caller the simple question, "Do you know what needs to be done?" Most always, the caller would have an answer and usually it was right on point. The executive would close by saying, "Just go ahead and do what you need to do, and drop me a note on my desk on any documentation that I need to see when I get back." As the executive pointed out, his job got easier over time and he really did believe that his people knew what to do in their specific area of responsibility. The autocratic coworker was left to field more and more calls where everything came through him and people wouldn't dare to think for themselves.

Performance coach, Tom Mitchell, relates this to a story about a coach who was facing a young know-it-all professional athlete who really needed help to up his game. The young star had answers for every question and every suggestion. The one question from the coach that got no snappy reply was simply, "How old were you when you realized that you knew everything?"[6] Don't fall into that trap as you ascend the management ranks. The best leaders learn something from everyone they meet. For example, they honestly listen to new hires because they have a fresh perspective, old-timers because they have a wealth of experience, and front-line employees because they see the day-to-day realities that customers see.

Get Real

At the root of the ability to serve as a transformational leader is how grounded you are, how authentic you are, how "real" you are. Rosa Perez, chancellor of a district overseeing two of Silicon Valley's community colleges, has been widely recognized for her work as a transformational leader in her field. She puts this ability in very clear terms as a personal challenge, "To transform an organization, you need to be willing to transform yourself. I feel the most powerful as a leader when I have alignment of the strength in my heart and openness in my thinking in my head. Too often, we try to just think our way through transformations, with everything in the head. You need a balance among the depth, intuition, openness, and listening that comes from strength within your heart and body as well as the thinking around goals, deliverables, and metrics that happens in your head."[7]

Your ability to connect deeply with your team correlates directly with the ability to build the trust and inspiration necessary for people to take the risks required to move into execution of the transformation. People know when you are playing full-out in an authentic way. And, they know when you're holding something back, calculating your moves, and manipulating the situation. You can sense the authenticity of your moves from observing the passion and commitment of all of the people around you. Say what's in your heart, keep it simple, act in a way that is true to who you are, and you'll show up as a "real" leader. You serve in this way as a leader and you'll put your transformation in motion.

Go For It!

The business world is constantly moving faster and the "new normal" has become a constant state of change, or transformation. Any winning formula today is copied, improved, or undermined too quickly to get stuck in one business model.

Many of the systems, approaches, and management programs that have been used for years are so overengineered in how they get deployed that they are rejected by organizations now sick of the program-of-the-month cycle. Moreover, if actually implemented they create gridlock as one program is layered on another in a patchwork of Band-Aids that actually sets up conflicting priorities and stretches resources too thinly to matter.

Now that you've finished reading this book, let's be clear that nobody really ever learned how to lead a transformation by reading about it. You need to go out and put what we've been talking about into practice. So, put down the book, reaffirm your personal commitment, engage your team, and then distill a version of the ACT process architecture that will work for your team to create both safe passage and an ongoing catalyst for transformation. Then engage with and learn from your people. It's that BIG commitment you make that will get you from your BIG ideas to BIG results.

Go for it!

Endnotes

[1] Based on an interview conducted by Michael Kanazawa on March 29, 2007 with Peter Darbee, CEO of a $16 billion market-leading, energy company. Reprinted by permission.

[2] Based on an interview conducted by Robert H. Miles with John Milton, executive vice president and CFO of Florida Rock Industries, on March 30, 2007. Reprinted by permission.

[3] Based on an interview conducted by Robert H. Miles with Dr. Bami Bastani, CEO of Anadigics, Inc. and former vice president and general manager of the Memory Products Division at National Semiconductor, on April 9, 2007. Reprinted by permission.

[4] Based on direct support of Bruce Nelson's transformation project while CEO at Office Depot. Reprinted by permission.

[5] Based on an interview conducted by Michael Kanazawa on June 1, 2007 with Gordon Eubanks, prior CEO of a market-leading, global software company and successful software start-ups. Reprinted by permission.

[6] Based on a conversation in 2006 with Tom Mitchell, performance coach to the National Basketball Association and business executives. Reprinted by permission.

[7] Based on an interview conducted by Michael Kanazawa on April 18, 2007 with Rosa Perez, chancellor of district overseeing two Silicon Valley Community Colleges. Reprinted by permission.

Afterword

Why Did We Write the Book?

Getting you from BIG Ideas to BIG Results is the promise of this book.

We would like to share with you some of the influences and career experiences that have shaped our thinking about what has become our joint practice. We hope when you put down the book you will grasp our simple but powerful process and principles, be emboldened by the insights you have gleaned, and share our passion for successfully leading organizations from BIG ideas to BIG results.

Mike Kanazawa

Going through business school in the late 1980s, my uncle and business mentor gave me some advice. He had both risen up the corporate ranks in oil companies and then built his own company that was sold to Computer Sciences Corporation. I trusted his input. He started with this advice, "You know, all of you MBAs coming out of school don't know anything (he used another word) about creating business value." He went on to point out that most MBAs skip learning about operations and want to move directly into making strategic decisions or into mergers and acquisitions. His advice, "Go take an operations job and find out what it truly takes to run something and create value. Take the gritty type of job that you will not want to go back later in your career to do. Now is your chance to learn." For good measure, he threw in more advice, "When you first get on the job, if you keep your mouth shut for the first couple of months, nobody will know that you don't know anything. If you focus more on listening to the people around you, you'll learn how things actually work, and then when you do open your mouth, you'll have something valuable to say." It has always been hard for me to sit quietly, but along the way I was able to learn quite a bit from the people around me.

With that seed of advice, I continued down my career path that took me from working in the guts of a telecommunications switching office with no windows, to a call center operation with rolled razor wire around the parking lot, and then to leading a team of 140 small business sales and service team members in Los Angeles. I learned why field operators can see corporate people as "staff weenies," rolling out programs and strategies that just don't play in the real world. Then, I moved into corporate headquarters to do product strategy for a $300 million product line and finally into corporate strategy, where I saw why corporate staffers sometimes think the field is full of "hard-headed dinosaurs," who don't get that the ice age is coming and that they need to change or become extinct.

During this time, I worked right down the hall from Scott Adams, the creator of the Dilbert comic strip, which captures perfectly the foibles of how many of us experience life at work. It is maddening to work in a bumbling, ineffective organization and the popularity of Dilbert is unfortunate proof that these experiences are all too common across businesses.

In my years as a corporate manager, I worked with most of the top consulting firms in the world. There were some consultants who were great, but too often my mentor proved to be right. There were a lot of people peddling advice who had never worked an operations job in their life. From the experiences of running operations, one lesson was clear: The analysis and planning are only about 10% of what is needed to drive a transformation or strategic shift. The other 90% is execution effort and about getting things done through peoples' day-to-day efforts.

Right near the end of my time as a corporate manager, I was running a corporate strategy group and was assigned to work with an outside advisor, Bob Miles, to implement a process to transform our company to better deal with major competitive and regulatory shifts impacting the business. By that time, I was a bit jaded on consultants, but he turned out to be quite different than the rest. He had a clear process that let us as business managers take the lead in the work. He worked with just a few other consultants, not the army that normally followed an initial partner in the door. The process he brought was simple and easy to replicate throughout all levels of employees. After seeing so many clumsy attempts at transformations and strategic shifts, this approach was clearly different and matched the principles of the most successful leaders I had been able to learn from at that point. The whole approach was no nonsense, grounded in reality, tough on business, inclusive with people, and results oriented. Simple.

Taking a risk to build something new, I left my corporate job and joined a strategy consulting firm that partnered with Bob Miles on corporate transformation projects. The firm's founder, Michael Norkus, had come out of the Boston Consulting Group and was based in Cambridge, Massachusetts. The firm worked with Bob in providing corporate strategy services to clients and was looking to launch and build a West Coast practice. In building the practice and becoming a partner in the firm, I initially worked with Bob on speeding up the pace of transformations with high-tech companies. Symantec Corporation's leaders were some of the first to greatly accelerate the process of engaging the full company with a rapid leader-led approach that was launched quickly and then followed up with rapid cycles of sharpening the strategies and realigning execution.

We also pressed the edges of speed by driving more rapid strategic assessments, based on many of the same approaches my team was using with private equity firms to complete due diligence projects on potential investments. We found through these experiences that analytical rigor and speed are not mutually exclusive, if you can make what seems complex, simple. This helped reduce the front-end cycle of the typical transformation launch. In one example, working with Dr. Bami Bastani at Anadigics, Inc., our strategy team worked with his executives to put a joint team together that completed full strategic assessments and developed business plans for each business unit in a matter of weeks. This was about a third of the time it would have taken with a traditional strategy consulting approach. This allowed the company to immediately begin shifting focus and execution toward the things that mattered most, and then to refine the plans over time as the markets reacted to the initial strategic moves. During that time, we began fine-tuning strategy tools for rapidly developing market-driven innovations that tied directly into the front end of our process.

Then, at the peak of the stock market bull-run in 2000, we sold the strategy firm to a national consulting company. I stayed with them for about a year and then stepped out to create a new form of consulting firm. To me, the traditional model of leveraged staffing, where a partner has the expertise and is surrounded by MBA and college analysts, was one that got in the way of the speed and impact for clients. In our projects, companies ran a leader-led process and provided their own staff resources to do the work. In these cases, the client teams owned the work, the recommendations were well grounded in their reality, and, therefore, the results were bigger and hit sooner.

It has now been more than ten years that Bob and I have been collaborating on continually refining and speeding up what we call our Accelerated Corporate Transformation, or ACT, process by delivering it with leaders of companies in all different industries and sizes of organizations. Through all of these experiences, I've had countless opportunities to work side by side with top executives and their teams in driving corporate transformations. Over time, we've found that the ACT process and the principles behind it apply to a wide range of business challenges and levels of management beyond just full corporate transformations, including the first 100 days for new leaders, aligning companies post-acquisition, and sparking organic growth. The process also solves one of the most challenging problems of today: driving the large-scale breakthroughs required for continuous growth while executing the short-term plans to generate results today.

One of my goals in writing this book is to make the complex simple, uncovering the essence of the ACT process and reasons why it works, so that more leaders at all levels can quickly and predictably get from BIG ideas to BIG results.

Bob Miles

It is fascinating to me that I and my partner and coauthor have taken such different routes to arrive at the same place in our thinking and practice. Whereas Mike purposively and progressively worked his way up the career ladder in business organizations to arrive at the place where our careers intersected, by a combination of circumstance and chance I arrived there by taking a very different path.

I was thrust into general management when my father and grandfather were no longer able to run the small family steel fabrication and precision machining business. In my early twenties, I was given the challenge of managing and eventually selling the family business while waiting on an indefinite deferment as a commissioned officer in the Army.

So, before I had an opportunity to explore more typical career options, I was meeting Friday payrolls and reassuring stockholders, who were family members and friends, while searching for a purchaser.

After the business was sold and my Army time was up, I pursued a very different career track than I had initially planned. Much to the amusement of all my friends, I opted for a Ph.D. in a brand-new field of business administration, called Organizational Behavior, and ended up as a charter faculty member at the new Yale School of Management.

Our first task as faculty members was to build a whole new curriculum for students who would begin graduate study there a year later. So I set about that task with all the vigor and naiveté of a newly minted assistant professor.

One day not too long after I arrived in New Haven, I read an article in the business section of the *Hartford Courant* that described how Aetna was going to put together a unit reporting directly to the president to enable this old-line insurance company and its business divisions to adapt more quickly to changing industry trends and public policies.

Thinking this might make a good teaching case, I called the president of the company. Bill Bailey picked up the phone in his eighth-floor office at the 150 Farmington Avenue headquarters on the second ring. (It didn't dawn on me until much later that this was a pretty exceptional event, even during America's Age of Aquarius!)

After introducing myself and explaining that I would like to come for a visit to write a case on what he was putting in place, Bill paused to open his copy of the paper before responding, "Bob, this story is about 'little' Aetna. We're 'big' Aetna. But this sounds like a very good idea. Would you come to Hartford and work with one of our top attorneys, a person I just hired from the White House and a couple of senior-line guys to build this capability for us?" The relationship lasted for over ten years. And that was how and why I started my corporate transformation practice.

Three years later when I moved to join the Harvard Business School faculty, the aberration of chance became a career-long pattern. A handful of innovative faculty members and senior executives on sabbatical at the school had come up with the idea that Harvard should invite *Fortune 500* CEOs and business presidents to come to campus to plan together how to tackle the major challenge confronting each of their enterprises. They asked me to join as the last of five faculty members. Three years later, I was appointed faculty chairman of the program.

The application process was very simple. A write-up of the major challenge was all they needed to do to complete the application form. For those accepted, we made certain that competitors were not invited and we allowed the successful applicants to bring two to three management team members with them. What followed was an intensive, two-week immersion into real-world practice. What they took back with them was what you would call a rudimentary plan for leading a transformation in their organization.

Most important, we decided to bring everyone back nine months later to a follow-up program to see what worked and what didn't. From that series of experiences came the foundations of what Mike and I now call Accelerated Corporate Transformation, or ACT.

That was how I initially got into the business of supporting leaders of transformation. The next step was to sign on with the transformation of General Electric under Jack Welch, which was followed by a wide variety of corporate transformation engagements over the next two decades.

Many things have subtly but powerfully shaped my thinking and practice over the years. But a few in particular stand out.

One was the advice of my grandfather, a practical genius who built his own company and who at the end of his long career made the mock-up manned capsules and space hooks for NASA's Mercury and Gemini Projects. On the eve of my decision to go for a doctorate, he didn't say much, but cautioned, "Don't get caught up with unworkable ideas. Be practical." Message: *Keep it simple*.

The second source of influence was my high school teacher, "Bloody Mary" Barnes, who put me in her senior honors class in British literature, but quite remarkably allowed me to do my senior thesis on Dostoevsky. After some casual summer reading, I had expressed to her a keen but naïve interest in Russian literature, about which she had little familiarity. Her simple concession to let me explore something of great immediate interest made all the difference to me. Twelve years later, I sent Bloody Mary a copy of my doctoral dissertation in business administration, which I had dedicated to her. Message: *Be flexible in exploring ways to engage people to perform at their best*.

The third major influence on my approach to transformation came from the simple fact that I had more than a full-time job as a faculty member, and later administrator, in leading business schools while plying my corporate transformation practice. Only in the past decade or so did consulting become a full-time job for me. For all those early years of practice development, I had to develop an approach that greatly leveraged my personal influence. As a consequence, I became more of a process architect and senior advisor while the leaders at all levels in the organization became the true builders of their transformations. As you will see later in the book, the approach to transformation consulting support that we have developed is not dependent on hordes of on-site consultants, and that has made all the difference in our success. Message: *Enable others to lead*.

The last major influence came with the shift in the center of gravity of my transformation practice from the East Coast to the West Coast. On the East Coast, I had mastered the disciplines of simplicity, focus, and execution. These were the pillars of the transformation work of Jack Welch at GE, and I had taken those insights and applied them far and wide east of the Mississippi. At the beginning of the 1990s, I shifted my practice to Silicon Valley, where I supported successful transformations at companies like National Semiconductor and Symantec.

To be sure, the young leaders of these nascent, high-tech companies sorely needed practical insights about focus and execution, and with the raging "War for Talent" in Silicon Valley, they had to develop powerful ways to engage their highly professional and mobile employees. But even more pressing was their need for speed. When compared to those of their more conventional corporate counter-parts, these high-tech firms had much more compressed cycle times. What could successfully take place over months or even years in more conventional firms often needed to take place in a matter of weeks in high-tech firms. And before too long, the proliferation of high-tech products in more conventional firms began to increase their need for speed as well. Message: *Master the need for speed in transformation.*

The other great thing about my shift to the West Coast during the roaring decade of the nineties is that I encountered a young man of enormous energy and talent who has become my senior colleague and partner in corporate transformation work. Mike was leading a corpo-rate strategy team in a large telecommunications company with which I was engaged to support a transformation launch. He was assigned to the support team within the company to help translate my transforma-tion framework and concepts for application in his company.

Although he came with a degree in mathematics, an MBA, and a director of strategy title, Mike quickly grasped the importance of the process architecture I brought with me and became a strong internal advocate. Before too long, he left the company to head up the West Coast division of a Boston-based strategy boutique with which I had been partnering for many years.

Soon, Mike and I were partnering on major corporate transforma-tion engagements in a variety of sectors, and eventually we joined forces to form a unique consulting firm, Dissero Partners, that focuses exclusively on the challenges leaders face in launching and sustaining transformations in a streamlined, high-engagement manner. After over a decade of work together, we finally made the time to share with you what we have learned. The rest is the grist of this book.

The inspiration to write this book came on a cold New York night as the two of us were sitting with the CEO of a company that had almost been decimated by missing a full technology cycle. We were relaxing by a fireplace at a lodge that had served as our home-away-from-home as we had worked with the CEO and his team over the prior several months. He said to us, "I have now worked with your process at a global company as a division head and now as CEO of a fast-moving high-tech company. I'm convinced it could work at any type of organization. You need to figure out how to get it in the hands of more businesspeople."

Our goal in writing this book is to do just that. Get the simple process and powerful lessons into more peoples' hands. We want more business leaders and operators to consistently and quickly get their teams from BIG ideas to BIG results. As you will see, it's really pretty straightforward after all.

Acknowledgments

The wisdom in this book represents the collaboration between its two authors and over three decades of direct involvement in the fundamental processes by which leaders have successfully responded to a wide variety of what we call transformation challenges—of converting BIG ideas to BIG results in an accelerated, high-engagement manner.

Many talented executives and professional colleagues have contributed to the successful completion of this book.

One person in particular deserves enormous credit for launching the project and keeping us on course. There isn't a formal title of "producer" in writing a book, but if there was, we owe a huge debt of gratitude to our business partner, John Dare. John got this whole process started, arranged for our literary representation, worked with our agent in negotiating the contracts, and put together the marketing plans.

Then, there were many others who contributed along the way…

Michael T. Kanazawa and Robert H. Miles

Because I have been at this the longest, I want to recognize first the executive leaders with whom I have been intensively involved as they have risen to these daunting challenges. Heading the list is Jack Welch, who welcomed me aboard his corporate transformation launch at GE in the early 1980s and invited me back again when the process shifted into high gear through the early 1990s; to Gil Amelio, Bami Bastani, and Rodger Smith, who in different settings offered me the opportunity to support each of them in two successful corporate transformation efforts, with Gil at Rockwell International and National Semiconductor, Bami as general manager at National Semiconductor and again when he became CEO at Anadigics, and Rodger, again at the general manager–level at Southern Company and later as president of the engineering solutions business of Black & Veatch; to Mike Daniels, who led the charge in the largest business division in

IBM Global Services when then CEO Lou Gerstner decreed that IGS had to become the growth engine of IBM Corporation; to Bruce Nelson, who brought Office Depot back from free fall after the Department of Justice denied a prolonged merger attempt by the top two competitors in office supplies; to Len Rodman, who transformed Black & Veatch, a $3 billion global engineering services enterprise from a partnership to a private company while busting business silos and quadrupling its stock price; and to John Baker and John Milton, who doubled the market capitalization of Florida Rock Industries, a company they jokingly referred to as being in the business of "making big rocks into small rocks!" There are countless other executives at all levels of enterprises in all manners of businesses who have also contributed to my practical and intellectual development in this challenging arena, and many of them have received mention in my previous books. But the executives named here have had and continue to have a profound impact on my professional development and on the practical insights revealed in this book.

I also want to thank the Harvard Business School for providing a once-in-a-lifetime platform early in my career for launching the forerunner of what we now call the Accelerated Corporate Transformation (ACT) process. The "Managing Organizational Effectiveness" program, which Mike Beer founded at HBS in the late 1970s and which later I was fortunate to serve as faculty chair, provided a platform— what we now call "safe passage"—for Harvard faculty and Fortune 500 senior executives to come together to help each other wrestle with major corporate transformation challenges. Each year, I along with my faculty colleagues were able to each become intensively involved with five such executive leaders and their teams, not only in the diagnosis of the challenges they brought with them and the formulation of a plan of action, but also in helping them mine the learnings from their transformation attempts when they returned to campus nine months later for an intensive three-day follow-up program called "Learning from Changing." All of these executives, and the faculty who assembled each year for this occasion—Mike Beer, Paul Lawrence, Jay Lorsch, Richard Walton, By Barnes, Len Schlesinger, Vijay Sathe, Jack Gabarro, Todd Jick, Barbara Toffler, and the late Cal Pava—were rich sources of insights, which eventually found their way into the ACT methodology. I also want to acknowledge the influence of Noel Tichy, with whom I worked closely on major action learning projects, as well as the redesign of all the senior executive programs at Crotonville during the first wave of transformation of GE under Jack Welch. Thanks also goes to Jay Conger and Mitch Galloway, who served at different times as research assistants to help me decipher the strong patterns of learning from participating executives. Mitch now serves as chief executive of Galloway Consulting Group, my healthcare consulting firm that partners with Dissero as a specialist firm.

Next, I must acknowledge my colleagues in the leading business schools and in the Academy of Management for the insights they have developed and freely shared—insights that inform every aspect of the ACT process we have synthesized in this book.

Finally, I owe a deep debt of gratitude to my coauthor, Mike Kanazawa, who was the first to master the ACT methodology and now is taking it to new levels, and to our other senior colleagues at Dissero Partners, John Dare and Chris Thorsen, whose insights along the way toward publication of this book have been invaluable.

Robert H. Miles

The foundation Bob created with ACT and his willingness to share all of that knowledge with me has opened incredible opportunities for which I am continually grateful. The experience started as a great learning experience and over a decade plus has turned into an amazing collaboration that has led to the creation of a new type of advisory firm in Dissero Partners and the writing of this book. These creations now serve as vehicles for bringing the ACT process to more leaders and organizations and platforms for continuing to evolve the process to meet the challenges of today and tomorrow.

In addition to those people and organizations Bob has already named from the history of ACT, there are a number of executive leaders who contributed directly to the book based on our direct work with them and in some cases by sharing deeply personal stories and insights. These people include Sam Araki, William Barnes, Mike Benjamin, George Coll, Peter Darbee, Bruce Diamond, Gwen Edwards, Gordon Eubanks, Bill Hopkins, Robert Luse, Bill Maddox, Tom Mitchell, Larry Mondry, Javed Patel, Rosa Perez, Enrique Salem, Walt Torgersen, Tony Weiss, and Brad Youmans. Each of them has had an imprint on our work that goes far beyond their quotes on the pages in the book.

We also have had the privilege of working with a wonderful and inspired set of colleagues who have collaborated on particular projects and directly supported our early growth at Dissero. These colleagues include Ethan Berkwits, Katharine Boshkoff, Heidi Goldstein, Hodge Golson, Todd Keleher, Lili Pratt-King, Roger Williams, and Josh Zaretsky.

We had a team of colleagues who volunteered in reviewing early drafts of the book and provided valuable feedback, including several people already mentioned in our acknowledgments as well as Barbara Hibino, Derek Idemoto, Stuart Ogawa, and Dan Salah.

Our book production team was fantastic and made this project possible. Helen Rees has served as our agent and found a great publisher for our work. Donna Carpenter and Mo Coyle helped us unlock our stories and get a few of them on paper to develop our book proposal. With that jump start, we were able to pick up and write the book from there. Michael Dare brought endless creativity and energy to establishing our online and multimedia presence. Judy Safern provided a great platform for announcing our work publicly. Tim Moore, Martha Cooley, Anne Goebel, Megan Colvin, and the team at Pearson Prentice Hall believed in us and helped turn our ideas and experiences into the reality of this book.

There are so many others who have shaped my thinking and who I am as a person today that I can't name them all, but they are a part of this work as well. And, special thanks to a true mentor, Ko Nishimura, who has encouraged me to think big, be bold, and take risks.

Michael T. Kanazawa

About the Authors

Michael T. Kanazawa, chief executive officer of Dissero Partners, serves as a business advisor to executives on the topics of corporate transformation, strategy, business execution, and leadership.

Early in his career, Michael worked in the same maze of cubicles as Dilbert's creator Scott Adams. As an operating manager who progressed to directing corporate strategy for Pacific Bell and later serving as vice president at Alliance Consulting Group, he saw the best and the worst of corporate life. Those experiences inspired Michael's professional quest to help corporations confront reality, focus their priorities, engage the full power of people, and align every part of an organization to transform great business ideas into bottom-line results.

Clients have included a wide range of organizations, including Silicon Valley start-ups, private equity investors, and global corporations, such as AT&T, Anadigics, Intel, PG&E, Schlumberger, Symantec, and Verizon.

Michael is frequently asked to serve as a guest speaker at corporations, associations, and universities and is a popular media guest on the topics of transformation, business growth, and leadership.

Michael holds a BA in mathematics and economics from U.C. Santa Barbara and an MBA from the Marshall School of Business at the University of Southern California.

Michael lives with his wife Lisa and their three boys in Danville, California. He may be reached at mike@bigideastobigresults.com or mtk@disseropartners.com.

Robert H. Miles, Ph.D., chairman of Dissero Partners, is a thought and practice leader in the fields of corporate transformation and executive leadership. He also serves as chairman of Galloway Consulting Group and president of Corporate Transformation Resources.

Over the past two decades, Bob has pioneered an **Accelerated Corporate Transformation (ACT)** methodology at such leading companies as Anadigics, Inc., Black & Veatch, Florida Rock Industries, GE, IBM Global Services, National Semiconductor, Office Depot, the PGA TOUR, PricewaterhouseCoopers, Rockwell International, Southern Company, and Symantec, as well as a number of emerging high-tech companies. He is the author of many books on corporate transformation and organizational effectiveness, including most recently *Corporate Comeback: The Story of Renewal and Transformation at National Semiconductor* and *Leading Corporate Transformation: A Blueprint for Business Renewal* (Jossey-Bass, 1997 and 1997).

Frequently serving as a process architect to executive teams as they plan, launch, and refocus corporate transformation efforts, Bob often helps new CEOs and division presidents take charge, a process that frequently involves launching or reenergizing a corporate transformation. At least half of his practice focuses on what happens *after* the planning is done. A hallmark of his approach has been the intensive, all-employee cascade. This high-engagement methodology quickly focuses everyone in the enterprise on a shared set of business and cultural stretch goals for quantum improvement.

As a part of the Harvard Business School and Yale School of Management faculties for many years, Miles taught in the MBA, doctoral, and residential executive programs. While at Harvard, he also was faculty chairman of the intensive Managing Organizational Effectiveness executive program, which helped CEOs, business presidents, and their teams plan major transformation efforts. He was Dean of the Faculty and Hopkins Professor at the Goizueta Business School of Emory University, where he also held the rank of University Distinguished Professor. He has frequently served as a member of the Stanford Executive Institute faculty at Stanford University and on the boards of several leading business schools, the Organizational Effectiveness Advisory Council of The Conference Board, and the Advisory Board of the U.S. Department of Energy. He is also special advisor on Execution and Corporate Transformation to Julius Baer, a Swiss investment bank.

Miles holds a B.S. from the McIntire School of Commerce at the University of Virginia and a Ph.D. in business administration from the Kenan-Flager School at the University of North Carolina at Chapel Hill.

He lives with his wife, Jane, in Charlottesville, Virginia, and Chatham, Massachusetts. He may be reached at CorpTransform@aol.com or rmiles@disseropartners.com.

Index

A

abdication, 179
absolute alignment.
   See alignment
Accelerated Corporate
   Transformation. *See* ACT
Accelerated Transformation
   launch road map, 121-122
accountability
   closed-loop accountability,
      156-159
   importance of, 156
   promises versus
      declarations, 160-164
   undermining with task
      overload, 16-17
acknowledging that you don't
   have all the answers, 201-203
ACT (Accelerated Corporate
   Transformation), 210-212
   acknowledging that you don't
      have all the answers, 201-203
   ACT Arrow, 56-58
   alignment, 73
      of budgets, 89-90
      corporate initiatives,
         limiting, 74-77

importance of, 90-92
individual Commitments to
   Action (CTAs), 83-84
reducing silos, 84-87
resetting action plans and
   priorities, 80-83
tips, 92
of values, 87-89
zombie projects, 78-80
breaking through gridlock
   event-driven versus
      process-driven
      management, 23-24
   prioritizing initiatives,
      19-20
   software industry case
      study, 20-23
   tips, 24
case studies, 8
challenges, 1-2
commitment, 196-197
confronting reality, 33-34
   confronting reality work
      sessions, 52-53
   dialogue versus
      discussion, 36-37
   employee interviews, 39-40

encouraging dialogue about taboo topics, 35

generating dialogue as a leader, 37-39

market maps, 48-52

opinions of customers and noncustomers, 47-48

outside-in perspective, 44-47

participation of lower-level employees, 41-44

tips, 53-54

cycle of failure, 3-5

cycle of success, 6-9

dangers of overhyping, 30-32

definition of transformation, 1

employee engagement, 95-96

failed attempts, 100-101

high-engagement, all-employee cascade, 101

importance of dialogue, 101-103

maintaining focus, 110-111

performance results, 96-100

tablework, 104-110

tips, 112

frustration with transformation, 1-2

importance of process, 31-32

leadership, 3

Power Curve, 136

sharing power, 147

strategic thinking within teams, 145-147

under-powered organizations, 137

origins and development, 6

personnel changes, 197-201

process map, 28-30

productive speed

Accelerated Transformation launch road map, 121-122

benefits of, 116-117

case study, 118-121

expanded launch road map, 124-125

explanation of, 113-116

launch efforts, 123-127

process architecture, designing for speed, 121-123

Quick Starts, 127-130

sense of time, managing, 131-133

speed as leadership discipline, 133-134

tips, 134

safe passage (clear transformation process)

creating, 32

importance of, 25-28

slumps, avoiding, 175-177

behavior and mind-set, 191-192

continuous transformation, 192-193

mid-course adjustment, 181-184

mini-cascades, 184-187

multi-year ACT process, 188-191

post-launch blues, 178-181

predictable slump points, 177-178

re-launch, 187-191
tips, 193-194
strategy, building, 55-56
  ACT Arrow, 56-58
  business success
    modeling, 63-64
  due diligence
    process, 65-70
  strategic vision,
    creating, 60-63
  tips, 70
  transformation planning
    funnel, 58-59
traction, building, 149-150
  accountability, 156-159
  committing with
    confidence, 150-151
  misguided incentives,
    168-171
  oversight of
    transformational
    initiatives, 151-155
  performance coaching,
    171-172
  promises versus
    declarations, 160-164
  results measurements,
    164-168
  tips, 172
transformation planning
  funnel, 58-59
value of following a proven
  routine, 9-11
ACT Arrow, 56-58
action plans, aligning, 80-83
Adams, Scott, 78, 208
Aetna, 211

alignment, 73
  of budgets, 89-90
  corporate initiatives,
    limiting, 74-77
  importance of, 90-92
  individual Commitments to
    Action (CTAs), 83-84
  reducing silos, 84-87
  resetting action plans and
    priorities, 80-83
  tips, 92
  of values, 87-89
  zombie projects, 78-80
Anadigics, Inc., 128-129,
  157-159, 209
Andreesen, Marc, 118
Apple, 49-50
Araki, Sam, 161-162
AT&T, 78
attitude, 191
authenticity, 203-204
avoiding slumps, 175-177
  behavior and mind-set,
    191-192
  continuous transformation,
    192-193
  mid-course adjustment,
    181-184
  mini-cascades, 184-187
  multi-year ACT process,
    188-191
  post-launch blues, 178-181
  predictable slump points,
    177-178
  re-launch, 187-191
  tips, 193-194

B

Bailey, Bill, 211
Baker, Jerry, 42
Baker, John, 159
ballast-and-keel role of leaders, 179-181
Barnes, Bill, 20, 82
Barnes, "Bloody Mary," 213
baseline funding, 81
Bastani, Bami, 128-129, 157-159, 198, 209
Benjamin, Mike, 145
"big box" retail case study (task overload), 15
Black & Veatch, 19, 85, 193
Boston Consulting Group, 209
breaking through task-overload gridlock
  event-driven versus process-driven management, 23-24
  prioritizing initiatives, 19-20
  software industry case study, 20-23
  tips, 24
budgets, aligning, 89-90
Business Success Cycle, 7, 10
business success modeling, 63-64

C

case studies
  "big box" retail (task overload), 15
  breaking through gridlock, 20-23
  software industry (task-overload gridlock), 20-23
Southern Company, 8
Symantec, 8
clear transformation process
  creating, 32
  importance of, 25-28
closed-loop accountability, 156-159
co-champions, 153-155
coaching performance, 171-172
Coll, George, 91, 115, 164
commitment, 150-151, 196-197
Commitments to Action (CTAs), 83-84
communication
  with customers and noncustomers, 47-48
  dialogue grounded in reality and facts, 102-103
  dialogue versus discussion, 36-37
  direct verbal communication, 102
  employee interviews, 39-40
  encouraging dialogue about taboo topics, 35
  generating as a leader, 37-39
  importance of, 101
  outside-in perspective, 44-47
  participation of lower-level employees, 41-44
  tablework, 104-110
compensation, performance-based pay, 170
Computer Sciences Corporation, 207
confidence, 150-151

confronting reality, 33-34
  confronting reality work
    sessions, 52-53
  dialogue versus
    discussion, 36-37
  employee interviews, 39-40
  encouraging dialogue about
    taboo topics, 35
  generating dialogue as a
    leader, 37-39
  market maps, 48-52
  opinions of customers and
    noncustomers, 47-48
  outside-in perspective, 44-47
  participation of lower-level
    employees, 41-44
  tips, 53-54
Corona project, 161
corporate initiatives,
  limiting, 74-77
cross-functional teams, 155
CTAs (Commitments to Action),
  83-84
customers, listening to, 47-48
cycle of failure, 3-5
cycle of success, 6-9

D

Darbee, Peter, 196
debate versus dialogue, 37
declarations versus
  promises, 160-164
delegation, 179
denial, overcoming, 33-34
  confronting reality work
    sessions, 52-53
  dialogue versus
    discussion, 36-37

employee interviews, 39-40
encouraging dialogue about
  taboo topics, 35
generating dialogue as a
  leader, 37-39
grounding dialogue in
  reality, 102-103
market maps, 48-52
opinions of customers and
  noncustomers, 47-48
outside-in perspective, 44-47
participation of lower-level
  employees, 41-44
tips, 53-54
dialogue
  compared to discussion, 36-37
  with customers and
    noncustomers, 47-48
  dialogue grounded in reality
    and facts, 102-103
  direct verbal
    communication, 102
  employee interviews, 39-40
  encouraging dialogue about
    taboo topics, 35
  generating as a leader, 37-39
  importance of, 101
  outside-in perspective, 44-47
  participation of lower-level
    employees, 41-44
  tablework, 104-110
Diamond, Bruce, 162-163
Dilbert comic strip, 78, 208
direct verbal
  communication, 102
discussion versus
  dialogue, 36-37

Dissero Partners, 6, 214
Draper Award, 162
due diligence process, 65-70

E

Eastern Airlines Flight 401, 165
Edwards, Gwen, 167
Eine Kleine Nachtmusik, 28-29
Einstein, Albert, 63
Eisenhower, Dwight D., 161
Emperor Has No Clothes
  syndrome
    dialogue versus
      discussion, 36-37
    encouraging dialogue about
      taboo topics, 35
    generating dialogue as a
      leader, 37-39
employees
  communication with
    *dialogue grounded in
      reality and facts, 102-103*
    *dialogue versus
      discussion, 36-37*
    *direct verbal
      communication, 102*
    employee interviews, 39-40
    *encouraging dialogue
      about taboo topics, 35*
    *generating as a
      leader, 37-39*
    importance of, 101
    *outside-in
      perspective, 44-47*
    *participation of lower-level
      employees, 41-44*
    tablework, 104-110

cross-functional teams, 155
engaging, 95-96
    failed attempts, 100-101
    *high-engagement, all-
      employee cascade, 101*
    *importance of dialogue,
      101-103*
    maintaining focus, 110-111
    *performance
      results, 96-100*
    tablework, 104-110
    tips, 112
  personnel changes, 197-201
enabling others to lead, 213
engaging employees, 95-96
  failed attempts, 100-101
  high-engagement, all-employee
    cascade, 101
  importance of dialogue, 101
    *dialogue grounded in
      reality and facts, 102-103*
    *direct verbal
      communication, 102*
    maintaining focus, 110-111
    tablework, 104-110
  performance results, 96-100
  tips, 112
Eubanks, Gordon, 31, 58, 200
event-driven
  management, 23-24
executive leadership, 3
  acknowledging that you don't
    have all the answers, 201-203
  authenticity and being
    "real," 203-204
  ballast-and-keel role, 179-181
  commitment to
    transformation, 196-197

delegation, 179
employee engagement, 95-96
    failed attempts, 100-101
    high-engagement, all-
        employee cascade, 101
    importance of
        dialogue, 101-103
    maintaining focus, 110-111
    performance results,
        96-100
    tablework, 104-110
    tips, 112
enabling leaders, 213
generating dialogue, 37-39
oversight of transformational
    initiatives, 151-155
personnel changes, 197-201
Power Curve, 136
sense of time,
    managing, 131-133
sharing power, 147
speed as leadership
    discipline, 133-134
strategic thinking within
    teams, 145-147
strategic vision, creating, 60-63
underpowered
    organizations, 137
**expanded launch road
map, 124-125**

F

failure, cycle of, 3-5
Fairchild, 163
firefighting versus fire
    protection, 23-24

flexibility, 213
Florida Rock Industries,
    159, 197
focus, 18, 110-111
followers/employees
    communication with
        dialogue grounded in
            reality and facts, 102-103
        dialogue versus
            discussion, 36-37
        direct verbal
            communication, 102
        employee interviews, 39-40
        encouraging dialogue
            about taboo topics, 35
        generating as a
            leader, 37-39
        importance of, 101
        outside-in
            perspective, 44-47
        participation of lower-level
            employees, 41-44
        tablework, 104-110
    cross-functional teams, 155
    engaging, 95-96
        failed attempts, 100-101
        high-engagement, all-
            employee cascade, 101
        importance of dialogue,
            101-103
        maintaining focus, 110-111
        performance results,
            96-100
        tablework, 104-110
        tips, 112
    personnel changes, 197-201
49ers, 108, 133

G

GE (General Electric),
   6, 200, 212
gridlock (task overload)
   breaking through
      *event-driven versus
         process-driven
         management, 23-24*
      *prioritizing
         initiatives, 19-20*
      *software industry case
         study, 20-23*
      tips, 24
   definition of, 13-14
   examples, 15-16
   impact on accountability, 16-17
   lack of focus, 18
   origins of, 14-15
ground truth, 166

H

Hartford Courant, 211
Harvard Business School, 212
high-engagement, all-employee
   cascade
   importance of dialogue, 101
      *dialogue grounded in
         reality and facts, 102-103*
      *direct verbal
         communication, 102*
   maintaining focus, 110-111
   tablework, 104-110
Hopkins, Bill, 66, 69

I

incentives, misguided, 168-171
individual Commitments to
   Action (CTAs), 83-84
initiatives
   accountability
      *closed-loop
         accountability, 156-159*
      importance of, 156
   oversight of, 151-155
   prioritizing, 19-20
initiatives, limiting, 74-77
interviewing employees, 39-40

J-K

Johns Hopkins University, 150

Kanazawa, Mike, career
   experience of, 207-210
Kelleher, Herb, 144
Kennedy, John F., 161

L

lack of focus, 18
launch efforts, 123-127
leadership, 3
   acknowledging that you don't
      have all the answers, 201-203
   authenticity and being
      "real," 203-204
   ballast-and-keel role, 179-181
   commitment to
      transformation, 196-197
   delegation, 179
   employee engagement, 95-96
      failed attempts, 100-101
      *high-engagement,
         all-employee cascade, 101*

importance of
  dialogue, 101-103
maintaining focus, 110-111
performance results,
  96-100
tablework, 104-110
tips, 112
enabling leaders, 213
generating dialogue, 37-39
oversight of transformational
  initiatives, 151-155
personnel changes, 197-201
Power Curve, 136
sense of time, managing,
  131-133
sharing power, 147
speed as leadership
  discipline, 133-134
strategic thinking within
  teams, 145-147
strategic vision, creating, 60-63
underpowered
  organizations, 137
listening to customers/former
  customers, 47-48
Luse, Robert, 102, 182

M

Maddox, Bill, 106
managers, 3
  acknowledging that you don't
    have all the answers, 201-203
  authenticity and being
    "real," 203-204
  ballast-and-keel role, 179-181
  commitment to
    transformation, 196-197

delegation, 179
employee engagement, 95-96
  failed attempts, 100-101
  high-engagement, all-
    employee cascade, 101
  importance of
    dialogue, 101-103
  maintaining focus, 110-111
  performance results,
    96-100
  tablework, 104-110
  tips, 112
enabling leaders, 213
generating dialogue, 37-39
oversight of transformational
  initiatives, 151-155
personnel changes, 197-201
Power Curve, 136
sense of time, managing,
  131-133
sharing power, 147
speed as leadership
  discipline, 133-134
strategic thinking within
  teams, 145-147
strategic vision, creating, 60-63
underpowered
  organizations, 137
Managing Organizational
  Effectiveness program
  (Harvard Business School), 6
maps, market, 48-52
market focus, 18
market maps, 48-52
Marketing Excellence, 145
McNeally, Scott, 58
measuring results, 164-168

Microsoft, 60
mid-course adjustment, 181-184
Miles, Robert H., career
  experience of, 6, 208-215
Miller, Edward, 149
Milton, John, 197
mini-cascades, 184-187
misguided incentives, 168-171
Mitchell, Tom, 203
Mondry, Larry, 74
Montana, Joe, 108, 133
Mozart's *Eine Kleine
  Nachtmusik*, 28-29
multi-year ACT
  process, 188-191

N

Napster, 49
Nassikas, Jim, 127
National Semiconductor,
  6, 41-43, 213
Nelson, Bruce, 8, 110, 199
Netscape, 118
noncustomers, listening
  to, 47-48
Nordstrom, 60

O

Office Depot, 6, 88, 110, 199
operational traction. *See*
  traction
outside-in perspective, 44-47
overhyping, danger of, 30-32
oversight of transformational
  initiatives, 151-155

P

Patel, Javed, 30
Perez, Rosa, 203
performance-based pay, 170
performance coaching, 171-172
personnel changes, 197-201
pilot tests, 81
Plato, 36
Pond, Kirk, 163
post-launch blues,
  avoiding, 178-181
Power Curve, 136
power, sharing, 147
priorities
  aligning, 80-83
  prioritizing initiatives, 19-20
process
  importance of, 31-32
  process architecture, designing
    for speed, 121-123
  process-driven
    management, 23-24
process map (ACT), 28-30
productive speed
  Accelerated Transformation
    launch road map, 121-122
  benefits of, 116-117
  case study, 118-121
  expanded launch road
    map, 124-125
  explanation of, 113-116
  launch efforts, 123-127
  process architecture, designing
    for speed, 121-123
  Quick Starts, 127-130
  sense of time,
    managing, 131-133

speed as leadership
   discipline, 133-134
tips, 134
promises versus
   declarations, 160-164
proven routines, value of, 9-11

Q-R

Quick Starts, 127-130

reality, confronting, 33-34
   confronting reality work
      sessions, 52-53
   dialogue versus
      discussion, 36-37
   employee interviews, 39-40
   encouraging dialogue about
      taboo topics, 35
   generating dialogue as a
      leader, 37-39
   grounding dialogue in
      reality, 102-103
   market maps, 48-52
   opinions of customers and
      noncustomers, 47-48
   outside-in perspective, 44-47
   participation of lower-level
      employees, 41-44
   tips, 53-54
reducing silos, 84-87
re-launch, 187-191
resetting action plans and
   priorities, 80-83
restacking the whole, 80-83
results
   ground truth, 166-168
   measuring, 164-166

retail case study (task
   overload), 15
Rice, Jerry, 108
Rockwell International, 6, 35
Rodman, Len, 19, 85, 193

S

safe passage (clear
   transformation process)
   creating, 32
   importance of, 25-28
Salem, Enrique, 124, 171
San Francisco 49ers, 108, 133
San Jose Mercury News, 118
sense of time, managing,
   131-133
sharing power, 147
silos
   reducing, 84-87
   silo approach to
      management, 154-155
simplicity, 213
slumps, avoiding, 175-177
   behavior and mind-set,
      191-192
   continuous transformation,
      192-193
   mid-course adjustment,
      181-184
   mini-cascades, 184-187
   multi-year ACT process,
      188-191
   post-launch blues, 178-181
   predictable slump points,
      177-178
   re-launch, 187-191
   tips, 193-194

Smith, Rodger, 45-47
software industry case study
(task-overload gridlock), 20-23
Southern Company, 8, 45-47
Southwest Airlines, 144
speed, productive
Accelerated Transformation
launch road map, 121-122
benefits of, 116-117
case study, 118-121
expanded launch road
map, 124-125
explanation of, 113-116
launch efforts, 123-127
process architecture, designing
for speed, 121-123
Quick Starts, 127-130
sense of time, managing,
131-133
speed as leadership
discipline, 133-134
speed in transformation, 214
tips, 134
Stanford Park Hotel, 127
strategic thinking within teams,
145-147
strategic vision, creating, 60-63
strategy, building, 55-56
ACT Arrow, 56-58
business success
modeling, 63-64
due diligence process, 65-70
strategic vision, creating, 60-63
tips, 70
transformation planning
funnel, 58-59
streamlined process
architecture, 124-125

success, cycle of
(transformation), 6-9
Sun Microsystems, 58
Symantec Corporation, 6-8,
58, 209, 213

T

tablework, 104-110
taboo topics, encouraging
dialogue about, 35
task-overload gridlock
breaking through
*event-driven versus
process-driven
management, 23-24*
*prioritizing initiatives,
19-20*
*software industry case
study, 20-23*
tips, 24
definition of, 13-14
examples, 15-16
impact on accountability, 16-17
lack of focus, 18
origins of, 14-15
teams, strategic thinking
within, 145-147
templates, transformation
initiative templates, 75-76
tests, pilot, 81
Torgersen, Walt, 142-143
traction, building, 149-150
accountability
*closed-loop
accountability, 156-159*
importance of, 156
committing with
confidence, 150-151

misguided incentives, 168-171
oversight of transformational
    initiatives, 151-155
performance coaching,
    171-172
promises versus
    declarations, 160-164
results measurements, 164-168
tips, 172
transformation (ACT), 210-212
acknowledging that you don't
    have all the answers, 201-203
ACT Arrow, 56-58
alignment, 73
    of budgets, 89-90
    corporate initiatives,
        limiting, 74-77
    importance of, 90-92
    individual Commitments to
        Action (CTAs), 83-84
    reducing silos, 84-87
    resetting action plans and
        priorities, 80-83
    tips, 92
    of values, 87-89
    zombie projects, 78-80
breaking through gridlock
    event-driven versus
        process-driven
        management, 23-24
    prioritizing initiatives,
        19-20
    software industry case
        study, 20-23
    tips, 24
case studies, 8
challenges, 1-2

commitment, 196-197
confronting reality, 33-34
    confronting reality work
        sessions, 52-53
    dialogue versus
        discussion, 36-37
    employee interviews, 39-40
    encouraging dialogue
        about taboo topics, 35
    generating dialogue as a
        leader, 37-39
    market maps, 48-52
    opinions of customers and
        noncustomers, 47-48
    outside-in perspective,
        44-47
    participation of lower-level
        employees, 41-44
    tips, 53-54
cycle of failure, 3-5
cycle of success, 6-9
dangers of overhyping, 30-32
definition of transformation, 1
employee engagement, 95-96
    failed attempts, 100-101
    high-engagement, all-
        employee cascade, 101
    importance of dialogue,
        101-103
    maintaining focus, 110-111
    performance results,
        96-100
    tablework, 104-110
    tips, 112
frustration with
    transformation, 1-2
importance of process, 31-32

leadership, 3
  Power Curve, 136
  sharing power, 147
  strategic thinking within
    teams, 145-147
  underpowered
    organizations, 137
origins and development, 6
personnel changes, 197-201
process map, 28-30
productive speed
  Accelerated
    Transformation launch
    road map, 121-122
  benefits of, 116-117
  case study, 118-121
  expanded launch road
    map, 124-125
  explanation of, 113-116
  launch efforts, 123-127
  process architecture,
    designing for
    speed, 121-123
  Quick Starts, 127-130
  sense of time,
    managing, 131-133
  speed as leadership
    discipline, 133-134
  tips, 134
safe passage (clear
  transformation process)
  creating, 32
  importance of, 25-28
slumps, avoiding, 175-177
  behavior and mind-set,
    191-192
  continuous transformation,
    192-193
  mid-course adjustment,
    181-184

mini-cascades, 184-187
multi-year ACT process,
  188-191
post-launch blues, 178-181
predictable slump
  points, 177-178
re-launch, 187-191
tips, 193-194
strategy, building, 55-56
  ACT Arrow, 56-58
  business success
    modeling, 63-64
  due diligence
    process, 65-70
  strategic vision,
    creating, 60-63
  tips, 70
  transformation planning
    funnel, 58-59
traction, building, 149-150
  accountability, 156-159
  committing with
    confidence, 150-151
  misguided incentives,
    168-171
  oversight of
    transformational
    initiatives, 151-155
  performance coaching,
    171-172
  promises versus
    declarations, 160-164
  results measurements,
    164-168
  tips, 172
transformation planning
  funnel, 58-59
value of following a proven
  routine, 9-11

U-V

under-powered
  organizations, 137

values, aligning, 87-89
vision statements, 60-63

W-X-Y-Z

Weiss, Tony, 140
Welch, Jack, 200, 212

Yale School of
  Management, 211
Youmans, Brad, 44, 51

zombie projects, 78-80

FINANCIAL TIMES

In an increasingly competitive world, it is quality
of thinking that gives an edge—an idea that opens new
doors, a technique that solves a problem, or an insight
that simply helps make sense of it all.

We work with leading authors in the various arenas
of business and finance to bring cutting-edge thinking
and best-learning practices to a global market.

It is our goal to create world-class print publications
and electronic products that give readers
knowledge and understanding that can then be
applied, whether studying or at work.

To find out more about our business
products, you can visit us at www.ftpress.com.